THE PSYCHOANALYTIC VOCATION:
RANK, WINNICOTT, AND
THE LEGACY OF FREUD

THE PSYCHOANALYTIC VOCATION

♦ RANK, WINNICOTT, AND THE LEGACY OF FREUD

PETER L. RUDNYTSKY

Yale University Press   New Haven   London

Designed by Nancy Ovedovitz and set in New Baskerville type by Keystone Typesetting, Inc., Orwigsburg, Pennsylvania. Printed in the United States of America by Hamilton Printing Company, Castleton, New York.

Library of Congress Cataloging-in-Publication Data

Rudnytsky, Peter L.
  The psychoanalytic vocation : Rank, Winnicott, and the legacy of Freud / Peter L. Rudnytsky.
  p. cm.
  Includes bibliographical references and index.
  ISBN 0-300-05067-4 (hard)
  1. Psychoanalysis—History. 2. Rank, Otto, 1884–1939.
  3. Winnicott, D. W. (Donald Woods), 1896–1971. 4. Freud, Sigmund, 1856–1939. I. Title.
  BF175.R83 1991
  150.19'52—dc20   91-9645
                                                  CIP

10 9 8 7 6 5 4 3 2 1

In memory of John F. Benton

Compared with the average professional man, the artist has, so to say, a hundred-per-cent vocational psychology. . . . For whereas the average man uses his ability chiefly as a means to material existence, and psychically only so far as to enable him to feel himself a useful member of human society—more or less irrespective of what his calling is—the artist needs his calling for his spiritual existence, just as the early cultures of mankind could not have existed and developed without art.—Otto Rank, *Art and Artist*

I think that the best part of it is that you start from a position of humility with the acknowledgement that we all have failures to our account. This is a great relief as compared with the tone of many speakers who seem to suggest that they can tackle everything. . . . It is certainly important for the [British Psycho-Analytical] Society to be reminded over and over again that man cannot live by bread alone—bread here meaning verbal interpretations.—D. W. Winnicott to Michael Balint, March 27, 1957

♦ CONTENTS

I n *Freud and Oedipus* (1987), I sought to situate psychoanalysis and to confront my own transferential relation to it by investigating the biographical, cultural, and literary dynamics of Freud's engagement with the Oedipus myth. The present book extends this project by taking up the history of psychoanalysis after Freud, which has in large measure been concerned with mapping the preoedipal realm.

As this description suggests, there is both a continuity and a shift of emphasis between this book and its predecessor. The shift has to do with the displacement of the father by the mother as the principal focus of my attention, as well as with a concomitant subordination of triangular issues of sexual conflict to dyadic ones of separation and individuation. The evolution is likewise reflected in my conversion to an object relations perspective, which entails a rejection of some key principles of classical analytic theory having to do particularly with the nature of the instincts or drives.

The continuity is manifested in my undiminished preoccupation with what it is no longer disreputable to call the self. The child enters human culture through the crucible of the Oedipus complex, but the oedipal stage cannot be reached unless a sense of existence has previously been instilled in the infant through adequate primary care. Although a reordering of priorities has undoubtedly accompanied my turn from the oedipal to the preoedipal realm, from another standpoint I have simply explored the origins of identity further in the same direction.

My orientation toward psychoanalysis thus remains fundamentally *humanistic* in inspiration. Although I encountered the work of Lacan in graduate school, his postmodern inflection of psychoanalysis left me dissatisfied, and I sought a figure through whom I could articulate an alternative vision of its possibilities. That alternative I have belatedly found in Winnicott and in the Independent tradition of British object relations theory.

Although I am not a psychoanalyst, by my title, *The Psychoanalytic*

Vocation, I mean to convey my sense that a psychoanalytic way of thinking can imbue existence with a meaning that is not less spiritual for being nonreligious. But the primary "vocation" is that of the mother who, by her love, calls her child into being. These two frames of reference coalesce in the transferential dialogue between analyst and patient.

Otto Rank (1884–1939) and D. W. Winnicott (1896–1971) may at first glance seem to form an odd collocation, and indeed I focus on them here largely because I have made a considerable personal investment in studying both. In 1984, I edited a special issue of *American Imago* commemorating the centenary of Rank's birth, and in 1985, I organized an international conference on Rank at Columbia University, where his papers are held. Reading Winnicott's *Playing and Reality* (1971) was revelatory, but not until 1987, when I attended a conference entitled "D. W. Winnicott and the Objects of Psychoanalysis" at the University of Massachusetts at Amherst and learned of the existence of the Winnicott archive at the New York Hospital–Cornell Medical Center, did I begin my work on him in earnest.

Rank was a member of Freud's early circle in Vienna. Winnicott never met Freud, and his analytic identity was consolidated in the context of the controversies between Anna Freud and Melanie Klein and their followers in the British Psycho-Analytical Society in the 1940s. Thus, Rank and Winnicott represent successive generations, and through them I hope to elucidate something of the larger history of the psychoanalytic movement from Freud's time to the present, in which each played a prominent part.

The patron saint of lay analysts, Rank pioneered in the application of psychoanalytic ideas to mythology and literature. Winnicott came to psychoanalysis from pediatrics, but, like Rank, he was keenly interested in art, play, and cultural experience, as well as in the role of the preoedipal mother and existential issues of the self. Rank eventually broke from Freud and became an opponent of psychoanalysis. Winnicott sought to preserve continuities at all costs but espoused a version of psychoanalysis that differed markedly from Freud's. In some ways, Rank's story is one of tragedy and Winnicott's one of triumph, though the greatness and complexity of both men belie such ready generalizations.

As in *Freud and Oedipus,* I assume in this book that the theory of psychoanalysis is intertwined with the fates of the men and women who have made it their lifework, so I shuttle back and forth between biography and intellectual history. In chapter 1, I sketch my reasons for casting my lot with Winnicott and object relations theory. In chapter 2, I deploy the ideas of both Rank and Winnicott to uncover the preoedipal dimensions of *Oedipus the King*. Chapters 3 and 4 are devoted to Rank. Chapter 3 examines the troubled relationship between Rank and Freud, and chapter 4 takes up Rank's neglected writings between 1924 and 1927 to argue that he is an unacknowledged progenitor of object relations theory. Chapter 5 polemically compares Winnicott to Lacan and Kohut, the leading figures of two rival traditions. In chapter 6, having asserted Winnicott's preeminence, I juxtapose his life and work with Freud's. Chapter 7 uses Guntrip's published account of his analyses with Fairbairn and Winnicott and his unpublished *Psycho-Analytical Autobiography* to probe the interactions among these three giants of British psychoanalysis. Finally, in chapter 8, I show how object relations theory provides a basis for questioning the postmodernism that dominates literary studies today.

The mid-1920s, when Rank made his painful break with Freud, was also when Winnicott began his ten-year analysis with James Strachey. (Winnicott later underwent a second analysis with Joan Riviere; Rank was never analyzed.) In 1926, Melanie Klein settled in London. In this moment of generational transition the center of gravity in the psychoanalytic movement began to shift from Vienna, via Budapest and Berlin, to London, following the trajectory of Klein's migrations. On November 11, 1924, Strachey wrote to his wife, Alix, in Berlin: "Our Rank letters crossed. Of course what *looks* so black about it all is that the bust-up should have been timed precisely for the moment at which the Professor was supposed to be kicking the bucket. If there was any conscious intention—and I really can hardly credit it—the whole affair was singularly mismanaged on Otto's part. Especially as he doesn't even seem to have succeeded in carrying off Ferenczi." Strachey astutely links Rank's "bust-up" with Freud to the onset of Freud's cancer, an aperçu I shall seek to substantiate in my own commentary on the affair. But what is most remarkable is that Strachey in the same letter goes on to mention Winnicott. "However, poor little Winnie seriously suggested to-day that perhaps he'd pumped [urinated] over his ma at the moment of his birth. I suggested that he may even have done it inside her. (The conversation arose from the enormous pleasure it gave him to pump while he was bathing in the sea.) I fancy he's cut out to be a Rankschüler" (Meisel and Kendrick 1985, 115). Strachey's designation of Winnicott as a potential "Rankschüler" is intended ironically, but in fact, Winnicott came to emulate Rank in his probing of the earliest traumas of life. Beneath its ostensible casualness, the conjunction of Rank and Winnicott in Strachey's letter evokes their submerged historical and theoretical affinities.

Inevitably, the vision of psychoanalysis I offer in this book is a personal one, and the vocation about which I speak is above all my own. But that which has private meaning is shaped by the circumambient culture and may in turn resonate with its larger patterns.

Pasadena
August 1990

♦ ACKNOWLEDGMENTS

This book was written during a period in which I could not find permanent academic employment. Among the rewards of a peripatetic existence has been my heightened appreciation for the generosity of those who have stood by me. I wish to thank Harold Bloom, Sander L. Gilman, Steven Marcus, and Edward W. Tayler, without whose support I would not have received a Fulbright Western European Regional Research Scholarship in 1988–89.

If psychoanalysis has not brought me a job, it has sustained me as a vocation, and I feel a special solidarity with my fellow heeders of the call. These include Ellen Handler Spitz, David Willbern, Antal Bókay, Patrizia Giampieri, Vera J. Camden, Karin Dannecker, John Kerr, Paul E. Stepansky, Mary Catherine Wimer, Norman N. Holland, and Christopher Bollas. Mark Kanzer gave me access to his library. Janis Butler Holm suggested that I title the book *The Psychoanalytic Vacation*. John Rickard was the noblest Tiger of them all. James P. Bednarz and Kathie Plourde have sheltered a homeless person in New York, as has Matthew S. Santirocco in both Atlanta and Philadelphia. The members of my family have patiently forborne what they could not get me to change.

I have been honored to present portions of this book to audiences in this country and abroad. I thank the following for their invitations: in Vienna, the Österreichische Gesellschaft für Literatur, the Sigmund Freud–Gesellschaft, the Wiener Psychoanalytische Vereinigung, and the sponsors of the 1989 International Symposium on Philosophy and Psychoanalysis; in Berlin, the Berliner Psychoanalytisches Institut and the Hochschule der Künste; in Freiburg, the Freiburg Psychoanalytisches Seminar; in Budapest, the Tündérhegy Psychotherapy Department; in Paris, the Societé Psychanalytique de Paris; in London, the Wellcome Institute for the History of Medicine; in Cambridge, the University of Cambridge Seminar on the History of Psychiatry, Psychoanalysis, and Related Disciplines; in New York, the Seminar on the History of Psychiatry at New York Hospital–Cornell Medical Center, the organizers of a 1990 conference at Cornell University entitled "Oedipus at the Crossroads: Psychoanalysis, Philosophy, and the Classics," and the University of Buffalo; in Massachusetts, the Group for Psychoanalytic Studies at the University of Massachusetts at Amherst and the Austen Riggs Center in Stockbridge; in Ohio, my hosts at Kent State University for the 1987 International Conference on Literature and Psychology; in Florida, the Seminar on the Applications of Psychology at the University of Florida; and in Washington, D.C., the American Society of Psychoanalytic Physicians and the organizers of a 1988 conference at the Washington School of Psychiatry entitled "The Kingdom of Oedipus." I was also pleased to be a visiting faculty member in the Object Relations Theory and Therapy Program at the Washington School in 1990. An earlier version of chapter 1 was published in *Philosophie und Psychoanalyse: Symposium der Wiener Festwochen*, ed. Ludwig Nagl, Helmuth Vetter, and Harald Leupold-Löwenthal (Frankfurt: Nexus, 1990), pp. 137–53; of chapter 3 in *American Imago*, 41 (1984): 325–41, and is reprinted by permission of the Johns Hopkins University Press; of chapters 6 and 7, in *The Psychoanalytic Study of the Child*, 44 (1989): 331–50 and 43 (1988): 423–32.

My quest for Winnicott has taught me how many people's lives were changed by having come into contact with this remarkable man. I owe a particular debt to Madeleine Davis for her personal integrity and intellectual standards. In my work on Rank, I have had the benefit of interviews with his widow, Estelle Buel Simon, and daughter, Helene Rank Veltfort, as well as the counsel of E. James Lieberman. Harry Slochower invited me to serve as guest editor of the 1984 Rank issue of *American Imago*. Herbert Kraus came from Vienna to New York in 1986 to interview me for his program about Rank on the Österreichische Rundfunk. At Yale University Press, Gladys Topkis showed confidence in this project from its earliest stages; Mary Pasti wrought alchemical transformations in my prose.

◆ NOTE ON SOURCES

Institutions and individuals have graciously granted me access to, and permission to use, unpublished sources. I have relied extensively on the Otto Rank collection in the Columbia University Rare Book and Manuscript Library, directed by Kenneth A. Lohf, and the D. W. Winnicott collection in the Archives of Psychiatry, New York Hospital–Cornell Medical Center, directed by Eric T. Carlson. Michael Balint's letter to Winnicott in chapter 5 is quoted by permission of Enid Balint. The letters to and from Winnicott cited without documentation and the excerpt from the manuscript "Applied Theory" in chapter 6 appeared by permission of the Archives of Psychiatry, New York Hospital–Cornell Medical Center, in the earlier version of the chapter published in *The Psychoanalytic Study of the Child*. David Ross, librarian of the New York Psychoanalytic Institute, provided me with the summary of the responses to Winnicott's paper "The Use of an Object." Kelly E. Burket, archivist of the Menninger Foundation, provided me with the manuscript of Harry Guntrip's *Psycho-Analytical Autobiography*. Both the autobiography and an unpublished letter from Guntrip to Winnicott are quoted in chapter 7 by permission of John D. Sutherland, literary executor for Harry Guntrip. The excerpts from Winnicott's poem "The Tree" and Winnicott's letter to Guntrip in chapter 7 are reproduced by permission of the Estate of D. W. Winnicott by arrangement with Mark Paterson and Associates, Colchester. I have likewise made use of the unpublished Freud-Ferenczi correspondence, the original manuscripts of which are at the National-Bibliothek in Vienna and copies of which are at the Freud Museum in London.

Appendix A, Rank's "Genesis of the Object Relation," a chapter from volume 1 of *Grundzüge einer genetischen Psychologie (Fundamentals of a Genetic Psychology;* 1927), is taken from a manuscript in the Marion E. Kenworthy collection of the New York Hospital–Cornell Medical Center and is published here in English for the first time. The translation, edited for readability, dates from 1926 and is unattributed. Rank delivered the paper as part of a private lecture series in New York. Appendix B, a June 1983 interview with Clare Winnicott, Winnicott's second wife, by Michael Neve, lecturer, History of Medicine, at the Wellcome Institute of the History of Medicine, is my transcription of a tape recording deposited in the Winnicott collection of the New York Hospital–Cornell Medical Center. It is published here for the first time by permission of Michael Neve and the Estate of Clare Winnicott by arrangement with Mark Paterson and Associates, Colchester.

Any otherwise unattributed translations from foreign languages are my own. All italics in quoted passages are found in the original texts.

THE PSYCHOANALYTIC VOCATION:
RANK, WINNICOTT, AND
THE LEGACY OF FREUD

1 ♦ A PSYCHOANALYTIC WELTANSCHAUUNG

It is the mark of an educated man to look for
precision in each class of things just so far as the
nature of the subject admits.—Aristotle,
Nicomachean Ethics

In proposing to define a psychoanalytic weltanschauung, I do so
deliberately with the indefinite article. I can offer only my own sense
of what it means to think psychoanalytically; I do not pretend to
speak with the voice of the discipline itself, as if such a prosopopoeia
were even possible.

The point of view that I shall espouse and whose implications I shall
seek to elucidate is one I would associate with the Middle Group of
British object relations theory. The leading light of the group is D. W.
Winnicott, but it can also boast the brilliance of W. R. D. Fairbairn, the
passion of Michael Balint, the synthetic gifts of Harry Guntrip, the
empirical bent of John Bowlby, and the creativity of Marion Milner, to
invoke only the most talismanic names. Through Balint, there is a
direct link to the Hungarian legacy of Sándor Ferenczi, and the neglected premonitions of Otto Rank must also be given their due. The
indispensable antecedent of Fairbairn's theoretical breakthrough, of
course, is Melanie Klein's work, though Klein herself remained tied to
the outmoded terminology of Freud's instinct theory, whose limitations
her pioneering exploration of internal objects did so much to expose.
The current state of object relations theory may be seen to best advantage in books by Christopher Bollas (1987, 1989), who continues to
exemplify the independence of the Independent tradition.

Anyone attempting to thread through the labyrinth of contemporary psychoanalysis must first gain his or her bearings in relation to
Freud. Freud remains the indispensable point of origin, the enabling

genius to whom everything is owed and whose work sustains interminable rereadings. At the same time, it is essential to be clear about
where one parts company with Freud. My effort at revision is bifold,
taking the measure of Freud the man as well as Freud the thinker.
Indeed, in the history of psychoanalysis, the realm of theory can never
be fully divorced from that of lived experience.

In considering Freud as a human being, I do not think it can be
denied that there was a tragic flaw in his personality. This flaw is
exhibited most clearly in his relationships with his male followers, to
whom he refused to grant true intellectual autonomy. The evidence for
this assertion lies in the repeatedly sundered friendships with those
men who mattered most to him—Wilhelm Fliess, C. G. Jung, and
Rank—with which Freud's career is scarred. Ferenczi, the best loved
and most gifted of all Freud's disciples, never broke ranks with Freud
but suffered no less acutely from the painful choice between subservience and defiance that was imposed on him. He writes in his posthumously published *Clinical Diary* of 1932: "The anxiety-provoking idea,
perhaps very strong in the unconscious, that the father must die when
the son grows up, explains [Freud's] fear of allowing any one of his sons
to become independent" (1988, 185). Ferenczi saw Freud in Vienna,
for what proved to be the last time, in August 1932 on his way to a
psychoanalytic congress in Wiesbaden. At this meeting, Freud urged
that Ferenczi refrain from publishing his seminal paper "Confusion
of Tongues between Adults and the Child" (1933).[1] Ferenczi, much
shaken, nonetheless delivered his paper and shortly thereafter suffered the attack of pernicious anemia from which he died in May 1933.
He records in the final entry of his diary: "In my case the blood-crisis
arose when I realized that not only can I not rely on the protection of a
'higher power' but *on the contrary* I shall be trampled under foot by this
indifferent power as soon as I go my own way and not his" (212). That
Freud's callous behavior played a part in Victor Tausk's suicide in 1919
has already been cogently argued (Roazen 1969), and it is not too much
to say that the death of Ferenczi was likewise hastened by his "indifferent power."

Ferenczi's unique position stems from his dual identity as Freud's

---

1. On this episode in the Freud-Ferenczi relationship, see Masson 1984,
145–87. As Jeffrey Masson notes, after Ferenczi's death the English translation
of his paper, which had been set in type, was removed from the *International
Journal of Psycho-Analysis*. It did not appear until 1949, in a translation by Balint.

analysand and as a master analyst of others in his own right. The awareness of what it means to see analysis *from the patient's point of view* was never lost on Ferenczi, and in this he differs radically from Freud, who not only was never analyzed by anyone else but also consistently resisted the efforts of his pupils to draw him into more genuinely reciprocal relationships. Ferenczi observes: "In his conduct Fr[eud] plays only the role of the castrating god, he wants to ignore the traumatic moment of his own castration in childhood; he is the only one who does not have to be analyzed" (1988, 188). Ferenczi went so far in his convictions about the dialectical nature of the analytic encounter as to experiment with "mutual analysis," in which time would be set aside for the analyst to be analyzed by the patient.

This technical innovation must be placed in the context of the broader divergence between Ferenczi and Freud on matters of therapy. Ferenczi quotes Freud's remark that "neurotics are a rabble [*Gesindel*], good only to support us financially and to allow us to learn from their cases: psychoanalysis as a therapy may be worthless" (1988, 186). In contrast to Freud's "therapeutic nihilism" (93) is Ferenczi's refusal to abandon his belief in the curative powers of analysis and his attempt to evince an attitude of compassion and even love toward the patients in his care.

Our discussion has moved from the personality of Freud to the nature of the analytic relationship. Masud Khan has justly contended that "the greatest invention of Freud will always be the invention of this unique human situation where a person can explore the meaning and experiential realities of his life, through a relationship with another, and yet not be intruded upon or manipulated in any way that is not true to his own self and values" (1972, 127). Although this "human laboratory" is Freud's greatest invention, he did not always avoid intrusiveness and manipulation in practice. Indeed, notwithstanding the wisdom of his papers on the subject, Freud's classical technique differs from the empathic technique derived by object relations theorists from Ferenczi and Rank in tending toward authoritarian closure rather than dialectical openness. In this regard, moreover, Melanie Klein remains much closer to Freud than to Ferenczi. One has only to contrast Klein's declaration that "the essential prerequisite for conducting an early analysis—and, indeed, a deep-going analysis of older children—is certainty in grasping the material presented" (1932, 30) with Winnicott's responsiveness to "the child's ability to 'think up'—in a way, to *create*—an analyst, a role into which the real analyst can try to fit himself" (1948, 169) to measure the gulf between dogmatic and tentative approaches to analysis.

As I shall argue at greater length below, one of the implications of a commitment to an object relations position is acceptance of the hermeneutic dimensions of the analytic encounter. In this connection, it is instructive to consider Serge Viderman's influential paper "The Analytic Space" (1979). On the one hand, Viderman embraces a radical hermeneutic relativism, insisting that analytic interpretations "cannot be contained in an alternative binary proposition of truth or untruth" (266). On the other hand—and this is the point I wish to stress—he combines this position with an analytic authoritarianism that is entirely indefensible. For Viderman, "the frame is set up by the analyst alone," and the analysis depends on "a formal, rigid, and unalterable situation with . . . a division of roles which demands that each remain strictly within his range from beginning to end" (288, 279–80). It is not necessary to respond to such high-handedness by going to Ferenczi's extreme and advocating that the analyst submit to analysis by the patient. A contemporary object relations position would simply note that, as in Winnicott's squiggle game, the play of analysis depends on the contributions of *both* partners to the dialogue and that, as Bollas has written, "the analyst is compelled to relive elements of [the analysand's] infantile history through his countertransference," which means that he "may for a very long time indeed exist in an unknowable region" (1987, 200).

After considering Freud's personality, then the analytic relationship, we come to questions of theory. As I have indicated, the decisive breakthrough was achieved by Fairbairn; it is condensed in his proposition that "libido is primarily object-seeking," not pleasure-seeking (1944, 126). (In his later formulations, Fairbairn avoided the apparent hypostatization of the notion of libido by saying that "it is the *individual in his libidinal capacity* . . . that is object-seeking"; Guntrip 1961, 305.) What this means, in essence, is that not only must Freud's speculative attempt in 1920 to go "beyond the pleasure principle" with the theory of the death instinct be discarded as an unprofitable fiction but the pleasure principle itself must be similarly abandoned. As Fairbairn elaborates, Freud's view of libido "follows directly from his divorce of energy from structure," whereas "once we conceive of energy as inseparable from structure, the only [psychic] changes which are intelligible are changes in structural relationships . . . and such changes are essentially directional" (1951, 176). Freud's hydraulic model of sexualized mental energy pressing blindly for discharge—what is known in psychoanalytic metapsychology as the economic point of view—is without empirical foundation and has, as I shall document below, been refuted by direct evidence.

What the Middle Group would offer in its place is a consistent object relations theory of the personality. (The American "interpersonal" school founded by Harry Stack Sullivan is in many ways similar but lacks the idea of internal objects, which is integral to an understanding of the dynamic unconscious; Guntrip 1961, 174–90.) In spite of minor divergences among its members, there exists a broad underlying agreement that Freud's emphasis on mechanistic drives operating within the individual considered in isolation must give way to the recognition that infants exist from the beginning in a state of *dependence* on their mothers or caretakers and that the predominant need in human beings is not for sex but for *attachment*. In addition to the pleasure principle and the death instinct, a further casualty of this recasting of psychoanalytic theory is Freud's concept of primary narcissism, which, as Balint (1937) has trenchantly shown, is enmeshed in contradiction and is better replaced with the concept of primary object love.

I have suggested that one consequence of an acceptance of object relations theory is a convergence between psychoanalysis and hermeneutics. It is only an apparent paradox to say that a further consequence is a closer fit between psychoanalysis and natural science. The scientific foundations of the contemporary understanding of attachment are laid down mainly in the work of Bowlby, who has dedicated himself to building a bridge between psychoanalysis and ethology.[2] Bowlby cites, for instance, the famous research of Harry Harlow on rhesus monkeys, in which four infant monkeys in cages were fed on demand from model "mothers" made of cylindrically shaped wire, and four others from similar cylinders covered by soft cloth. The experiments showed that animals in *both* groups spent most of their time clinging to the cloth model (Bowlby 1969, 213–14). Bowlby quotes

2. See also the pioneering papers of the Hungarian analyst Imre Hermann (1933, 1936), who appealed to ethological data to support his hypothesis of a "clinging instinct." Susan Deri (1984) brings the work of Hermann into conjunction with contemporary object relations theory.

(214) from Harlow's conclusion: "These data make it obvious that contact comfort is a variable of critical importance in the development of affectional responsiveness to the surrogate mother and that nursing appears to play a negligible role. . . . These findings are at complete variance with a drive-reduction theory of affectional development." As Bowlby notes (211), the refuted "secondary drive" theory is that espoused by Freud, who asserted as late as *An Outline of Psycho-Analysis* that "love has its origin in attachment to the satisfied need for nourishment" (1940, 188).

In assessing both the historical unfolding and the theoretical achievement of object relations thought, special mention must be made of Ian Suttie's *Origins of Love and Hate*. This book, largely neglected at the time of its publication, has increasingly been hailed as a classic and indeed contains the kernel of virtually every idea elaborated by subsequent analysts. Suttie distills Winnicott's (1967d) entire thesis concerning the location of cultural experience when he writes that "play . . . and culture-interests generally are substitutes for the mutually caressing relationship of child and mother. *By these substitutes we put the whole social environment in the place once occupied by the mother*" (1935, 16). Suttie likewise anticipates Bowlby in seeking "to put the conception of altruistic (non-appetitive) love on a scientific footing" by drawing on research in animal behavior, and he explicitly makes the methodological claim that these facts are important because they "are objective and can be checked by several observers, *unlike evidence derived from the analysis of patients*" (3, 8).

Moreover, although Suttie recognized that he was working within a Freudian tradition, he did not hesitate to take Freud to task for the shortcomings he found. Like Ferenczi, who speculates about the "personal aversion" that underlies "the unilaterally androphile orientation of [Freud's] theory of sexuality" (1988, 187–88), Suttie quotes (71) Freud's declaration in *Civilization and Its Discontents* (1930) that "the derivation of a need for religion from the child's feeling of helplessness and the longing it evokes for a *father* seems to me incontrovertible. . . . There may be *something else behind this, but for the present it is wrapped in obscurity*" and adds a crushing rejoinder: "There *is* something else 'behind this,' namely the child's need for the *mother's* love; and the 'obscurity' to which Freud refers exists only in his own mind." This blind spot with regard to the mother and female sexuality is a corollary to Freud's refusal to grant autonomy to his male followers, and it

underscores what Ferenczi brands the "personal causes for the er-
roneous development of psychoanalysis" (1988, 184).[3]

A major reorientation in psychoanalytic thinking has, then, been effected by object relations theory. With the recognition, in Winnicott's
words, that "there is no id before ego" (1962a, 56), it follows that life "is
more nearly about BEING than about sex" (1967a, 35). As these quotations make clear, one effect of the paradigm shift has been to align
psychoanalysis more closely with existentialism. The proper study of
psychoanalysis is the development of the *whole person*, beginning in earliest infancy, as this is facilitated or impinged upon by interactions with
key figures in the family and the outside world. Strictly speaking, even
the use of the term *id* is inconsistent within an object relations framework; and in Guntrip's judgment, the decisive question is whether
psychoanalysis is to adhere to a notion of the "system ego" as set forth
by Freud and refined by Heinz Hartmann or to a notion of the "person
ego" as this emerges from the work of Fairbairn and Winnicott (1968,
390–426; 1971, 103–41).

In stressing discontinuities, it is no less important to bear in mind
how much has been retained from Freud's legacy. Roughly speaking,
whereas many of Freud's explanatory *theories* have undergone modification, the *observations* upon which he based these theories have stood
up remarkably well (Guntrip 1971, 7–8). The formative role of early
experience, the conflicts that often arise among emotions, the way that
these emotions can be repressed and yet continue unconsciously to
exert a powerful effect on a person's thoughts and behavior, the role of
dreams as a means of reliving unresolved problems of past life, the way
that human beings live in an internal world of fantasy as well as in
external reality—all these discoveries (and more) were made by Freud
and have proved to have lasting validity. And, I hasten to add, a shift to
object relations thinking does *not* mean a disregard of sexuality and
aggression as experiential components of human life.[4] Granted the
priority of ego structures and the basic human need for attachment,
sexuality nonetheless retains a secondary autonomy of its own and is

3. On the suppression of the role of the preoedipal mother in Freud's
writings, see the powerful recent studies of Madelon Sprengnether (1990) and,
with reference to Freud's Jewish origins, Estelle Roith (1987).

4. On the distinction between a psychoanalytic emphasis on sexuality and
Freud's drive-reduction theory, see G. Klein 1976.

admitted by object relations theorists of all stripes to have a biological basis. With aggression, there is a division between those who assign it to an innate source (Klein, Winnicott) and those who impute it to an internalized reaction to deprivation and frustration (Fairbairn, Guntrip). In either set of theories, however, aggression—like sexuality—is far from slighted, and it assuredly figures prominently in the analysis of all individuals whose ego is basically intact.

In advancing a psychoanalytic weltanschauung consistent with object relations theory, it is imperative to confront Freud's own views on the subject and the controversies to which they have given rise. In the *New Introductory Lectures,* Freud disposes of the matter with the assertion that psychoanalysis is "quite unfit to construct a *Weltanschauung* of its own: it must accept the scientific one" (1933, 158)—the alternatives being those of religion and philosophy. Freud's effort to confine psychoanalysis within the parameters of natural science has been challenged by a range of analysts and thinkers from the hermeneutic school, who rally around Jürgen Habermas's contention that Freud initiated the "scientific self-misunderstanding of psychoanalysis" (1968, 214). This position, in turn, has been vehemently attacked by Adolf Grünbaum, who seeks to clear away the hermeneutic reading of Freud as a preliminary to showing that Freud's own claims for the scientific standing of his enterprise cannot be sustained. Since Grünbaum's *Foundations of Psychoanalysis* (1984) has gained notoriety as a formidable critique of psychoanalysis, it behooves me to explain why I believe this reputation is inflated.

Although Grünbaum's work is presented as a coolly reasoned intellectual argument, in fact its most conspicuous feature is the unrelenting scorn Grünbaum heaps upon those with whom he disagrees. He wonders "whether Habermas himself knows just what he wishes to claim" (12); Gadamer makes "grandiose assertions" (16); Ricoeur is guilty of a "willful impoverishment" of the issues he discusses (45); Grünbaum doubts "whether Ricoeur has decided just what he wants to maintain" (48); Habermas "is incoherent on the face of it" (12) and "has entrapped himself in an absurdity" (41); to follow George Klein would be to "aver [an] inanity" (52); Roy Schafer is "simply oblivious" to fundamental principles (74); and even Karl Popper is "highly unfair and misleading" in his exegesis of Freud (129).

Such passages, which could easily be multiplied, establish the tone in which Grünbaum goes about presenting his case. Ironically, whereas the advocates of the hermeneutic position question Freud on certain points in order to vindicate psychoanalysis, Grünbaum purportedly defends Freud in order to demolish psychoanalysis more effectively. At the core of the dispute between Grünbaum and his opponents is that he wishes to regard Freud purely as a natural scientist; for members of the hermeneutic school Freud's work is fraught with potentially rich and productive contradictions. For example, in *On the History of the Psycho-Analytic Movement,* Freud asserts that "psycho-analysis is my creation. . . . Even to-day no one can know better than I do what psycho-analysis is" (1914, 7). Conversely, in a letter to Fritz Wittels, his first biographer, he insists: "The public has no concern with my personality, and can learn nothing from an account of it" (1924b, 286). When it suited him, then, Freud could maintain that his life was irrelevant to psychoanalysis; at other times he arrogated the proprietary right to legislate on its behalf. This contradiction goes to the heart of the status of psychoanalysis as a hybrid discipline, inhabiting an intermediate area between humanistic and scientific modes of knowledge.

Grünbaum chastises Habermas because he "cites tendentiously" from Freud's work (1984, 32), but it is rather his own use of sources that is conspicuously one-sided. Nowhere, for instance, does Grünbaum quote Freud's pronouncement in *Studies on Hysteria* that "it still strikes me myself as strange that the case histories I write should read like short stories and that, as one might say, they lack the serious stamp of science" (1895, 160), for to do so would be to admit that Freud recognized at times that his discovery of the "talking cure" led him beyond the positivistic heritage in which he had been trained into a domain of literary truth. Grünbaum rebukes Habermas and Gadamer for drawing a "pseudocontrast" between the natural and human sciences, adducing the example of an electrically charged particle moving through a magnetic field to prove that physics "features laws that embody a far more fundamental dependence on the history and/or context of the object of knowledge than was ever contemplated" in psychoanalysis (17). That Grünbaum could suppose the history of a particle is comparable to that of a human being attests to his incomprehension of the essential insight of hermeneutics since Wilhelm Dilthey (J. Phillips 1987, 600).[5] To borrow Grünbaum's own words, the reader "may well

---

5. "A person and an atom are not the same kind of object, and it seems clear that metapsychology springs from the assumption that the only type of scientific study that is truly scientific is one that reduces all phenomena to their lowest, physical terms" (Guntrip 1961, 130).

be forgiven for wondering" whether he himself has "decided just what he wants to maintain."

It is also disappointing that Grünbaum should belittle those who have attempted to work critically in the psychoanalytic tradition. In spite of their "fundamental defects," he tells us, Freud's arguments are "mind-boggling" in their superiority to those of his "neo-revisionist epigoni, let alone of their apologists" (247). In the opinion of Frederick Crews, Grünbaum has "irremediably exposed" psychoanalysis as a "speculative cult," and analysts "have not proved capable of subjecting Freudian ideas to the unsparing criticism that would typify a genuinely empirical discipline" (1986, 81, 24). But nowhere do Crews or Grünbaum cite the work of ethologically oriented analysts such as Suttie, Bowlby, and Daniel Stern, all of whom have truly subjected Freud's ideas to "unsparing criticism." Indeed, in his major synthesis of psychoanalysis and developmental psychology, Stern explicitly warns that when these two perspectives conflict, "it is psychoanalysis that will have to give way" (1985, 17). If, as Crews claims, Grünbaum's book is distinguished by its "fairness and exhaustive rigor" (1986, 82), then perhaps the work of Stern should be dismissed as that of a member of a "speculative cult"; but I think it is rather the heirs of Freud whose thinking is genuinely critical and the opponents of psychoanalysis who are wearing self-imposed blinders.

My own position, as I have tried to make clear, is that there is a complementary relation between psychoanalysis and natural science. The achievement of the object relations school has been precisely to clear away the detritus of Freud's instinct theory—a relic of nineteenth-century psychophysics—and to place the psychodynamic understanding of human development on a sound empirical foundation. Stern's (1985, 39) citation of proof that three-day-old infants turn their heads in the direction of breast pads smelling of their mother's milk must impress us with its demonstration of the intertwining of cognitive and affective processes beginning at birth.[6] Harlow's empirical finding that an adult female rhesus monkey reared in isolation habitually sucked her own breast, as a male did his own penis (Bowlby 1969, 219), strikingly corroborates Fairbairn's emphasis on the primacy of the

6. Stern's work refutes Margaret Mahler's (1968) hypothesis that the newborn infant exists in a state of "normal autism." This conclusion extends Balint's (1937) critique of Freud's theory of primary narcissism.

libidinal object: "Thumb-sucking thus represents a technique for deal-ing with an unsatisfactory object relationship; and the same may be said for masturbation" (1941, 33). As Winnicott has contended, "When a child is stealing and after the therapeutic consultation there is no more stealing, then there is a strong presumption that the work done in the consultation was effective and therefore based on a theory which is not altogether incorrect" (1971e, 215).

Although compatible with natural science, psychoanalysis can by no means be reduced to it. On the contrary, in clinical practice psycho-analysis is inextricably bound up with hermeneutics. After all, neither a particle nor an animal can be analyzed, because both are incapable of language, and this distinction between human and nonhuman objects of knowledge must be maintained if we are not to fall into the absurdity of Grünbaum's conception of history. As Stanley Leavy has written: "In the dialogue with persons one is never in the position of putting nature to the question, when the observer is a subject examining an outside object. For as soon as we talk together we are not strange to one another; we acquire one another's words and accordingly live in one another's world" (1980, 31). Rank defines psychoanalysis as a "science of relations" (1929b, 20), and this phrase cannot be bettered as a summation of the double-edged quality of object relations theory.

To justify the reconciliation of psychoanalysis with hermeneutics, however, a further objection needs to be addressed. Morris Eagle, who sees that object relations theory requires a revision of Freud's concepts of drives and psychic structure, nonetheless rejects the view of psycho-analysis as a hermeneutic discipline because it founders on the prob-lems of "reliability" and "criteria for knowledge" (1984, 164).[7] (This mixed position can be compared with that of Viderman, who embraces hermeneutics but remains rigidly orthodox in his attitude to the psy-choanalytic situation.) According to Eagle, if a Kohutian and a classical Freudian analyst "each claims that, on the basis of empathy, he has achieved the knowledge that the primary bases for his patient's diffi-culties are, respectively, self-defects and oedipal conflict" (164), there is

7. See also André Green, who does not "share the views of some who see psychoanalysis as a branch of hermeneutics. . . . I do not believe that all inter-pretations have the same value, or that their relation to truth depends solely on one's point of view" (1986, 14). As I argue in the text, this objection reflects a misconception of the nature of hermeneutics.

no way to arbitrate the dispute. What is more, since hermeneutics holds that "different interpretations or formulations are only constructions," then all such constructions are "equally effective," and "the issue of reliability can be bypassed" (165).

But Eagle's case against hermeneutics rests on a fallacy, for it is not a reliance on empathy in clinical practice that prevents the Kohutian and the classical analyst from settling their differences but their initial theoretical assumptions. In addition, as Eagle acknowledges, it is not intrinsic to a hermeneutic point of view, but only to "the extreme relativistic version of it" (165), to suppose that all interpretations are equal. This untenable brand of hermeneutics is advocated by Donald Spence, who maintains that "interpretations are persuasive . . . not because of their evidential value but because of their rhetorical appeal; conviction emerges because the fit is good, not because we have made contact with the past" (1976, 32). But Spence assumes a set of false dichotomies, for it is only when a reconstruction "makes contact with the past" that it is likely to offer a "good fit" in the present, and the "rhetorical appeal" of interpretations is inseparable from their "evidential value."[8] Surely an abuse of the hermeneutic position does not constitute an argument against its proper use. Above all, Eagle goes astray when he contends that "the accuracy of interpretations is not so much defined by the patient's response . . . as by such criteria as whether the interpretation is in accord with what is known about the syndrome from which the patient is suffering" (167). Although an analyst must possess a coherent theory of human development and pathology, no a priori diagnostic label can offer more reliable grounds for assessing the validity of an interpretation than the response of a specific patient.[9]

To the extent that interpretations are always constructions, Eagle's

8. See also Paul Ricoeur, who argues against the similarly extreme hermeneutic position of Roy Schafer. If there were no external validation for interpretations, Ricoeur contends "psychoanalytic statements [would turn] into the rhetoric of persuasion under the pretext that it is the account's acceptability to the patient that is therapeutically effective" (1977, 862).

9. "It has always been taught that the right time to interpret is the moment when the patient is nearly seeing something important and just needs a bit of help over the last bit of resistance. But you cannot teach a candidate how to know when that moment has come" (Guntrip 1971, 183).

rejection of hermeneutics goes to the heart of psychoanalysis itself. Here we return to Grünbaum (1984, 127–72), who gives the name of the "tally argument" to Freud's assertion that the analyst's interpretations will be effective only if they "tally with what is real" in the patient (1916–17, 452). Grünbaum dismisses this claim as insufficient to exempt psychoanalysis from the charge of being a form of suggestion treatment, but the underlying problem is what the word *real* can mean in a psychoanalytic context. One of Freud's reasons for abandoning the seduction theory, expressed in his letter to Fliess of September 21, 1897, was that "there are no indications of reality in the unconscious" (Masson 1985, 264). Elsewhere Freud writes: "The second phase [in a sequence of three scenes] is the most important and the most momentous of all. But we may say in a sense that it has never had a real existence. It is never remembered, it has never succeeded in becoming conscious. It is a construction of analysis, but it is no less a necessity on that account" (1919a, 185). If a scene that has no "real existence" can be the "most momentous of all," then the issue of "reliability" is faced as acutely by Freud as by any avowedly hermeneutic analyst.

Freud, however, escapes the dangers of extreme hermeneutic relativism, for even a countertransferentially reconstructed scene must indeed "tally with what is real" in the experience of the patient if it is to possess therapeutic efficacy. To say that the criterion for validity of interpretations in the analytic dialogue is an intersubjective fit is not, it bears repeating, to say that all interpretations are equal. Nor does it follow that psychodynamic therapy is merely the result of suggestion, for this leaves out of account both sides of a paradoxical truth: although only the patients themselves possess the answers to their own problems (and hence interpretations that are off the mark ultimately will not take), a continuous phenomenon of resistance still interferes with the gaining of insight. Nor is it any serious objection to psychoanalysis that therapists of various theoretical persuasions should arrive at various kinds of insight with their patients. Since therapy is a process of dialogue, in which the most important curative factor is the personal relationship between analyst and patient, no two analyses will unfold alike, and the power to do good or ill is not restricted to the members of any single school.

In conclusion, it is essential to distinguish between the evidence for psychoanalytic propositions that can be gathered inside and outside the clinical session. Whereas outside evidence is subject to empirical corroboration, inside evidence is necessarily context-bound and non-repeatable.[10] These are the two faces of psychoanalysis: science and hermeneutics. To draw an analogy from literary criticism, some questions are in principle capable of definitive resolution—for instance, those involved in establishing a reliable text. But other questions are inherently unanswerable—those that ask what the text means. The data drawn from empirical research, whether on human or nonhuman subjects, have led to revisions in psychoanalytic theory, just as Freud's secondary drive model of the infant-mother bond has been refuted by the experiments of Harlow. But no externally measured demonstration of the effects of maternal deprivation on a child can give us direct access to how that experience actually felt or enable us to exercise the therapeutic skill that might begin to heal it. For this reason, there is still no substitute for case histories, provided most notably by the members of the Middle Group—Winnicott (1971e), Milner (1968), and Patrick Casement (1985, 1990)—as an instrument of communicable psychoanalytic knowledge.

The life and works of Freud can never be equaled as a source of psychoanalytic inspiration and insight. Yet in the years since Freud's death many of his ideas have been called into question, and psychoanalytic theory has undergone extensive modification. This paradox whereby Freud is at once insuperable and out-of-date encapsulates the ineradicably ambiguous character of psychoanalysis as a discipline partaking equally of the "two cultures" of science and humanism (Khan 1972). Whereas there is a progressive dynamism in science, one discovery rendering a previous one obsolete, in the humanities the creation of a new masterwork does not diminish the authority of the old. In this respect, Freud is as ageless as Shakespeare and as time-bound as Newton.

The central issue in psychoanalysis today is the elusive but indispensable concept of the self. Grounded in the theory of Fairbairn and the practice of Winnicott, it receives its most explicit formulation in the writings of Guntrip: "The problem of having an unquestioned possession or else a lack of sense of personal reality and selfhood, the identity problem, is the biggest single issue that can be raised about human existence" (1971, 119). Likewise, although Stern errs in asserting that

10. See, however, the paper by David Mark (in press), who has shown that Freud's theory of motivated forgetting can be tested experimentally using audiotapes of psychotherapeutic sessions.

object relations theorists "never considered the self as the primary organizing principle" (1985, 26), he focuses his synthesis of psychoanalysis and developmental psychology on "the development of the sense of self, not encumbered or confused with issues of the development of the ego or id" (19).[11] Finally, as Oliver Sacks has written: "If a man has lost a leg or an eye, he knows he has lost a leg or an eye; but if he has lost a self—himself—he cannot know it, because he is no longer there to know it" (1987, 35–36). The "neurology of identity" that Sacks expounds with such poignance in his "clinical tales" (viii) is the culmination of the fusion of science and hermeneutics in a psychoanalytic weltanschauung.

11. In the French psychoanalytic tradition, Didier Anzieu has drawn on infant research to explore the origins of "the sense of being a unique Self" in early experience of a "skin ego" (1985, 58).

2 ♦ THE BIRTH OF OEDIPUS

Oedipus the King sustains more than one reading for
psychoanalysts, too.—André Green, "Oedipus, Freud,
and Us"

My concern with the theme of birth in *Oedipus the King* is part of
a broader focus on pregenital or "preoedipal" issues in the
play. In a recent paper, Robert Michels has drawn attention to
the role of preoedipal dynamics in shaping Oedipus's character.

> It is important to separate what Oedipus did not consciously know about his
> past into two categories: one involves that which he knew but was desper-
> ately disavowing—the murder of his father Laius and his marriage to his
> mother Jocasta, both of which occurred after he was able to register them
> mentally; the other includes those major traumas that occurred before he
> was able to remember or register them—his abandonment by his parents,
> his physical mutilation, and his adoption. Oedipus (and we) may have been
> preoccupied with his oedipal sins, but it was these preoedipal traumas that
> shaped his characterologic pathology. (1986, 614)

Michels's distinction between Oedipus's actively repressed knowledge of his deeds of incest and patricide and his not even recollected
earlier traumas of exposure and mutilation precisely registers the contrast between the triangular stage of oedipal conflict and the prior
dyadic stage of infantile dependence on the mother. When disturbances (almost always due to a failure of environmental provision)
interfere with development in this earliest period, an individual is
unlikely to reach the neurotic harbor of the Oedipus complex but will
rather remain in the borderline condition of fractured selfhood that
Michael Balint (1968) has indelibly named the "basic fault." Because of
his massive infantile traumas, Oedipus exhibits the severe psychopathology associated with preoedipal dynamics, which Michels identifies as his "impulsive" behavior and his susceptibility to attacks of
"narcissistic rage" (1986, 600).

But Michels does not extend this valuable exploration of the pre-oedipal realm to a consideration of the motif of birth in the play. In the discussion that follows I shall proceed on the assumption that the analysis of a myth or literary text may disclose intricacies as subtle as those met with in any clinical case. I thus disagree with the contention of Stanley Leavy (1985) that the Oedipus complex must undergo a "demythologizing" in order for its conceptual richness to be appreciated. On the contrary, Sophocles' tragedy qualifies as a classic because it will invariably be found to anticipate and contain the insights painstakingly elaborated by theory. According to Leavy, "Freud's supplementary doctrine of the 'complete' Oedipus complex is, in effect, his own early demythologizing of the concept. He did not allow the myth to restrict his vision" (451). But as I have previously argued (1987, 257–59), it is precisely by portraying Oedipus as a man who loves and identifies with his father (his predecessor on the throne of Thebes) and seeks to kill his mother (upon learning that it was she who exposed him in infancy) that Sophocles shows his grasp of the complete Oedipus complex, and in a manner that strikingly replicates not only the theory but also the life of Freud.[1] Far from "restricting our vision," literary texts and artistic images offer inexhaustible sources of inspiration for the inward gaze needed in clinical work (Spitz 1988).

For better or worse, the name of Otto Rank is indelibly linked with the concept of the birth trauma. As the work that precipitated Rank's break with the psychoanalytic movement, *The Trauma of Birth* (1924b) has from the time of its first publication been enmeshed in controversy. I do not propose to reopen those debates here but will rather simply take for granted that birth, like the loss of the nipple in weaning and of feces in bowel movements, constitutes an experience of separation underlying the castration complex (Stärcke 1921). It was, after all, Freud who first asserted in a footnote added in 1909 to *The Interpretation of Dreams* that "*the act of birth is the first experience of anxiety, and thus the source and prototype of the affect of anxiety*" (1900, 400–1); and Rank initially regarded his own work as building upon the foundation Freud

1. To my earlier analysis I would add that a similarly complete Oedipus complex is present in the character of Hamlet, whose heterosexual fantasies of patricide and incest underlie the idealization of the memory of his deceased father and friendship with Horatio and his violently aggressive behavior toward both Gertrude and Ophelia.

had established. Accordingly, I shall treat *The Trauma of Birth* as a contribution to classical psychoanalysis that anticipates developments in contemporary theory.

From the first, Rank's discussion of the birth trauma possessed a double focus. In addition to highlighting its importance as the paradigm for anxiety, he related the birth trauma to the analytic situation. Indeed, Rank begins his work by remarking that birth symbolism frequently accompanies the end phases of a successful analysis and by arguing that the patient's separation from the analyst therefore constitutes a reenactment of the infant's earliest separation from the mother. Rank equates healing with rebirth and draws attention to the spiritual and infantile meanings of this equation, but he remains (at this phase of his career) firmly psychoanalytic in stressing the primacy of the regressive dimension. "I was struck on the one hand by the infantile character of the 'rebirth-phantasy,' and on the other hand by its 'anagogic' character, which has been valued to excess by Jung to the neglect of its libidinal tendencies, and hence has been misleading theoretically" (1924b, 3). In turning now to *Oedipus the King*, I shall retain this double focus of the concept of birth trauma, examining its recapitulation in the action of the play before treating birth as an event in the life of the infant Oedipus.

Oedipus the King is important for psychoanalysis not only because it depicts the incest and patricide that make up the contents of the classical Oedipus complex but also because, as Freud noted in *The Interpretation of Dreams,* its action resembles the "work of a psychoanalysis" (1900, 262). What vitally contributes to this effect is that key characters in the play participate simultaneously in Oedipus's present and past. The Messenger who arrives from Corinth with the news that Oedipus's foster father, Polybus, is dead happens to be the same man who gave the infant Oedipus to the king and queen of Corinth for adoption. Similarly, the old Herdsman initially summoned because he was the sole surviving witness to the murder of Laius is also the man who took the infant Oedipus from Jocasta and gave him to his Corinthian counterpart.

Compressing the functions of characters in *Oedipus the King* may be artistically economical, but it is also thematically integrated into the play: the same redundancy extends to Jocasta, who has a dual identity as Oedipus's wife and mother. Indeed, the central fact of incest, which confounds generations and arrests the passage of time, gives rise to this blurring of past and present, for which Sophocles has provided so brilliant a structural correlative. Transference, or the reliving of past experiences in the present, arises in any analysis but has a literal applicability to the case of Oedipus; for him the present *is* his past. Oedipus at once blinds himself when he makes the connection between himself as a grown man and as a child: "I am he."

The sense of the play as an analytic process is reinforced by the manner in which it enacts a return to Oedipus's infancy. The Messenger and then the Herdsman take Oedipus increasingly further back into his past. The climax of this regressive movement comes when the Herdsman discloses that he received the newborn Oedipus from Jocasta to be exposed to die but gave him instead to the Corinthian Messenger. (Sophocles' specification of the mother as the one responsible for exposing the child represents a departure from traditional sources.) Oedipus then calls for a sword and rushes into the palace in search of Jocasta. Upon discovering that she has hanged herself, Oedipus seizes the brooches from her robe and puts out his own eyes.

Oedipus's bursting into the palace, which is recounted in the climactic speech by the Second Messenger, permits an elaboration of the pattern of regression depicted in the play.[2] In addition to becoming an infant once again, Oedipus specifically reenters his mother's womb, first passing through the doors of the palace and then through the doors of the bedchamber. I follow here the powerful reading of John Hay.

> It may be pointed out, at the risk of seeming too clinically exact, that the two doorways through which [Oedipus] passes . . . symbolize both vaginal and cervical entrances respectively, and thus *the bedchamber symbolizes precisely the womb*. Oedipus is symbolically retracing the route of his own incestuous seed, and that of his father before him, to the homosporic (same-sown) womb— there to confront his beginnings; there to die; there to be reconceived; thence to be reborn and to issue forth, once again through the same gates, transfigured. (1979, 103)

In *Thalassa*, Ferenczi argues that human life is motivated by the compulsion to return to the womb and outlines the "threefold manner" in which regression to the womb takes place in the male during sexual intercourse. "The whole organism attains this goal by purely

---

2. The argument in this section draws upon that previously advanced in my *Freud and Oedipus* (1987), 259–62.

hallucinatory means, somewhat as in sleep; the penis, with which the organism as a whole associates itself, attains it partially or symbolically; while only the sexual secretion possesses the prerogative, as representative of the ego and its narcissistic double, the genital, of attaining *in reality* to the womb of the mother" (1923, 18). In an earlier essay Ferenczi first proposed publicly the now canonical interpretations of Oedipus's self-blinding, considered a displaced act of castration, and his name, Swollen Foot, considered an allusion to an erect penis. If, as Ferenczi affirms, "the myth completely identifies with a phallus the man who achieved the monstrous feat of sexual intercourse with the mother" (1912, 263), following the evolution of his thought to *Thalassa* leads us to concur that Oedipus—upon reentering the palace and the bedchamber—also becomes identified with the "sexual secretion" and exercises its "prerogative" of "attaining *in reality* to the womb of the mother."[3]

This interpretation of Oedipus as not only a phallus but also a spermatozoon finds confirmation in the language of Sophocles' play. After Jocasta disappears into the palace, having grasped the truth from the Corinthian Messenger, Oedipus vows: "Burst out what will! However small it be, / I shall will to see my seed" (ll. 1076–77). On one level, Oedipus resolves not to be deterred by what he mistakenly believes to be Jocasta's fears concerning the lowliness of his birth. As I have literally translated them, however, the final words express at another level Oedipus's desire to "see my seed"—a desire he achieves when he revisits the bedchamber representing Jocasta's homosporic womb.

The sexual symbolism of Oedipus's entrance into the palace amplifies the sexual symbolism subtending the central motif of the crossroads. The crossroads where Oedipus slays Laius is described as both a "narrow pass" and a "split road." Karl Abraham, who notes the terms, interprets them as allusions to distinct aspects of the female genitalia: the narrow pass to their shape, and the split road, or "trifurcation," to their location at "the two thighs which join together at the trunk" (1922, 85). Most interestingly, Abraham proceeds to correlate the two references to the crossroads with divergent infantile fantasies: whereas the trifurcation, "the place of heavy traffic, clearly represents the mother as a prostitute," the narrow pass "gives expression to another

---

3. Ferenczi's enthusiasm interferes here with his logic, since it is of course the womb of the sexual partner—and not that of the mother—that the "sexual secretion" normally reaches. In the case of Oedipus this distinction falls away.

fantasy, that of encountering the father inside the mother's body before birth; the fantasy of observing coitus from within the womb" (85).

Of these two fantasies, "observing coitus from within the womb"
bears particular relevance to Oedipus's breaking into the palace. When
Jocasta withdraws, as the Second Messenger reports, she execrates the
marriage bed and calls not on Oedipus but on her former husband, the
long-dead Laius. Thus, when Oedipus arrives at the bedchamber, he
encounters his father, as it were, inside his mother's body. This moment
in *Oedipus the King* may be glossed by Freud's exegesis of the concept of
the primal scene in the case of the Wolf Man. When "there is a wish to
be back in a situation when one was in the mother's genitals," Freud
writes, "the man is identifying himself with his own penis and using it
to represent himself" (1918, 102). For the bisexual Wolf Man, moreover, the fantasy is not simply one of engaging in sexual intercourse
with the mother; it is also a fantasy of returning to the womb "in order
that he might be copulated with there by the father . . . and might bear
him a child" (101).

In *The Trauma of Birth*, Rank seizes on this passage from Freud to
bolster his own contention that the origin of primal scene fantasies lies
in the "intrauterine Oedipus situation," where the paternal phallus
disturbs the "blessed peace" enjoyed by the fetus in its mother's womb.
Indeed, he goes so far as to characterize this prenatal occurrence as the
"nuclear complex of the neuroses," of which the later Oedipus complex is merely the "psychosexual elaboration" (1924b, 194). Rank's
extension of the Oedipus complex to the intrauterine state is a theoretical fantasy, but it strikingly corresponds to the dynamics not only of
Freud's most celebrated case history but also of *Oedipus the King*.

If Oedipus's entrance into the palace culminates his return to his
origins, then his reemergence is a symbolic rebirth. Through his self-
blinding, an act of desperation, Oedipus comes to accept the knowledge of himself that had eluded him as long as his vision was directed
outward. Like Teiresias, he accedes to a higher—indeed, religious—
level of awareness. In an uncanny dovetailing with Christian myth,
Oedipus answers Nicodemus's query to Jesus concerning the mystery
of rebirth in John 3:4: "How can a man be born when he is old? Can he
enter the second time into his mother's womb, and be born?"[4] In
seeking to provide for the welfare of his daughters, Oedipus exhibits a

4. Jung penetratingly discusses the dialogue between Jesus and Nicodemus
in his treatment of the symbolism of rebirth (1912, 252–54).

hitherto untapped capacity for altruistic love. This breakthrough heralds what Balint (1932) has called the moment of "new beginning" in analytic treatment. The entire myth may be said to move between infantile and anagogic poles, and Oedipus's reappearance marks the moment of peripeteia between the two aspects of the rebirth-fantasy.

The birth symbolism in the analytic drama of *Oedipus the King* is paralleled by the actual importance of birth in the life of Oedipus. As Winnicott observes in "Birth Memories, Birth Trauma, and Anxiety": "When there has been a normal birth experience, birth material is not likely to come into the analysis in a way that calls attention to itself. . . . When, however, birth experience has been traumatic it has set a pattern. This pattern appears in various details which will need to be interpreted and dealt with each in its own right, at the appropriate time" (1949, 180). Rank had earlier reached the same conclusion: "As to the aetiological significance of the birth trauma . . . there are only quantitative factors which decide" (1930a, 23). A birth trauma, then, is properly spoken of only when there has been a birth experience of unusual severity, which, in Winnicott's language, has resulted in an insupportable interruption of continuity of being. It is, I would add, a tragicomic commentary on Rank's neglect by later psychoanalysts that Winnicott's sole mention of Rank, to my knowledge, occurs in this paper when he recounts the dream of a young psychotic female patient (whose birth had indeed been traumatic), dreamed in reaction to reading *The Trauma of Birth*.

That Oedipus, too, had a traumatic birth is indisputable—especially if it is permissible to consider the piercing of his ankles and his threatened exposure as an extension of the birth process. In the Moses story, as Rank contends in *The Myth of the Birth of the Hero*, "the exposure in the water signifies no more and no less than the *symbolic expression of birth*" (1909, 69). Even though the amniotic element of water is lacking in the Oedipus myth, the perilous experience of exposure remains bound up with that of birth.[5]

Beyond question, the parents of Oedipus attempted to prevent his birth and survival. As Rank points out, there is in myths a "tendency to represent the parents as the first and most powerful opponents of the hero." He continues: "The entire family romance owes its origin to the

5. As Rank (1912, 259) notes, in the earliest versions of the legend the infant Oedipus was in fact put out to sea in a small chest.

feeling of being neglected—namely, the assumed hostility of the parents. In the myth, this hostility goes so far that the parents refuse to let the child be born" (1909, 72). Set against this backdrop, the scene at the crossroads in which Oedipus meets and slays his father, Laius, can justly be seen as a reenactment of the birth trauma at the oedipal level.

The theme of birth in *Oedipus the King* is bound up with the Sphinx's riddle, which Freud interprets as an allusion to "the oldest and most burning question that confronts immature humanity," that is, the "origin of babies" (1907, 135).[6] Rank identifies the Sphinx, whose name means "strangler," as "the nuclear symbol of primal anxiety," resulting from the act of birth (1924b, 143): "The Oedipus saga is certainly a duplicate of the Sphinx episode, which means psychologically that it is the repetition of the primal trauma at the sexual stage (Oedipus complex), whereas the Sphinx represents the primal trauma itself" (144). In other words, the birth trauma is to the Oedipus complex what the Sphinx episode is to the action of *Oedipus the King*. In drawing this parallel, Rank provides a metaphor for the ideal balance between his perspective and that of Freud.

Rank's recognition in *The Myth of the Birth of the Hero* that "the future hero has actually overcome the greatest difficulties by virtue of his birth" (1909, 73) foreshadows his formulation of a full-fledged theory of the birth trauma fifteen years later. Ironically, *The Trauma of Birth,* which heralded Rank's own traumatic struggle for intellectual autonomy, was at first not merely dedicated to Freud but offered to him as a *birthday* present (Menaker 1982, 63). As I have already intimated, Rank's theory of the birth trauma—beyond its limited literal scope— remains important for contemporary psychoanalysis as an early attempt to grapple with the vital issues of separation and individuation.

Rank comments that the father's "refusal to let the son be born . . . is frequently concealed by the contrasting motif, the wish for a child . . . , while the hostile attitude to the future successor on the throne and in the kingdom is projected to the outside—it is attributed to an oracular verdict" (1909, 73). As mythographers know, the account of the oracle

6. In a related attempt to link the Sphinx to parental intercourse and birth, Géza Róheim suggests that her riddle, which delineates a "being with an indefinite number of legs," evokes the "combined body" glimpsed by the child in the primal scene, "father and mother in one person" (1934, 8). For a recent interpretation, which concludes that the Sphinx's riddle has to do with the denial of the importance of the mother, see Lidz 1988.

given to Laius in *Oedipus the King* differs considerably from that found in Sophocles' legendary sources. According to these earlier versions, Laius incurred the wrath of Hera by abducting and committing homosexual rape upon Chrysippus, the son of King Pelops. In retaliation, Hera warned him not to have intercourse with his wife, because the child of that union would grow up to kill him. In a drunken stupor, or seduced by Jocasta, Laius disregarded the prohibition and begat Oedipus.

Elsewhere I have stressed that the distinctiveness of Sophocles' treatment resides precisely in his *suppression* of this material, thereby making *Oedipus the King* into a universal tragedy of self-knowledge told from the son's point of view (1987, 255–56). Nonetheless, in a study of the myth, the motif of regression I have traced back to Oedipus's birth may legitimately be extended to take in the history of his entire family. Everything depends on whether we wish to adopt the individualistic outlook of classical psychoanalysis or a collective orientation.[7] From the latter perspective, even Laius is finally not to blame, since the oracle may signify not so much his private filicidal desires as the burden of inherited guilt that oppresses the entire Labdacid line.

In *Modern Education,* Rank frontally attacks Freud's theory of the Oedipus complex as "an expression of the individual psychology of the son" and reinterprets the myth from the standpoint of his own later thought. The heart of the matter is now said to inhere in the desire for immortality exhibited in complementary ways by Laius and Oedipus.

> The boy was immediately exposed after birth, because the father wanted no successor but wanted to be his own immortal successor, a desire which the myth presents in the incest of Oedipus with his mother. . . . For as little as the father wants to continue to exist only in his sons, just as little has the son an inclination to play only the part of a successor to the father. . . . This inner resistance of the man against any kind of racial [i.e., biological] role, whether that of the father or that of the son, is presented in the Oedipus saga as an external strife between father and son. (1932b, 193–94)

This sociological approach to the Oedipus myth, which polemically reduces the themes of both patricide and incest to epiphenomenal status, seems far removed from psychoanalysis, but it may be assimilated to a contemporary Freudian reading. A bridge is furnished by Rank's declaration in *Will Therapy.*

---

7. See Krüll 1979 for a biographical study of Freud that employs this theory of family systems.

The fear in birth, which we have designated as fear of life, seems to me actually the fear of having to live as an isolated individual, and not the reverse, the fear of the loss of individuality (death fear). That would mean, however, that primary fear corresponds to a fear of separation from the whole, therefore a fear of individuation, on account of which I should like to call it a fear of life, although it may appear later as fear of the loss of this dearly bought individuality, as fear of death, of being dissolved again into the whole. Between these two fear possibilities, these poles of fear, the individual is thrown back and forth all his life, which accounts for the fact that we have not been able to trace fear back to a single root, or to overcome it therapeutically. (1929–31, 124)

Rank here extends his concept of the birth trauma beyond its biological parameters to address the tasks of separation and individuation that each human being faces throughout life. His polarity of "life fear" and "death fear" strikingly prefigures Margaret Mahler's definition of the rapprochement subphase as "the mainspring of man's eternal struggle against both fusion and isolation" (1972, 231). An intermediate link between Rank and Mahler is provided by Fairbairn, who found in his patients "the most striking evidence of a conflict between an extreme reluctance to abandon infantile dependence and a desperate longing to renounce it" (1941, 39). Fairbairn adds: "Although one of these attitudes may come to predominate, there is in the first instance a constant oscillation between them owing to the anxiety attendant on each" (43).

As Esther Menaker has written: "To be born means to be responsible for one's own separate existence and survival; and in this separateness man experiences his own finiteness; he comes to know death, to fear the loss of his hard-won individuality, and to perceive the connection between birth and death" (1982, 64). To this Rankian insight I would append only the psychoanalytic proviso that the knowledge of the connection between birth and death is inevitably mediated by the discovery of sexuality. As Teiresias warns Oedipus in *Oedipus the King:* "This day will give you birth and will destroy you" (l. 438). Oedipus, whose birth was the greatest obstacle to his existence, indeed comes to perceive the inseparability of birth and death by confronting his own deeds of incest and patricide in the course of the single day's analytic work of the play.

Having established the role played by the birth trauma in the life of Oedipus, I now return to *Oedipus the King* as an analytic process and to the therapeutic dimension of Rank's contribution. As is well known, a cornerstone of the collaborative work of Ferenczi and Rank is that it is "not only absolutely unavoidable that the patient should, during the cure, repeat a large part of his process of development, but . . . it is a matter of just those portions which cannot be really experienced from memory, so that there is no other way open to the patient than that of repeating" (1923, 3). By raising the issue of the proper balance between recollection and repetition and stressing particularly those developmental phases "which cannot be really experienced from memory," Ferenczi and Rank join Michels, who contrasts the two categories of events outside Oedipus's consciousness: his oedipal crimes of incest and patricide about "which he knew but was desperately disavowing" and those preoedipal traumas of mutilation and abandonment "that occurred before he was able to remember or register them."

If we combine Ferenczi and Rank's "active" view of therapy with Michels's comments on the unremembered traumas of Oedipus's earliest years, we arrive at a fresh understanding of the analogy between the action of *Oedipus the King* and the work of psychoanalysis: the analytic process undergone by Oedipus consists not only in the *gain of intellectual insight* but also in the *emotionally charged reliving of his infantile traumas*. (This distinction may also be applied to the spectator of Sophocles' drama, whose theory—psychoanalytic or otherwise—of the meaning of Oedipus's fate must accommodate the pity and fear produced by Oedipus's sufferings as they are enacted on the stage.) Fairbairn observes that "the Oedipus situation is one that has its roots in the vicissitudes of infantile dependence." He elaborates his revisionist view: "It is a remarkable fact that psychoanalytical interest in the classical story of Oedipus should have been concentrated so preponderantly upon the final stages of the drama, and that the earliest stages should have been so largely ignored. . . . The same Oedipus who eventually killed his father and married his mother began life by being exposed upon a mountain, and thus being deprived of maternal care in all its aspects at a stage when his mother constituted his exclusive object" (1954, 116).

This passage makes it clear how deeply we have penetrated into the territory of object relations theory. In the case of a severely regressed patient, Winnicott insists, the essential ingredient is not interpretation but the analyst's provision of a reliable holding environment. "In the treatment of *schizoid* persons the analyst needs to know all about the interpretations that might be made on the material presented, but he must be able to refrain from being sidetracked into doing this work that is inappropriate because the main need is for an unclever ego-support, or a holding. This 'holding,' like the task of the mother in infant-care, acknowledges tacitly the tendency of the patient to disintegrate, to cease to exist, to fall forever" (1963f, 241). The reason the analyst needs to concentrate on the holding function, of course, is generally that the schizoid patient's mother failed to perform her task of infant-care in "good-enough" fashion. Balint makes the similar point that the patient at the level of the basic fault, unlike the neurotic oedipal patient, is unable to internalize verbal interpretations *as interpretations* but rather responds to them as attacks or seductions. From this realization, Balint proceeds to discuss the technical problems inherent in "managing" the severely regressed individual (1968, 11–17).

In exploring the linguistic gulf that opens up between the analyst and the schizoid patient, Balint cites Ferenczi's final paper, "Confusion of Tongues between Adults and the Child." Ferenczi is concerned with the difference between verbal and preverbal experience, as well as with the pathogenic role of actual sexual traumas suffered in childhood. His formulations anticipate not only those of Balint but also those of Winnicott: "The patient gone off into his trance is a *child indeed* who no longer reacts to intellectual explanations, only perhaps to maternal friendliness; without it he feels lonely and abandoned in his greatest need, i.e. in the same unbearable situation which at one time led to a splitting of his mind and eventually to his illness" (1933, 160). Ferenczi's recommendation that analysts exhibit a "maternal friendliness" toward deeply disturbed patients may have seemed suspiciously radical when first advanced, but by reformulating it in terms of the holding environment, Winnicott enables us to discern its inevitable rightness and integrate it into contemporary psychoanalytic theory.

In differentiating between the oedipal level of analytic work and the level of the basic fault, Balint observes that "Oedipus was an adult man" (1968, 16). But as Oedipus's preoedipal traumas make clear, his chronological age does not preclude his being an emotional child, more in need of "maternal friendliness" than "intellectual explanations." From this perspective, the traditional identification of Teiresias with the figure of the analyst—like the identification of the play as a whole with a psychoanalysis—requires modification. If Teiresias is indeed an analyst, he is a bad one, who gives way to countertransferential anger and advances prematurely intellectualized interpretations (Michels 1986, 601).

In pursuing the clinical implications of Oedipus's severely regressed state, I have derived great clarification from Winnicott's posthumously published paper "Fear of Breakdown." Winnicott points out that "what we see clinically is always a defence organization, even in the autism of childhood schizophrenia. The underlying agony is unthinkable" (1974, 90).[8] It is suggestive to consider all the characters in *Oedipus the King*—Teiresias, Creon, Jocasta, the Messenger, the Herdsman—as manifesting various forms of "defence organization," though only that of Oedipus may properly be termed psychotic.

Winnicott's most brilliant idea in this paper is that the breakdown feared in the analysis has *already taken place* but has *not yet been experienced*, because it occurred before the ego was sufficiently mature to master it.

> There are moments . . . when a patient needs to be told that the breakdown, a fear of which destroys his or her life, *has already been*. It is a fact that is carried round hidden away in the unconscious. . . . In this special context the unconscious means that the ego integration is not able to encompass something. . . . In other words the patient must go on looking for the past detail which is *not yet experienced*. This search takes the form of a looking for this detail in the future. (90–91)

The analysis therefore aims to enable the patient to *experience* what has already *happened* and thereby relegate it definitively to the past. "If the patient is ready for some kind of acceptance of this queer kind of truth, that what is not yet experienced did nevertheless happen in the past, then the way is open for the agony to be experienced in the transference, in reaction to the analyst's failures and mistakes" (91). Winnicott's emphasis on the analyst's "failures and mistakes" as the inevitable catalytic agent allowing the patient to recollect "the original failure of the facilitating environment" (91) is characteristically modest. He was preceded in this wisdom by Ferenczi, an equally great therapist, who speaks of "the willingness to admit our mistakes" as an indispensable ingredient in building the disturbed patient's confidence "*that establishes the contact between the present and the unbearable traumatic past*" (1933, 160).

Winnicott's exposition of the way analysis can permit the patient to experience, and hence remember, a breakdown that took place in early childhood serves as a precise gloss on the action of *Oedipus the King*.

> The patient needs to "remember" this but it is not possible to remember something that has not yet happened, and this thing of the past has not happened yet because the patient was not there for it to happen to. The only way to "remember" in this case is for the patient to experience this past thing

8. According to Winnicott's editors, this paper was probably written in 1963.

for the first time in the present, that is to say, in the transference. . . . This is
the equivalent of remembering, and this outcome is the equivalent of the
lifting of repression that occurs in the analysis of the psychoneurotic patient.
(1974, 92)

For Winnicott, as for Ferenczi and Rank, repeating takes the place of
remembering in the treatment of the schizoid patient; and as we know,
Oedipus is a severely regressed character whose most important traumas occurred "before he was able to remember or register them."

Oedipus's return to childhood and infancy as enacted in the course
of the play, culminating in his reentry into the maternal womb of the
palace bedchamber and his ensuing rebirth, entails just such a reliving
of the earliest traumas of birth and abandonment. Teiresias may be a
bad analyst, but his technical blunders of premature interpretation and
the rest, if only he could admit them, might then paradoxically represent those inevitable mistakes through which "the original failure of
the facilitating environment" is re-created in the transference and
thereby brought under the patient's control. What Oedipus needs
above all, of course, is adequate therapeutic holding; although this is
not forthcoming from either Teiresias or Creon, to whom he responds
with anger and defensiveness, it is offered by Jocasta, whom he loves
and who alone treats him with compassion and "maternal friendliness." Fittingly, whereas his exchanges with his male antagonists only
drive him deeper into resistance, Oedipus recalls and divulges his
repressed memory of what happened at the crossroads while talking
with Jocasta (Lesser 1967, 162).

Even though, at the preoedipal level, Oedipus undergoes a repetition of his infantile traumas, he succeeds by the end of *Oedipus the King*
in transforming his emotional experience into intellectual insight. I
cannot, therefore, agree with Michels that Oedipus's "quest for truth"
condemns him merely to "blind repetition" (1986, 616). (The irony in
Michels's use of the word *blind* appears to be inadvertent.) Still less can I
agree with Rank's wholly unpsychoanalytic contention that the Oedipus myth is "a warning against intellectual pride," an adjuration not "to
seek behind appearances for the true being of things, for the more one
experiences of truth, the more one knows, the unluckier one becomes"
(1929–31, 51).[9] This reading not only strips Oedipus of his heroism

9. For a restatement of this Rankian interpretation of the Oedipus myth, see
Lieberman 1985, xxviii–xxxi.

but also overlooks a key point: that a failure on his part to heed the injunction of the Delphic oracle to expose the murderer of Laius and thereby lift the plague on Thebes would scarcely have been a "luckier" alternative. Still, by attacking Freud's idealization of Oedipus (and that of an entire misogynist tradition epitomized by Schopenhauer) Rank reminds us that there is a truth of relationship, as well as of knowledge, and that Oedipus's "masculine" ruthlessness needs to be balanced by Jocasta's "feminine" capacity for tenderness.

Repudiating their earlier close association, Ferenczi insists in a critical review (1927) of Rank's *Technique of Psychoanalysis* (1926c) that emotional experience alone is not enough to effect therapeutic change. Ferenczi protests that he never meant to derogate the primacy of intellectual understanding: "But all such experiencing during an analysis was regarded by me as no more than a means for arriving rather more rapidly or more deeply at the roots of the symptoms, and this latter part of the work—the real guarantee against a relapse—was always thought of as something intellectual, the raising of an unconscious process to the preconscious level" (94). As so often, Winnicott arrives independently at the same conclusion: "One way out is for the patient to have a breakdown (physical or mental) and this can work very well. However, the solution is not good enough if it does not include analytic understanding and insight on the part of the patient" (1974, 92).

Until his self-blinding, Oedipus is a victim of the insolent behavior and the proclivity to narcissistic rage that the Greeks called hubris. As we have seen, the developmental cause of this emotional arrest lies in the conjoined traumas of birth and abandonment he suffered in early infancy. In the course of the drama, through a combination of emotional experience and intellectual insight, Oedipus overcomes his grandiosity and accepts responsibility for the incest and patricide he has unwittingly committed. As Hans Loewald has written: "Unless the oedipal level of his psychic life is available to the patient and he comes to understand it as a genuine step in his human development and not as a tragic decline from a state of grace, he remains a victim of the selfobject stage and its narcissism" (1985, 443). Through the work of his psychoanalysis, which is ultimately a self-analysis, Oedipus confronts his guilt and takes the heroic step from the basic fault to the Oedipus complex.

3 ◆ DAVID AND GOLIATH

I didn't mean to tear Freud down. We were friends
and colleagues, but I didn't realize that I was
beginning to separate from him. Although I was very
close to Freud and followed his ideas, there came a
time when I began to branch out myself and our ideas
began to differ. This was a painful experience for
both of us!—Otto Rank, reported in Ethel
Seidenman, "In Therapy with Otto Rank, 1936–38"

The story of Otto Rank is in many respects a tragic chapter in the
history of psychoanalysis. Dominated by his break from Freud
following the publication of *The Trauma of Birth,* Rank's career
has largely faded from view except as an object lesson in deviancy,
and his writings are little known today apart from such early applied
classics as *The Myth of the Birth of the Hero.* To be sure, Rank has always
had his partisans, particularly among social workers, and the sympathetic study by Esther Menaker (1982), the authoritative biography by
E. James Lieberman (1985)—supplementing the still indispensable
account by Jessie Taft (1958)—and the special issue of *American Imago*
commemorating the centenary of Rank's birth (Rudnytsky 1984) all
give grounds for hope that we are experiencing something of a Rank
revival. Nonetheless, Rank's neglect by psychoanalysts remains widespread, even though many important developments in contemporary
theory are unacknowledged elaborations of his ideas.

Rank's revolt, which took place after the cancerous malignancy was
discovered in Freud's jaw in the spring of 1923, belongs to the succession struggles of the psychoanalytic movement. Indeed, Freud's career
may be divided into three major stages, each marked by a painful
quarrel: with Fliess in the late 1890s, as psychoanalysis came into
being; with Jung (on the heels of the rift with Alfred Adler and Wilhelm Stekel) in 1912–13, as the movement reached maturity; and with

Rank in the mid-1920s, toward the close of Freud's life. Each rupture left its own bitter residue, but that with Rank was especially distasteful to Freud because it came so late and seemed to be unprovoked by anything that he himself had done.

Freud's response to the challenge posed by Rank was doubtless hardened not only by the onset of his cancer but also by the death, in 1923, of his beloved grandchild Heinele (the younger son of Sophie Halberstadt, who had herself died three years earlier, and brother of Ernst, renowned for his fort-da game, reported in *Beyond the Pleasure Principle*). On March 20, 1924, Freud wrote elegiacally to Ferenczi about the dissolution of the Committee—the cabal of his closest followers originally formed in 1913 in response to the secession of Jung—which was precipitated by Rank's backsliding. "I have survived the Committee that was to be my successor, perhaps I shall yet survive the International Association. I only hope that psychoanalysis will survive me. But taken altogether it makes a sad ending to life" (Taft 1958, 91). This idea of "surviving his successor," which could be applied equally to the death of Heinele, reveals the inseparability of familial and professional loss in Freud's mind.[1]

That Rank's relationship with Freud should have had a filial component is readily comprehensible in light of Rank's personal history. Born in 1884 and thus the youngest member of Freud's inner circle, Otto was the third of three children born to Simon and Karoline Rosenfeld. His brother, Paul, was born in 1881; his sister, Elisabet, born the following year, died in infancy. Because Simon Rosenfeld, by trade a jeweler, was an alcoholic, the family was both economically and emotionally deprived. In an autobiography written in 1903 at the precocious age of nineteen, Rank refers ironically to "an idyllic family life," in which a "deep rage" seethed inside everyone (Taft 1958, 14). The "chief antagonists" were Otto's father and brother, but he, like his mother, "could not bear a row," and the two of them "fled accordingly." (Otto eventually joined Paul, with whom he had a close yet ambivalent bond, in refusing even to speak to their father.) Although Paul was permitted to enroll in the Gymnasium, Otto was forced to attend a technical school and then to work for a pittance in a machine shop.

This toil was especially onerous to Rank because within him burned the soul of a writer. His notebooks of the time attest to his omnivorous

---

1. Compare Jacques Derrida's discussion of *Beyond the Pleasure Principle* and the prospect that "the speculator can survive the legatee" (1978, 121).

reading and innumerable literary projects. In his autobiography he charts his intellectual development in terms of his discovery of three principal authors—Schopenhauer, Ibsen, and Nietzsche—and in his diary (*Tagebuch*) he offers an astute appreciation of Darwin. Rank's course of study constituted an ideal preparation for the reading of Freud, and in October 1904 a quotation from *The Interpretation of Dreams* "appears without comment" in his notebook, "as if what he reads . . . comes naturally and is instantly put to use" (Taft 1958, 33). In Rank's reception of Freud's ideas, the connection of psychoanalysis to nineteenth-century literature and philosophy is vividly enacted. Indeed, the humanistic (and specifically romantic) roots of psychoanalysis are even more perspicuous in Rank than they are in Freud, whose avowed intellectual allegiance was to the scientific materialism of his masters Hermann von Helmholtz and Ernst Brücke.

The turning point came in 1905 when Adler, whom Rank had consulted medically, introduced him to Freud. This meeting was for Rank a dream come true on every level. Recognizing the promise shown in *The Artist,* a manuscript inspired by the twenty-one-year-old Rank's reading of Freud's early works, Freud aided in its publication in 1907 and rescued the impecunious autodidact from his loathed job. He financed Rank's studies at the University of Vienna, which granted Rank a doctorate in 1912 for a thesis on the Lohengrin legend—the first to employ a psychoanalytic methodology. Through Freud, Rank escaped his oppressive familial and cultural background and gained entry to a world of unbounded intellectual breadth and excitement. For his part, Freud secured for psychoanalysis the benefits of Rank's prodigious erudition and industry. These benefits continue to be reaped by posterity, not least because Rank kept the minutes that preserve for us what went on at the historic Wednesday evening meetings of the Vienna Psychoanalytic Society.

Unfortunately, however, the same factors that initially drew Freud and Rank together sowed the seeds of their eventual discord. Rank— who legally adopted in 1909 the non-Jewish pen name he had begun to use in 1903—turned his back on his natural father and revered Freud as his idealized surrogate.[2] Reciprocally, Freud cherished Rank as an

2. As Ellen Handler Spitz has observed, Rank's change of name reflects, in Lacanian terms, "a turning away from paternal law and prohibition altogether to an imaginary relation with the mother," a move which is later "partly enacted in the case of Rank's own theoretical writing" (1989, 99). Ironically,

adopted son. But this comfortable arrangement depended on Rank's acceptance of his filial role, which fostered in him an exaggerated submissiveness while reinforcing Freud's paternalistic tendencies. Revealing testimony about Rank's public persona during the first decade of his association with Freud is provided by Lou Andreas-Salomé in her journal. In her entry of February 12–13, 1913, Andreas-Salomé considers the threat posed to Freud's "noble egoism as investigator" by the "aggression" and "independence" of Victor Tausk and contrasts it with the docility of Rank, "who is a son and nothing but a son." She reports Freud's comment: "Why can't there be six such charming men in our circle instead of only one?" Of course, as Andreas-Salomé points out, "even in his wish for a half-dozen the individuality of the man referred to is put in doubt." During a lecture by Rank on regicide, Freud scribbled a note to Andreas-Salomé: "R. disposes of the negative aspect of his filial love by means of his interest in the psychology of regicide; that is why he is so devoted" (1964, 97–98).

The unhealthy situation created by Rank's status as Freud's amanuensis and loyal right-hand man exemplifies even as it is explained by the father-son emphasis of classical psychoanalytic theory. To be sure, oedipal dynamics governed the bond between the two men, and these dynamics eventually brought to the fore the "negative aspect" of the ambivalence that inheres in the attachment between sons and fathers. Although the centrality of the Oedipus complex to the conflict between Freud and Rank is beyond dispute, its very prominence as a personal and theoretical issue suggests that it may have screened a deeper level of emotional conflict. For Rank, the break with Freud proved in retrospect to be not merely an oedipal rebellion but a struggle for separation, a "trauma of birth" vital to his quest for autonomy both as a thinker and as a human being.

In view of the underlying maternal significance of his tie to Freud, it is ironic that Rank himself offered the most blatantly oedipal interpretation of his actions. In a circular letter (*Rundbrief*) of December 20, 1924, written at the moment of acutest crisis, Rank confesses that his behavior toward Freud and his fellow members of the Committee was motivated by his oedipal and fraternal complexes.

---

however, by 1906, Rank had moved to a Viennese street called Simon Denkgasse, which (although Simon Denk is a proper name) may be rendered as Simon Memorial Lane, and thereby inscribes a symbolic return of the repressed Name-of-the-Father (Lieberman 1985, 69).

Obviously certain things had to *happen* before I could gain the insight that my affective reactions toward the Professor and you, insofar as you represent for me the brothers near to him, stemmed from unconscious conflicts. . . . Not only have I recognized the actual cause of the crisis in the trauma occasioned by the dangerous illness of the Professor, but I was able also to understand the type of reaction and its mechanism from my childhood and family history—the Oedipus and brother complexes. I was thus obliged in reality to work out conflicts that would probably have been spared through an analysis, but which I believe I have now overcome through these painful experiences. (Taft 1958, 110)

The interpretation of this letter has proved a thorny problem for Rank's biographers. Taft maintains that at no other time did Rank "yield so completely to the dictates of emotion, at the expense of his own integrity" (1958, 110), whereas Lieberman contends that Rank's contrition may have been "at least partly an act" (1985, 250). But these accounts may be to some extent reconciled by recognizing that Rank was offering his final and most impassioned plea for readmittance to the psychoanalytic fold and hence allowed himself to frame his apology in language that he had already rejected intellectually.

Whereas Rank interpreted his collision with Freud in terms of the Oedipus complex only at one critical juncture, for Freud it remained the key to why Rank had gone astray. Hanns Sachs quotes Freud as having said of Rank, "When one has forgiven someone everything, one has finished with him" (1944, 150), but the increasingly severe criticisms of Rank scattered in Freud's writings, from "The Dissolution of the Oedipus Complex" (1924a) through *Inhibitions, Symptoms and Anxiety* (1926) to the *New Introductory Lectures* (1933) and "Analysis Terminable and Interminable" (1937), attest that he was far from having either "forgiven" or "finished with" his wayward disciple. Finally, in *Moses and Monotheism* (1939), Freud offered the vignette of "a young man whose fate it was to grow up beside a worthless father, [and who] began by developing, in defiance of him, into a capable, trustworthy and honourable person. In the prime of life his character was reversed, and thenceforward he behaved as if he had taken this same father as a model" (125). Asked by Sachs whether this was intended as a portrait of Rank, Freud confirmed it shortly before his death.

To the extent that their relationship conforms to an oedipal pattern, this tendency says at least as much about Freud as about Rank. In a memorable passage from *Beyond the Pleasure Principle,* Freud discusses the operation of fate in the lives of supposedly "normal" people.

Thus we have come across people all of whose human relationships have the same outcome: such as the benefactor who is abandoned in anger after a time by each of his *protégés,* however much they may otherwise differ from one another, and who thus seems doomed to taste all the bitterness of ingratitude; or the man whose friendships all end in betrayal by his friend; or the man who time after time in the course of his life raises someone else into a position of great private or public authority and then, after a certain interval, himself upsets that authority and replaces him by a new one. (1920, 28)

Although Freud neglects to say so, this account of the workings of the repetition compulsion is transparently autobiographical. He himself is abandoned by his protégés and betrayed by his friends, and he replaces the person he has installed in a position of authority. Indeed, these are three variations of the same basic experience, and drawing a distinction among them merely manifests the phenomenon in question. When Freud brands the repetition compulsion a "daemonic" power because what individuals take to be an externally imposed fate "is for the most part arranged by themselves and determined by early infantile influences" (21), he diagnoses his own recurrent history of oedipally charged betrayal and rebellion by his closest friends and followers as, in truth, a "fate neurosis" whose origins lie in his own early childhood.[3]

If Rank's break with Freud needs to be viewed in relation to the succession struggles of the psychoanalytic movement, its most important prototype is Jung's earlier schism. The parallel between Rank and Jung is an overdetermined one and may be approached in terms ranging from the biographical to the theoretical to the psychoanalytic-political. Biographically speaking, it is noteworthy that both Rank and Jung as boys suffered sexual seduction by an older man (Lieberman 1985, 87). Both then surely looked to Freud as an admired savior while simultaneously fearing a reprise of their earlier experience of seduction. But the analogy between Jung and Rank takes on its deepest meaning when seen from the point of view of Freud's unconscious attitude toward his potential successors. Freud's unacknowledged self-reflection in *Beyond the Pleasure Principle* was written before his rift with Rank, but its applicability to that episode underscores the extent to which Freud was himself responsible for the uncanny patterns of recurrence that shaped his life.

During the early years of psychoanalysis, of course, Freud regarded

3. For a fuller discussion of Freud's repetition compulsion, including its infantile determinants, see my *Freud and Oedipus* (1987), 18–53.

Jung as his favorite disciple. After their first meeting, he wrote to Jung, on April 7, 1907, in a hyperbolic vein: "I now realize that I am as replaceable as everyone else and that I could hope for no one better than yourself, as I have come to know you, to continue and complete my work" (McGuire 1974, 27). Freud's idealization of Jung, which was due in large measure to the latter's non-Jewish origins, as well as to his eminent position at the Burghölzli Clinic in Zurich, is regularly coupled with disparagement of his Viennese adherents, among whom he considered Rank the best of a bad lot. He continues in the same letter: "I feel sure that Rank will not get very far. His writing is positively autoerotic. . . . It goes without saying that we shall expect far more of your manner of treating the material" (28).

Even in praising Jung, however, Freud raises the specter of a potential rival. Both Jung and Rank specialized in applying psychoanalysis to the sphere of mythology, and as Jung fell from grace, Rank ascended into it. Freud saw in him his sole remaining follower whose learning could match that of the apostate angel. That this seesawing between his two most erudite disciples had an unsavory ethnic dimension emerges from a letter to Rank on August 22, 1912, in which Freud invited Rank to join him and Ferenczi on a trip to London (which was never taken) as a reward for having completed his magnum opus, *The Incest Theme in Literature and Legend:* "What is most regrettable about the changes in Zurich is the certainty that I did not succeed in bringing together Jews and anti-Semites, whom I hoped to unite on psychoanalytic ground." Freud added that his disappointment was mitigated because he did not think that the tension with Jung would lead to an open rupture, such as he had recently endured with Adler. "But who knows? In any event it is now time that we bring ourselves closer together, to which end the London trip should contribute" (Lieberman 1985, 137–38). When Jung strayed from the fold, the Aryanism that had formerly counted in his favor now stigmatized him as an "anti-Semite," and Freud instead harped to Rank on their common bond of Jewishness to cement his loyalty.

After the loss of Jung, the choice of a successor was never again clear-cut for Freud. Each contender had advantages and disadvantages. Rank's liabilities included his comparative youthfulness and his lack of medical training. But to understand the crisis of 1924, it is essential to recognize the fact—too often overlooked in histories of psychoanalysis—that Rank had reason to regard himself as Freud's probable heir. All sides agree that the war years wrought a decisive change in his personality. Whereas Rank had previously struck Ernest Jones—much as he had Andreas-Salomé—as "a weedy youth, timid and deferential, much given to clicking of heels and bowing," at their reunion in Switzerland in 1919 "in stalked a wiry, tough man with a masterful air" (1957, 12). In January 1916, Rank was dispatched to Kraków, where he became editor of the *Krakauer Zeitung,* the official newspaper of the armed forces and the only German-language daily in the territory of Galicia. He thus had an opportunity to exercise his considerable literary and administrative talents independently of Freud. While in Kraków, Rank met Beata ("Tola") Mincer, whom he married in November 1918. To have come home from the front, as Taft has remarked, "with a beautiful young wife, whose intellectual attainments rivaled her charm, must have done much to establish Rank on a new footing as a man of family" (1958, 70). Their daughter, Helene, was born in August 1919. Upon his return Rank for the first time began to practice psychoanalysis, and he resumed and solidified his position as Freud's trusted lieutenant and the only member of the Committee living in Vienna.

The high-water mark of Freud's affection for Rank was reached in a letter of August 4, 1922, written while Freud was on holiday in Salzburg. After confiding some apprehensions concerning the state of his health, Freud adds: "I think perhaps you did not value completely in their motivation my recently expressed regrets that I had not permitted you to study medicine. I thought that under those circumstances I would not now be in doubt as to whom I would leave the leading role in the psychoanalytic movement. As it now stands I cannot help but wish that Abraham's clarity and accuracy could be merged with Ferenczi's endowments and to it be given Jones's untiring pen" (Taft 1958, 77–78). Although this letter is cast in the subjunctive mood and treats Rank's lack of a medical degree as an impediment to his assuming the "leading role," it nonetheless dangles before Rank the vision that he is a model disciple and Freud's sentimental favorite. The way that Rank must have perceived matters is made clear by the testimony of Anaïs Nin, who, although she occasionally errs on details of fact, received Rank's version of events at first hand. "[Freud] gave Rank a ring (which Rank showed me and was wearing) and wanted him to marry his daughter, to be his heir, and continue his work. . . . Like all fathers he wanted a duplicate of himself. But he understood Rank's explorative mind, and he was objective. Even their disagreements on theories would not have separated them. The real cleavage was achieved by others, who wanted a group united by a rigid acceptance of Freud's theories" (1931–34, 279). This passage confirms Rank's expectation that he would be Freud's heir, sealed by the not inherently absurd idea (prior to his own marriage to Tola) of a union with Anna. As Nin reports Rank's later account, the ultimate cause of his falling out with Freud—beyond Freud's desire for a "duplicate of himself"—lay in the jealousy of those more doctrinaire colleagues who could not tolerate his creativity and rise to eminence.

Rank's assumption that he would emerge as Freud's successor, coupled with the discovery of the cancer in Freud's jaw in the spring of 1923 (about which Rank had been informed even before Freud), permits a reconstruction of the events that casts Rank in an unflattering light. Rank evidently believed that *The Trauma of Birth*, the manuscript of which he presented to Freud as a birthday gift in 1923, would usher in a new era in psychoanalysis with himself at the helm. Seen from this standpoint, Rank's act of homage in dedicating the work to Freud is a classically ambivalent gesture that conceals a wish for patricide. Ernest Jones reports that at the fateful meeting of the Committee in San Cristoforo in August 1923, when the news of Freud's illness was publicly discussed for the first time, "to our amazement Rank broke out in a fit of uncontrollable hysterical laughter" (1957, 93).[4] To compound the symbolism, Freud—who was vacationing in Rome at the time—saw a clipping from a newspaper in Chicago that announced he was dying and transferring his pupils to Otto Rank.

The theme of death had already played a prominent part in Freud's earlier attachments to Fliess and Jung (Kerr 1988, 13–15). Anxiety about a possible heart condition drew Freud closer to Fliess during 1893–94, and under the spell of Fliess's theories of periodicity, Freud superstitiously came to believe that he would die in either his fifty-first or fifty-second year. With respect to Jung, it suffices to recall the famous incident in the Park Hotel in Munich, on November 24, 1912, when Freud—after reproaching his Swiss colleagues for failing to cite his name in their publications—fainted in Jung's arms. His first words upon awakening were "How sweet it must be to die!" (Jones 1953, 317).

If the preoccupation with death clouded Freud's friendships with

---

4. There is no reason to doubt Jones's account of Rank's "hysterical laughter" at San Cristoforo. Jones fails, however, to mention that the meeting was largely devoted to thrashing out a personal quarrel between himself and Rank and that he deeply offended not only Rank but also other members of the Committee by making anti-Semitic remarks. See Lieberman 1985, 189–90.

Fliess and Jung, how much more severely it must have afflicted his relationship with Rank after his cancer was discovered in 1923, when there could have been no way of knowing that he would survive another sixteen years. The psychodramas of fantasied murder and survivor guilt, hitherto enacted on a purely symbolic plane, took on a somberly literal dimension when their leading actor was smitten by a terminal illness. The inner dynamism of Rank's intellectual and emotional development and Freud's intimation of his own mortality brought the two men into a collision at the most fateful of times.

The conflict between Freud and Rank was fueled by ambivalence. As Freud's behavior toward Jung shows—first anointing him his successor, then accusing him of harboring a death wish against him when Jung failed to cite his work—Freud looked upon his potential heirs with an ineradicable duality. He at once loved them as extensions of himself and as a means of attaining immortality and hated them as his replacements and the harbingers of death. (This same paradox inheres in the idea of the soul or double, explored theoretically first by Rank [1914] and later by Freud [1919b].) For his part, Rank could not subordinate his ambitions except to secure Freud's unqualified approval, thereby assuring his eventual accession to the psychoanalytic throne; when this approval was not forthcoming, he felt bitterly slighted.

Subterranean tremors of Rank's strivings for independence during the early 1920s may be detected in *The Don Juan Legend*.[5] In this wholly psychoanalytic work, Rank focuses on the Don Juan–Leporello relationship, an implicit commentary on his own master-servant tie to Freud. In the final chapter, "The Psychology of the Poet," Rank explains how "the poet creates a new personal ideal for the masses."

> Dissatisfied with the ideal of the group, he forms his own individual ideal in order to proffer it to the group, without whose recognition his creation remains very unsatisfactory. The impetus to his formation of an individual ideal obviously comes from a very strong narcissism, which prevents him from accepting the common ideal and makes it necessary for him to create an individual one. Seen from the inside, the pressure that the poet feels to solicit recognition of his new ideal from the group reveals that he created it

5. My comments on *The Don Juan Legend* show my debt to the introduction and notes to the English edition by David G. Winter, esp. pp. 21, 124. Rank's original article, virtually identical to the later book, was published in 1922 and hence precedes *The Trauma of Birth* by over a year.

not only to satisfy his own narcissism, but also to replace the old common ideal with a new one. In a psychological sense the poet thereby repeats the primal crime, for the new ideal which he has created is his own—it is himself in identification with the primal father. (1924a, 121)

Drawing on Freud's (1921) theory of the ego ideal, Rank presages with uncanny accuracy the effect of his publication of *The Trauma of Birth*. This manifesto indeed embodied his "individual ideal," proffered to other members of the group, deprived of whose "recognition" it "remained very unsatisfactory." His statement that the poet is motivated by a "very strong narcissism" is likewise a telling self-diagnosis.[6] That Rank's desire "to replace the old common ideal with a new one"— that is, to replace the Oedipus complex with the birth trauma—constituted a repetition of the "primal crime" through an "identification with the primal father" is confirmed by the dedication of *The Trauma of Birth* to Freud. The paragraphs in which this passage appears were, moreover, reprinted as the conclusion to the foreword to the fourth (1925) edition of *The Artist*, dated "Vienna, Easter 1924," one week prior to Rank's first departure for the United States and the beginning of his open break with Freud.

Freud's attitude toward *The Trauma of Birth* gradually hardened, and tension escalated on both sides with painful inexorability. After its publication, Freud wrote on December 1, 1923, to accept Rank's dedication "with cordial thanks." After alluding to his health problems—he had recently undergone a second operation—Freud went on: "Handicapped as I am, I enjoy enormously your admirable productivity. That means for me, too: '*Non omnis moriar*' ['I shall not altogether die'— Horace]" (Taft 1958, 85). Several months later, Freud retroactively reported his first reaction to *The Trauma of Birth* in a March 4, 1924, letter to Abraham. "When Rank first told me about his findings, I said jokingly: 'With an idea like that anyone else would set up on his own'" (Lieberman 1985, 216).

Jesters do oft prove prophets, and Freud's hope of being immortalized through Rank's work is, as in the case of Jung, the obverse of his fear of being superseded or killed. The truth of this assertion is borne out by a letter of November 26, 1923, in which Freud responds to Rank's interpretation of one of Freud's dreams (the transcript of which is now lost): "It is a long time since you have tried to interpret one of my

6. For an astute psychobiographical assessment of Rank from a self psychological perspective, see Stolorow and Atwood 1979, 131–71.

dreams in such a powerful analytical way." Speaking with the voice of his superego, Freud reverses the roles of David and Goliath in his associations: "'Attention here, the old one and the young one are interchanged, you [Freud] are not David, you are the boasting giant Goliath, whom another one, the young David will slay.' And now everything falls into place around this point that you [Rank] are the dreaded David who with his *Trauma of Birth* succeeds in depreciating my work" (Taft 1958, 78–79). During the trip to America in 1909, Freud had refused to permit Jung to interpret his dreams, a refusal that became a bone of contention between them at the time of their rift. In this letter, however, Freud not only submits his dream to Rank's "powerful" analytic gift but equates this inversion of roles with his apprehension that the younger man is the "dreaded David," who will slay him, the "boasting giant" Goliath, with *The Trauma of Birth*.

Rank's interpretation of Freud's "David and Goliath" dream completes a circle begun at the inception of their relationship. Even prior to his first meeting with Freud, Rank had drafted an eight-page letter, dated May 12, 1905, in which he challenged the meaning of Freud's dream of "Frau Doni" in *The Interpretation of Dreams*. Boldly questioning Freud's assertion that "my satisfaction was with the fact that my marriage had brought me children" (1900, 447), Rank singled out the appearance in the dream of Freud's eldest son, Martin—like himself, a budding poet—and contended that this interpretation was a "scientific disguise" concealing the wish to achieve immortality through his own work. Rank characterized *The Interpretation of Dreams* as a whole as an "unconscious defense" against Freud's fear of being a neurotic and glossed its epigraph from Vergil's *Aeneid,* "Flectere si nequeo superos, Acheronta movebo" (If I cannot bend the higher powers, I will raise hell), to mean: "If I cannot convince people of the correctness of my theory, I will at least soothe my 'unconscious'" (D. Klein 1981, 127–28). In view of the direct thematic links—father-son struggle and Freud's desire for immortality—between the "Frau Doni" and the "David and Goliath" dreams, Freud's 1923 comment that "it is a long time" since Rank had tried to interpret one of his dreams looks like a rueful allusion to Rank's letter of 1905.[7]

7. D. Klein, who first drew attention to this letter, argues that "there is no evidence that Rank ever sent it to Freud" (1981, 126), but I cannot believe that Rank would have failed to impart his insights. The version preserved in the Otto Rank collection in the Columbia University Rare Book and Manuscript Library may be a rough draft of that mailed to Freud.

As late as March 24, 1924, Freud wrote to Ferenczi of Rank's book: "I don't know whether 66 or 33 percent of it is true, but in any case it is the most important progress since the discovery of psychoanalysis" (Jones 1957, 59). Even such praise was not enough to satisfy Rank; he could only separate from Freud by physically striking out on his own. The crisis came on April 27, 1924, five days after his fortieth birthday, when Rank left for New York with the intention of practicing there for a time. Rank's proximity to Freud had been a source of abiding unease to more distant members of the Committee, and his absence from Vienna left Freud susceptible to the hostile influences emanating from Abraham in Berlin and from Jones in London.

In particular, Rank and Jones had long been at loggerheads over their need to collaborate in matters of publication when Austrian currency lost all value after World War I, and this practical strain was compounded by Jones's and Abraham's principled objections to the active therapy advocated by Ferenczi and Rank in their joint work, *The Development of Psycho-Analysis* (*Entwicklungsziele der Psychoanalyse;* 1923), and elaborated by Rank in *The Trauma of Birth*. Freud had formerly sided with Rank, but his allegiances began to shift, especially when analysts in New York leaked word of Rank's doctrinal divagations. Seeking to maintain affective ties, Freud wrote frequently; Rank seldom responded. In exasperation, Freud unleashed his growing doubts about Rank's innovations on July 23, 1924: "The exclusion of the father in your theory seems to reveal too much the result of personal influences in your life which I think I recognize and my suspicion grows that you would not have written this book had you gone through an analysis yourself" (Taft 1958, 99).

After this direct assault, the breach between Freud and Rank could never be mended, although its finality became apparent only over the course of time. Abraham and Jones had previously leveled accusations that Rank's unorthodoxy was the consequence of "personal influences," but this is the first time that Freud endorsed them. Freud's attitude toward Rank's unanalyzed status represents a complete and important reversal. When Jones, whose analysis with Ferenczi was exploited by Freud as a means of keeping him in check, had made insinuations against Rank on this score in 1922, Freud brusquely dismissed them in a Rundbrief of December 22: "In 15 years of consistently intimate working relationship with Rank the idea scarcely occurred to me, that *he* needed an analysis" (Lieberman 1985, 185). Now, however, in an attempt to exert control over Rank, Freud, too, unworthily descended to ad hominem accusations.

In his reply on August 9, 1924, Rank struck back forcefully. First, he wisely, if belatedly, retracted his emphasis on the literal act of birth in favor of the more extended notion that "the transference libido is a purely maternal one and that the anxiety basic to all symptoms was originally tied to the maternal genital and was transferred to the father only secondarily." Next, he voiced the suspicion that Freud's objections sounded "as if you had not read at all or heard what I really said." This was a telling blow, since Freud had earlier been forced to admit that he had not finished reading *The Trauma of Birth* when he passed judgment on it. Third, Rank denied that he had "excluded the father" and claimed rather "to give him the correct place." Most importantly, he denied the imputation that his ideas stemmed from not having been analyzed. Rank called his condition "fortunate" and pointed out profoundly that Freud's objection "says nothing of the truth or value of this insight," invoking the precedent of psychoanalysis itself to affirm that "the greatest achievements themselves result from complexes and their overcoming." Finally, Rank vented some spleen of his own, branding Abraham a "noisy ranter" of "abysmal ignorance" (Taft 1958, 100–102).

Rank's separation from Freud did not become final until nearly two years later, when in May 1926 he settled in Paris. The stormy interim included his return to Vienna in the autumn of 1924, a second attempt to journey to New York, aborted in Paris, another return to Vienna, where he prostrated himself before Freud and his colleagues in the Rundbrief of December 20 from which I have quoted, and a voyage to New York in January 1925, cut short by yet another return to Vienna in February due to the death of his brother. Before moving to Paris, Rank presented Freud on his seventieth birthday with an elegantly bound set of Nietzsche's works—a fittingly ambivalent gesture of farewell that at once conveyed thanks for all that Freud had done for him and reminded Freud of his own unacknowledged intellectual debts (Roazen 1971, 412).

In spite of the theoretical and personal justifications for Rank's decision to break away from Freud, their parting of ways was a human tragedy. The sense of fatality that hangs over the proceedings stems largely from the oedipal complexes that the quarrel activated in both men. Rank, as we have seen, was consumed by a long-suppressed ambition and, after the discovery of Freud's cancer, attempted (like Prince Hal) to seize the crown of psychoanalysis prematurely, before the primal father had actually passed away. Freud, for his part, scripted events according to his own repetition compulsion, first by casting Rank as "nothing but a son" and then by assimilating his inevitable strivings for independence to the David and Goliath pattern of youth slaying age, thereby leaving himself to play the part of the benefactor tasting the "bitterness of ingratitude" after being abandoned by yet another protégé.

4 ◆ RANK AS A PRECURSOR OF CONTEMPORARY PSYCHOANALYSIS

This error must mean something, as does every error,
including these views of mine, should they prove to be
such. For even an error contains a possibility of thought,
and every possibility of thought contains a possibility of
being.—Otto Rank, *Art and Artist*

I n "The Psychology of the Poet," the final chapter of *The Don Juan Legend*, Rank observes that "whenever we find distinct periods in the work of a poet . . . a process of devaluation of the poet's previous ego ideal formation is at work" (1924a, 123). Reprinted in the foreword to the 1925 edition of *The Artist*, this passage comments self-consciously on Rank's own intellectual development. But the subjective implications of this phenomenon of "devaluation" are more unsettling than Rank appears to have realized, for they point to the central fact of his career: the radical disjunction between his work before and after his break with Freud.

This caesura receives divergent interpretations from Freudians and Rankians. To the former, Rank's enduring contributions are those he wrote as a member of Freud's school, whereas the texts following *The Trauma of Birth* are summarily dismissed. To the Rankians, in contrast, in the twenty years Rank spent with Freud he deviated from his true self, which he discovered only in repudiating psychoanalysis; seeds of Rank's later ideas are nonetheless detected as early as *The Artist* (1907), concealed within a husk of Freudian terminology. No matter which half of Rank's oeuvre the assessors prefer, they concur that one cannot embrace both simultaneously. To some extent, this problem of reconciling Freudian and post-Freudian periods was also faced by earlier renegades, such as Adler and Jung, but it is especially acute for Rank, because of the sheer brevity of his life and because the great proportion of it spent with Freud made his influence more difficult to shed. An antithesis to Rank's self-imposed devaluation of his past is provided by Freud's writings, which fall readily into early, middle, and late periods but nonetheless retain the inner coherence of an organic whole.

Although Rank's partisans often take psychoanalysis to task for ostracizing him after *The Trauma of Birth,* and there is much in the way he was treated that is truly reprehensible,[1] I think it important to stress the degree to which Rank himself must share the responsibility for his isolation. As Ira Progoff has remarked, the split from Freud left a "psychological wound" in Rank, who internalized his former mentor as a "psychic adversary," and the attacks on psychoanalysis mounted in *Will Therapy* (1929–31) and *Truth and Reality* (1929c) arose from a sensibility that was "fundamentally negative in its inspiration" (1956, 195–96). Only in his subsequent writings concerned with art and religious experience, particularly *Psychology and the Soul* (1930b) and *Art and Artist* (1932a), according to Progoff, does Rank's negativity come "full circle, culminating in an affirmative and original contribution to modern thought" (196).

Progoff's schema has the virtue of conceiving Rank's career in implicitly dialectical terms, with the Freudian period as thesis, the treatises on will psychology as antithesis, and the final celebrations of art and the urge to immortality as synthesis. Although the relation between Rank's Freudian and post-Freudian periods is undoubtedly polarized, and, as Progoff is likewise correct to detect, Rank's emphasis shifted between his writings on will psychology and creativity, I am unable to share his Jungian enthusiasm for the mystical flights of Rank's final books. Rather than a distinct third period, these late works constitute in my judgment simply the second phase of his period of independence. Like most commentators, Progoff neglects Rank's writings from 1924 to 1927, when he had broken free of Freud's direct influence but still continued to think of himself as a psychoanalyst. Only during these years, which I am convinced are Rank's anni mirabiles, did he escape from the choice between subservience and defiance

1. In the most egregious episode, at the First International Conference on Mental Hygiene, held in Washington, D.C., in 1930, A. A. Brill from the podium branded Rank an "idiot" whose views were the result of "maladjustment" (Lieberman 1985, 291–92).

of both his pro-Freudian and anti-Freudian periods and arrive at a genuine dialectical synthesis that makes him the unacknowledged precursor of contemporary object relations theory.

The writings of Rank's transitional period have been slighted not only because they fail to appeal to either Freudians or Rankians but also because they are available in English only in scattered form. The richest veins, which I shall only begin to mine here, are the first volumes of *Technique of Psychoanalysis* (1926–31) and *Fundamentals of a Genetic Psychology* (1927–29).[2] Before scaling the heights of Rank's accomplishments between 1924 and 1927, however, we must gain our bearings with respect to Rank's career as a whole. At the conclusion of this chapter, I shall return to his final period and elaborate my reasons for thinking—in common with orthodox Freudians—that it was a period of decline.

The break between Rank's Freudian and post-Freudian periods is demarcated by a single work—*The Trauma of Birth*. In the preceding chapter, I argued that, beneath its ostensible homage to Freud, the work betrays Rank's desire to emerge as the leader of the psychoanalytic movement and that the anxieties (predominantly, but not exclusively, oedipal) aroused in both Rank and Freud by the onset of Freud's cancer in 1923 eventuated in their split. These psychological dynamics provide an indispensable context for understanding the place of *The Trauma of Birth* in Rank's intellectual development.

In *The Trauma of Birth*, Rank aggressively takes up the cudgels on Freud's behalf to attack all those, beginning with Josef Breuer, who have faintheartedly refused to recognize the importance of "the sexual factor." The secessions of Adler and Jung, Rank goes on, "led to new theories based not on observation but on opposition"; "one does not know which to admire most, Freud's courage in discovery, or the fighting tenacity with which he defended himself against the resistance of the whole world" (1924b, 184).

As we saw in chapter 2, Rank specifically reproaches Jung for neglecting the libidinal underpinnings of the rebirth fantasy. Because of this error, he asserts, Jung "has slipped into the opposite ethical analogical direction, . . . which is only an intellectualized ramification" of

2. Neither was translated by Jessie Taft. *Will Therapy* is her 1936 translation of volumes 2 and 3 of *Technique of Psychoanalysis*. *Truth and Reality* is her 1936 translation of volume 3 of *Genetic Psychology*.

the biological role of the mother (27). Rank directs his criticism against Jung's *Psychology of the Unconscious (Wandlungen und Symbole der Libido)* and, in particular, against the chapter "Symbolism of the Mother and Rebirth." In the offending passage cited by Rank (24), Jung interprets the longing to return to the mother's womb: "It is not incestuous cohabitation which is desired, but the rebirth. . . . Thus the libido becomes *spiritualized in an imperceptible manner*" (1912, 251).

Psychology of the Unconscious marks a watershed in the history of psychoanalysis because in it Jung challenged the primacy of the incest taboo and Freud's sexual conception of the libido, thereby sundering the psychoanalytic movement. Little more than a decade later, *The Trauma of Birth* played a similarly pivotal role in the defection of Rank, and again the relative importance of the Oedipus complex and the validity of Freud's libido theory were crucial issues. The irony of Rank's polemics in *The Trauma of Birth*, however, is that within a few years he would adopt a position virtually indistinguishable from that which he had so vehemently reprehended in Jung. Thus, Rank's attack against Jung—that he had "spiritualized" sexual meanings—became a boomerang that recoiled against his own later writings.

The categorical nature of Rank's subsequent change of heart is made clear by the following passage from *Psychology and the Soul (Seelenglaube und Psychologie)*. "Symbolic and anxiety dreams . . . can be understood only in relation to that 'unconscious' which never becomes conscious, and which Jung has properly called 'collective' because of its identity with the spiritual. The typical sexual symbols of serpent, mouse, and bird originally had spiritual meanings" (1930b, 126). In keeping with his conversion to a "collective" unconscious with "spiritual" meanings, Rank in *Art and Artist* scores Freud's "concrete" view of the mother and the birth trauma, which he now disdains "only as typical and ideological," and cites with approval Jung's *Psychology of the Unconscious* on "the symbolic significance of the mother" (1932a, 378).[3] The preface to *Beyond Psychology* lays bare Rank's final embrace of a religious outlook: "Man is born beyond psychology and he dies beyond it, but he can *live* beyond it only through vital experience of his own—in religious terms, through revelation, conversion and rebirth" (1941, 16).

3. Rank qualifies his approval by stating that Jung has understood this symbolism "one-sidedly, with emphasis on passive rebirth and without recognition of the active self-creative force" (378), but he nonetheless markedly prefers Jung to Freud.

In light of these pronouncements, Progoff can justly claim that from his standpoint Rank's late works echo Jung's "profound insight" into the collective nature of the unconscious (1956, 233).[4] Ironically, the same evolution also vindicates Jones and Abraham for warning Freud throughout the crises of the mid-1920s that Rank's freethinking tendencies would culminate in a full-blown heresy along the lines of Jung's. Indeed, the leitmotif of Jones's portrayal of Rank in his biography of Freud is a comparison to the earlier defection of Jung, though the bias that warps Jones's version of events is evident in his statement that this parallel is in one important respect unfair to Jung: "The outstanding difference between the two cases is of course that Jung was not afflicted by any of the mental trouble that wrecked Rank and so was able to pursue an unusually productive and fruitful life" (1957, 77). To enumerate the books written by Rank during the last thirteen years of his life—*Technique of Psychoanalysis* (1926–31), *Genetic Psychology* (1927–29), *Psychology and the Soul* (1930b), *Art and Artist* (1932a), *Modern Education* (1932b), and the posthumously published *Beyond Psychology* (1941)—to say nothing of his therapeutic, lecturing, and teaching duties, demonstrates at once his awesome productivity and the absurdity of Jones's contention that Rank was "wrecked" by "mental trouble" following his emergence from Freud's shadow.[5] In spite of its tendentiousness, however, Jones's analysis of Rank remains fundamentally valid at least on the intellectual plane, since by the end of his life Rank did arrive at a position very close to Jung's. Above all, Rank's metamorphosis with respect to Jung highlights the devaluation of his past and the impossibility of reconciling his Freudian and post-Freudian periods.

In retrospect, Rank's attacks on Jung and the other backsliders in *The Trauma of Birth* are clearly symptoms of the ambivalence underlying his militant championing of Freud. In Melanie Klein's (1946) terms, Rank used projective identification to split off the hostile components of his feelings toward Freud and deposit them into the "bad objects" of the opponents of psychoanalysis, where they could be safely destroyed by the conscious portion of his ego, which still saw itself as Freud's loyal

4. Interestingly, in spite of being repeatedly asked late in life by Progoff for his opinion of Rank, Jung refused to give any answer (Lieberman 1985, 401).

5. An animus no less severe than that exhibited toward Rank is evident in Jones's portrayal of Ferenczi, his former analyst, who, he claims, "toward the end of his life" developed "psychotic manifestations that revealed themselves in, among other ways, a turning away from Freud and his doctrines" (1957, 45).

disciple. Only when Freud failed to bestow his unqualified approbation and anoint Rank his heir did Rank defect from the cause and channel his aggression against the now-hated paternal imago of Freud.

In keeping with Rank's emotional ambivalence, *The Trauma of Birth* foreshadows both the best and the worst features of his later thought. On the one hand, Rank's insights into the role of the mother, the theme of separation, and the experiential aspects of psychoanalytic therapy are invaluable contributions that he continues to elaborate during his immediately ensuing three-year transitional period. On the other hand, however, Rank's more dubious pronouncements look ahead to his antipsychoanalytic final phase. He proclaims in the last chapter of *The Trauma of Birth:* "Analysis is now in the position to free itself to an extensive degree from the work of investigation, since we know from the outset . . . the whole content of the unconscious and the psychical mechanisms" (1924b, 213). Rank's confidence that his theory could supersede Freud's schema of "different places of fixation, which are supposed to determine the choice of neurosis, by *one* traumatic injury" (211), likewise leads him to recommend that the significance of the birth trauma be immediately disclosed to the patient.

But, as Freud objected in a Rundbrief to members of the Committee on January 9, 1924, "it is not clear to me how the premature making-conscious of the therapeutic transference as a tie to the mother can contribute to a shortening of the analysis" (Taft 1958, 88). Freud's criticism is telling, for if the preoedipal realm precedes the oedipal one, it is illogical for Rank to suppose that an awareness of its importance would lead to a shortening rather than a lengthening of treatment (although his advocacy of a briefer psychotherapy may be justified on separate grounds). What is more, it runs counter to Rank's own commitment to analysis as an experiential process to claim that the analyst's elucidation of the birth trauma as a theoretical principle could take the place of the patient's coming to apprehend the trauma as an emotional reality in his or her own life.[6] Rank takes his disdain for the "work of

---

6. See Guntrip, who criticizes Rank's "superficial idea" that issues of dependence can "be quickly brought to consciousness in a short analysis of a few months by what could only be merely intellectual explanation." Guntrip, however, at least takes Rank seriously, and his contention that "Fairbairn's Infantile Dependence is the correct answer to the problems with which Rank's Birth Trauma theory first sought to grapple" (1961, 320) would be justified if it did not leave out of account Rank's writings from 1924 to 1927, in which Rank anticipates many of Fairbairn's insights.

investigation" in analysis to its illogical conclusion in *Will Therapy*, where he holds that "there is no use in searching out past events and experiences for the understanding of the present" and that "the therapeutic factor lies in the verbalizing of conscious emotion" (1929–31, 31, 23). Even more sweepingly, he insists in *Truth and Reality* that "the whole of psychology becomes of necessity a psychology of consciousness" (1929c, 25).

As I argued in chapter 1, object relations theorists have successfully challenged some of Freud's most cherished assumptions about drives and the primacy of sexuality as a motivating force of human behavior. To differentiate between legitimate and illegitimate forms of revisionism is imperative, however; the unconscious and genetic explanation are not similarly negotiable principles of psychoanalysis. By casting aside these cornerstones in *Will Therapy* and *Truth and Reality*, Rank undermines the edifice of his later thought.

In volume 1 of *Technique of Psychoanalysis*, Rank addresses the therapeutic implications of his reorientation from an oedipal to a preoedipal level of analysis. His declaration that "the transference is thus the nuclear problem of analytic therapy" (1926c, 2) may likewise be taken as a reappraisal of his tie to Freud, which at the time of their break he had construed purely in oedipal terms. The cogency of Rank's entire argument warrants extended quotation.

> Freud's conception [of the analyst as father] neglects, however, the principal meaning of the analytic situation, which goes beyond the manifest relationship of the sexes to determine the given role of the analyst from the sexually independent psychic situation. . . . Much that has long been recognized theoretically—such as the meaning of anxiety as birth anxiety, the fantasy of the maternal body, the maternal attachment of the homosexual, anxiety in the presence of women, and the sibling complex—could not be utilized therapeutically as long as the analyst placed the father-transference at the center of the analysis.
>
> In keeping with his theoretical findings, *Freud's* therapeutic conception was the analytic tracing of the transference back to the Oedipus situation, which the patient strives to reproduce after his individual fashion in the analytic situation but on the other side of which he often enough does not emerge. Many years ago now I have made the attempt *systematically* to pursue the analysis of the transference into the time before the development of the Oedipus complex and to turn this uncovering of the *pre-Oedipus situation* in the analytic transference relationship to account as a therapeutic agent. . . . (3–4)

The analytic situation is essentially a maternal situation for the libido of the patient; the analyst must first raise the libido through analysis to a paternal adaptation and finally, going even beyond this, lead the patient to his own ego. . . . The actual work consists in the analysis of the deepest maternal attachment on its various levels (birth, weaning, siblings, castration) up to the Oedipus situation, which therapeutically represents the *first* adaptation situation, which is then followed in turn by the overcoming of oedipal dependency in the development of one's own ego. . . .

This transposition of my technical point of view into therapeutic accomplishment may perhaps be characterized as "activity," if by this one understands not the imparting of prohibitions and orders to the patient (in *Ferenczi's* sense), which I have never systematically practiced, but rather only a braver application of our knowledge, especially of the deepest psychic layers, access to which remains forever closed off even to the patient. (6)

Rank's conception of the analytic situation principally in maternal terms arises from his attempt to trace the origins of the transference "into the time before the development of the Oedipus complex." As late as *Civilization and Its Discontents,* as we saw in chapter 1, Freud attributed the need for religion to "the infant's helplessness and the longing for the father aroused by it" and affirmed that whatever lay behind this was "wrapped in obscurity" (1930, 72). He thereby failed to profit from the emphasis placed by Jung, Rank, and many others on the role of the mother. By putting the mother in the foreground, on the other hand, Rank is able to approach the experiences of weaning, sibling rivalry, and castration anxiety as parts of a series of separations beginning with birth and—in consonance with both Kleinian and Independent schools of object relations theory—to view the Oedipus complex itself as a developmental achievement.

In the domain of technique, furthermore, Rank's advocacy of "a braver application of our knowledge" that permits contact with "the deepest psychic layers, access to which remains forever closed off even to the patient himself," anticipates the most exciting recent work in object relations theory—Christopher Bollas's (1987) conceptualization of the analyst's task as the articulation of the patient's "unthought known," that existential memory of earliest psychic life which stems from the preverbal infant-mother relationship and is fundamentally an operational, not a representational, form of knowledge. By examining maternal transference as both a theoretical and a technical issue, Rank stakes out the terrain that continues to be explored by object relations analysts to the present day.

The intrinsic interest of the *Technique of Psychoanalysis* is heightened by the fact that it elicited a review by Ferenczi, which, however, as we saw in chapter 2, was adverse. Ferenczi's critique singles out Rank's neglect of "the historical standpoint" of psychoanalysis (1927, 93), his concentration on the mother at the expense of the father, and his one-sided emphasis on the emotional aspects of the therapeutic relationship. These charges are cogent, if not wholly justified, but the Freud-Ferenczi correspondence reveals that Ferenczi's attack on Rank was at bottom motivated by affective considerations. Ferenczi had long been closely associated with Rank, especially since their joint publication of *The Development of Psycho-Analysis* (1923), and after Rank's defection he wished to tell the world that he was not contaminated by heresy. In a letter to Freud of May 30, 1926, Ferenczi announces that he plans to use the appearance of Rank's book as an occasion to break publicly from his erstwhile collaborator.

The rupture of the friendship between Ferenczi and Rank is one of the most unhappy aspects of Rank's departure from the psychoanalytic movement. When Ferenczi accidently met Rank in New York's Pennsylvania Station in 1926, he refused even to speak to him (Taft 1958, xvi). Not only did Ferenczi feel impelled to sever his ties with Rank, but he also evidently needed to bolster his identification with Freud. Ferenczi's neurotic inability to tolerate even slight divergences of opinion from Freud forms a leitmotif of their correspondence. And just as, in *The Trauma of Birth*, Rank had projected the negative component of his ambivalence toward Freud upon the opponents of psychoanalysis, so did Ferenczi, in his review of *Technique of Psychoanalysis,* strive to confirm his identity as Freud's devoted son by castigating the wayward Rank.

The psychic toll exacted by Ferenczi's unceasing efforts to propitiate Freud in both fantasy and reality is evident from his posthumously published *Clinical Diary* of 1932. As I noted in chapter 1, Ferenczi described himself as "trampled under foot" by Freud's "indifferent power" as soon as he sought to assert his independence. Taken together, Rank and Ferenczi embody the two sides of a single ambivalent filial relationship to Freud. Whereas Rank is the rebellious son who seeks to supplant and kill the father, Ferenczi is the docile son who submits to castration and death at the father's hand. As in the two main portions of Rank's career, neither subservience nor defiance leads to genuine autonomy, for both are reactive solutions to the oedipal dilemma imposed by Freud on his male heirs. The public opprobrium heaped on Rank in the wake of his rebellion, moreover, finds its counterpart in Ferenczi's private anguish, stemming from his inability to stand up to Freud.

The brilliance of Ferenczi's final papers, combined with his decision to remain within the psychoanalytic fold, has largely eclipsed the posthumous reputation of Rank. But in a letter to Freud on September 1, 1924, Ferenczi credits Rank with having been the first to grasp the maternal function of the analyst. In the *Clinical Diary*, Ferenczi likewise admits that he was so "dazzled" by Rank's "new insight" into the transference situation that he followed him too far in various errors of technique (1988, 186). Ferenczi's genius is beyond question, but it is a salutary corrective to received versions of the history of psychoanalysis—which unfailingly cast Ferenczi in the leading role—to discover that he himself paid tribute to Rank as the more dominant and innovative member of their intellectual partnership.

In 1927, the same year that Ferenczi reviewed *Technique of Psychoanalysis*, Rank published a review of Freud's *Inhibitions, Symptoms and Anxiety* (1926).[7] This piece is notable for being the only place Rank expatiates in writing about a work of Freud's. What is more, since Freud had been prompted to write *Inhibitions, Symptoms and Anxiety* largely to refute *The Trauma of Birth*, Rank's rejoinder afforded an opportunity at once to amplify his own position and to rebut the criticisms of Freud.

Leo Rangell has contended that the common element in all the various "alternative theories" of psychoanalysis is their "down-playing of the castration-danger and an attempt to eliminate this nuclear anxiety from the reservoir of neurosogenic factors" (1982, 40). Indeed, Rank criticizes Freud precisely for his overemphasis on castration anxiety. Citing Freud's retrospective commentary on the animal phobias of two famous patients, Little Hans and the Wolf Man, both of which are said to be "substitutes by distortion for the idea of being castrated by the father" (1926, 108), Rank calls attention to the fear of being bitten or devoured that is exhibited by both patients. He reproaches Freud for refusing to see "the primary relation of the sadistic-oral 'language' to the mother-object" and for failing to "put the castration fear in its proper place as connected only with the later (genital) Oedipus stage" (1927c, 182). According to Rank, the issue is not—as Rangell would

7. The importance of this review was signaled by Lieberman (1985, 264–67).

have it—"eliminating" castration anxiety from the theory of neurosis but rather giving it its "proper place," so that it does not preempt the attention that should be paid to genetically earlier sources of anxiety arising in the child's relation to the mother.

Concerning his own theory, Rank affirms that he "took a distinct step beyond Freud" in *The Trauma of Birth* when he "linked the *physiological* birth-anxiety"—which Freud himself had acknowledged, in a footnote added in 1909 to *The Interpretation of Dreams,* to be the prototype of anxiety—"to the separation from the mother as a trauma of great *psychological* importance" (1927c, 181). Rank's reorientation from physiological to psychological concepts of anxiety, above all his recognition of "separation from the mother" as the essential component of anxiety, strikes the keynote for subsequent relational theorists from Fairbairn to Mahler.[8]

In *Inhibitions, Symptoms and Anxiety,* Freud abandons his earlier theory of anxiety as repressed libido, but Rank notes that he continues to confuse matters by insisting that the mother is not experienced by the newborn infant as an "object." Freud writes that "during its intra-uterine life the mother was not an object for the foetus," hence "the striking coincidence by which the anxiety of the newborn baby and the anxiety of the infant in arms are both conditioned by separation from the mother does not need to be explained along psychological lines" (1926, 138). By maintaining that the anxiety not only of the "newborn" but even of the "infant in arms" requires biological rather than psychological explanation, Freud seeks at once to preserve the primacy of the castration complex against the encroachments of the birth trauma (and its sequelae) and to put the new wine of his definition of anxiety as a danger signal into the old bottle of the libido theory. Because Freud persists in defining danger in terms of unsatisfied libidinal needs, he attributes the infant's desire for the mother's presence not to anxiety provoked by the "loss of object" but to "the economic disturbance caused by an accumulation of amounts of stimulation which require to be disposed of" (137).

Rejecting this unwieldy attempt to reduce relationships to drives, Rank sensibly urges caution in interpreting the sensations of the infant

8. See chapter 2, where I have linked Rank's (1929–31) polarity of "life fear" and "death fear" to Fairbairn's exegesis of the vicissitudes of infantile dependence and to Mahler's emphasis on the rapprochement subphase of the separation-individuation process.

and remarks that whether or not the mother is defined as an object "amounts to nothing more than a quibble over words." He continues: "For it is certain that the newborn infant loses something as soon as it is born, indeed even as soon as birth begins—something that we can express in our language in hardly any other way than as the loss of an object or, if one wants to be more precise, the loss of a milieu. The characteristic quality of the birth act is that it is a transitional phenomenon κατ᾽ ἐξοχήν [in the highest degree], and that very fact may determine its traumatic character" (1927c, 183).

This passage has numerous resonances for object relations theory. Most notably, Rank anticipates the guiding premise of Melanie Klein, that "the infant has from the beginning of post-natal life a relation to the mother . . . which is imbued with the fundamental elements of an object-relation" (1952, 49). Winnicott, too, sides with Rank and against Freud in a crucial respect when he asserts that "at full term, there is already a human being in the womb, one that is capable of having experiences and of accumulating bodily memories and even of organising defensive measures to deal with traumata" (1988, 143). In describing birth as the loss not simply of an object but of a *milieu,* moreover, Rank concurs with all those—Winnicott, Balint, Sullivan, and Mahler—who from various angles have stressed that the infant's well-being depends on the sheltering environment provided by the mother, from whom it must gradually learn to separate. Finally, Rank's attribution of the "traumatic character" of birth to its being a "transitional phenomenon" evokes not only Winnicott's emphasis on transitionality in his classic paper (1953) but also Fairbairn's earlier delineation of a "transition stage" between "infantile" and "mature" dependence (1941, 38–39).[9]

To account for Freud's confusion, Rank suggests that in *Inhibitions, Symptoms and Anxiety,* "perhaps for the first time, Freud does not speak from his own analytic experiences, but uses my experiences deductively and critically" (1927c, 185). He shrewdly questions whether Freud's confession of fundamental difficulties in the work may not be "partly due to a resistance on his part to accepting any idea that originates from others" (187). Whatever the defects of *The Trauma of Birth,* he goes on, "it certainly has not the fault that has been ascribed to

9. Fairbairn's transition stage, however, occurs between what Freud's libido theory would term the oral and phallic phases of development and, unlike Winnicott's transitional object, is not a function of the earliest mother-child relationship.

it in analytic circles—that of being too radical in attempting to substitute new concepts for old." Rather, only "in criticizing my presentation, which implies an attempt to save the libido theory," has Freud
"been compelled to give up this libido theory, a step that I did not yet
trust myself enough to take completely in *The Trauma of Birth*" (188).

That *Inhibitions, Symptoms and Anxiety* marks a turning point in
Freud's thought is universally recognized by scholars of psychoanalysis,
and Rank's role in goading Freud into making his breakthrough is
occasionally given a perfunctory nod. In fact, Rank at once grasped
that nothing less than *Freud's abandonment of his libido theory* was at stake,
although his insight has remained unacknowledged to the present day.
Because Rank not only compelled Freud to take this step in the first
place but also immediately expounded its significance, on the basis of
this review alone he deserves to be hailed as the first object relations
psychoanalyst.

The line of thought staked out by Rank in his review of *Inhibitions,
Symptoms and Anxiety* receives its most comprehensive elaboration in
volume 1 of *Genetic Psychology* (1927a). The very title of this book
signals Rank's continued adherence to a developmental perspective,
which he would shortly abandon in *Will Therapy* and *Truth and Reality.*
As Taft has observed, Rank's principal achievement in *Genetic Psychology* is to have looked "at the normal development of the child positively
and constructively" (1958, 117). Two excerpts, "The Genesis of Genitality" (1926a) and "Psychoanalytic Problems" (1927b), were published
in English in *The Psychoanalytic Review,* and these provide a useful
compendium.

In "The Genesis of Genitality," Rank points out that the theme he
proposes to discuss is a familiar psychoanalytic one, but only in the
"narrow sense" of referring to "the sexual *impulse* as such" (1926a, 129).
He, however, is concerned with "not only the energetic problem of
libido displacement from one erogenous zone to another" but also "the
traumatic privations which apparently are necessary to start the phy-
logenetically preformed mechanism of displacement, and so to guarantee the continuity of the biologic development" (13). In other words,
Rank redirects his focus from the intrapsychic processes of libidinal
development to the obstacles faced by the growing child in the interpersonal realm.

In particular, he notes that for children of both sexes, "the mother
represents the first and, in the beginning, the only libido object" (130).
Although the transfer of cathexis from the mother to the father on the

part of a girl complicates her experience of the Oedipus complex, a boy, too, must accomplish a displacement, for his oedipal aim consists in the desire *"to possess the mother (woman) on the genital instead of the original oral level."* For Rank, then, it is the suckling's "oral-sadistic subjugation of the mother" that is the master key to sexual development (131). He generalizes: "Both sexes attempt to regain at the genital stage the oral sadistic pleasure originally experienced at the mother's breast." Not only does this sound like Klein, but Rank expressly invokes her to bolster his contention that feelings of guilt in the infant are present in the relationship to the mother "long before any father identification and the subsequent erection of the super-ego has taken place" (141).[10]

Of the various "traumatic privations" that trigger development, Rank highlights weaning as the event that "signifies the definite emancipation from the maternal nourishment" and induces the infant to abandon the oral stage (137). Although he thereby qualifies his theory of the birth trauma, Rank stresses that he does not mean to substitute one form of literalism with another but rather to draw attention to the "displacement processes" whereby a trauma *only then becomes effective at the next biologic stage."* Accordingly, that which is pathogenic "actually lies between the traumata" and depends on the "displacement mechanism," which "already is set going before the trauma" (138). In this dense but brilliant discussion, Rank tacitly appropriates Freud's (1895) concept of "deferred action," wherein the meaning of an earlier event is held to depend upon a later one, and extends this psychoanalytic model of temporality to the entire separation-individuation process.

"The Genesis of Genitality" is the opening chapter of *Genetic Psychology,* but "Psychoanalytic Problems" (1927b) forms part of the introduction and hence distills Rank's thinking at this time more purely. Rank underscores his critique of the libido theory, saying that his genetic

10. On Rank and Klein, Phyllis Grosskurth says: "They were the first figures in the psychoanalytic movement to emphasize the importance of the mother-child relationship," but Klein "no longer quoted him in her papers" after his *Trauma of Birth* because Rank became an "object lesson" in the excommunication that Klein wished at all costs to avoid. Grosskurth's comparison is apt, but, like Guntrip on Rank and Fairbairn, her claim that Rank "never traced" the vicissitudes of oral guilt "through the developmental phases of infancy and childhood as Melanie Klein was to do" reflects a lack of familiarity with his writings from 1924 to 1927 (1986, 127).

point of view "deals with impulses which are not assumed to be constant" but "again and again manifest themselves anew from actual occasions" (12). He reiterates that the vital feature of his theory of birth anxiety—insufficiently appreciated by Freud—is its emphasis on the "*psychical anchoring* of this affect to the mother and the loss of the libido-object so important for the ego" (14). Accordingly, the "real theme" of *Genetic Psychology* is a study of "the relation of the ego to its milieu in its biological, psychological and social" aspects and, above all, of the "fundamental problem" of "the relation of the ego to objects" (15). There could be no more forthright declaration of an object relations position, and Rank concludes by affirming that "this problem of the relation of the ego to the object and to reality represents the essential theme of genetic psychology, which is constructed on the results of the analytic method of investigation" (19).

Thus, in spite of having broken with Freud, Rank continues in *Genetic Psychology* to adhere to "the analytic method of investigation," and this blend of intellectual rigor with personal independence, which characterizes his entire period from 1924 to 1927, accounts for the richness of this book and for its kinship to contemporary object relations theory. In "Psychoanalytic Problems," Rank traces the vicissitudes in Freud's views concerning the interplay between fantasy and reality. On Freud's abandonment of his early seduction theory, Rank comments: "If one has overestimated reality in the original trauma-theory, then the next and most essential phase of the analytic development clearly represented an overestimation of the phantasy-life characterized by the concept of 'psychical reality'" (17). Without denying the "great merit" of this inward turn brought about by the libido theory, Rank criticizes Freud's increasing reliance on phylogenetic explanations, maintaining: "The great and not fully estimated importance of my concept represented in my *Trauma of Birth* among other things lay in this, that it endeavored to replace the so-called primal phantasies by tangible, individual, real experiences" (17). By paying renewed attention to "real experiences," Rank rehabilitates Freud's pre-1897 seduction theory, though without discarding the insight into the role of unconscious fantasy cultivated during the intervening years.

How to strike a balance between the claims of the inner and outer worlds is a perennial problem in psychoanalysis, and the value of a given theorist's work can be measured by the degree to which these two contradictory points of view are held in productive tension. Rank's return at a higher level to Freud's original point of departure strikingly presages Ferenczi's better-known reversal in his final papers. Ferenczi writes: "Having given due consideration to fantasy as a pathogenic factor, I have of late been forced more and more to deal with the pathogenic trauma itself" (1930, 120). More recently, Winnicott recapitulates the theoretical evolution of both Rank and Ferenczi by characterizing his abiding preoccupation as "how to get back to the environment without losing all that was gained by studying the inner factors" (1967b, 577). In his commentary on Freud in "Psychoanalytic Problems" as in his review of *Inhibitions, Symptoms and Anxiety,* Rank shows himself to be at once the earliest proponent and the intellectual historian of object relations theory.

Rank most uncannily anticipates contemporary psychoanalysis in a chapter of *Genetic Psychology* entitled "The Genesis of the Object Relation" (app. A).[11] Foreshadowing both Freud, who examines the way that the infant at the breast comes to "set over against the ego an 'object,' in the form of something which exists 'outside'" (1930, 67), as well as the more recent work of Mahler, Winnicott, and others, Rank begins by considering how the child "gradually learns to accept the mother as an object of the external world that can be denied him." His entire paper is a meditation on "maternalization," that is, on the way that the tie to the mother forms the prototype for all later object relations. As he does throughout this period, Rank insists that "one must go beyond the libidinal explanation and take up the genetic, evolutionary point of view," and the relational paradigm he proposes closely resembles that of Melanie Klein.

Notably congruent with Klein's argument is Rank's emphasis on the split produced by "the child's original idea of the mother as both good (vouchsafing) and bad (depriving) object." Klein writes: "Frustration and gratification from the outset mould the infant's relation to a loved good breast and a hated bad breast" (1945, 408). As in "The Genesis of Genitality," Rank in "The Genesis of the Object Relation" traces the process by which the penis substitutes for the breast in the unconscious fantasy of the child. This symbolic equation is pivotal to the thought of Klein, who terms the breast and the penis "the primary objects of the

11. In 1926, at the invitation of Dr. Marion E. Kenworthy, Rank presented several chapters from *Genetic Psychology*, including "The Genesis of the Object Relation," as a series of English-language lectures in New York under the title "Practical Social Applications of Psychoanalytic Viewpoints." Page references to this chapter will be omitted in the text.

infant's oral desires" and holds that "the two conflicting attitudes to the mother's breast are carried forward into the new relation to the father's penis" (408).

The tenet that the mother and her breast are subjectively experienced by the infant as both good and bad is taken over from Klein by Fairbairn, and much of Rank's analysis of the fate of internalized objects has a distinctively Fairbairnian cast. According to Fairbairn, "Guilt thus resolves itself into a defence against relationships with bad objects" (1949, 156). Rank amplifies the same idea: "The depriving mother, through identification with the inner inhibitions, is set up in the ego as a feared and punishing element, which . . . manifests itself as anxiety or a guilt feeling." In place of Freud's structural division of the mind into id, ego, and superego, Fairbairn proposes a model on strictly object relations lines, consisting of the central ego, the libidinal ego, and the persecutory ego (or internal saboteur; 1944, 101). Citing the analysis of a female patient's dream, Fairbairn observes: "The situations depicted in dreams represent relationships existing between endopsychic structures" (99). Rank, too, in "Projection and Object Relation," a later chapter of *Genetic Psychology*, holds that the ego's positive or negative projections onto objects can "best be studied in the dream, in the interpretation of which we are accustomed to consider all figures as finally representing one's own ego or as personifications of the split ego" (1927a, 129). In "The Genesis of the Object Relation" he directly adumbrates Fairbairn's schema when he posits that the ego's bifold relation to objects is structured by "three possible mechanisms and outlets," in which "one may project as true an image as possible, an idealised image, or a depreciated image."

As a result of his study of the mother-child bond, Fairbairn concludes that "the role of ultimate cause, which Freud allotted to the Oedipus situation, should properly be allotted to the phenomenon of infantile dependence" (1944, 120). "The Oedipus situation," he elaborates, "is essentially built up around the internalized figures of the exciting mother and the rejecting mother" (1951, 175). Similarly, Rank asserts in "The Genesis of the Object Relation" that "the Oedipus complex is only a transient phase of development and that its success or failure has been decisively determined beforehand by the original relation to the mother."

With these pronouncements, we return to Rangell's objection that departures from orthodox psychoanalytic theory eliminate the Oedipus complex and castration anxiety. I shall address this issue in greater detail in the following chapter, but for now it suffices to recognize that in looking upon the Oedipus complex as part of a genetic sequence, Rank is at least in the vanguard of an important trend in psychoanalytic theory. The projection into the Oedipus situation of the ambivalence arising originally in relation to the mother, Rank explains in "The Genesis of the Object Relation," enables "the ego to find again in objects gratifications and inhibitions which the maternal deprivations had forced within the ego." In normal development, he adds, "the two mother roles, the good and the bad, are divided up between the father and the mother, the role assigned to each depending upon the sex of the child." Rank's further comment that "the boy must, so to speak, make the father bad, in order to keep the picture of the good mother clear," has a biographical application to Freud, whose discovery of the Oedipus complex, as I have argued elsewhere (1987, 85–89; see also Swan 1974), was made possible by just such a split between the good and bad images of the mother—*mater* and Nannie—and the subsequent transfer of the bad image onto his father, which thereby enabled him to "keep the picture of the good mother clear."

Given that the relationship between mother and child shapes everything that follows and that the mother may be experienced either as predominantly good or bad, the formation of character depends, in Rank's view, on "whether an individual plays in life the good mother or looks for her in the object, or plays the bad mother or looks for her in the object." (These constitute four alternatives.) Because the ego develops out of the tie to the mother, the decisive factor for relationships in later life is whether "the original *object* is sought and found or whether one's *ego* is objectified." Rank here anticipates Edith Jacobson's insight that "because of the child's early symbiotic relationship with the mother, she is for both male and female child the first object of love as well as of primitive identifications" (1964, 116). Jacobson is in the mainstream of post-Freudian theory, but her exegesis of the interplay between identification and object-love in the infant's fantasies of merging with the mother's breast unknowingly echoes ideas originally put forward by Rank.

Rank observes that the ego's attempts to free itself from attachments to bad objects often bring "a new secondary guilt-feeling reaction with them, since the moral ego cannot bear the idea of making use of 'the other' (in the Kantian sense) as a means to an end." Rank's understanding of the guilt that arises from "making use of 'the other'" may be derived from Kant, but his terminology accords with that of Winnicott in "The Use of an Object" (1969). Nor is this connection a fortuitous one, since Winnicott, thus far faithful to his Kleinian heritage, likewise emphasizes the theme of oral sadism. His thesis in this paper is that "it is the destruction of the object that places the object outside the area of the subject's omnipotent control" (90), just as Rank contends that "every object relation . . . holds destructive elements within it" and refuses to underestimate "the destructive side of love."

In his review of *Technique of Psychoanalysis,* Ferenczi declares that "we are justified in regarding the view which it maintains as a relapse into the pre-analytic way of thinking without any scientific basis" (1927, 95). Although premature with respect to the writings of Rank's transitional period, this judgment does apply to his works after 1927. Indeed, turning Ferenczi's strictures on their head, Rank defiantly proclaims in *Will Therapy* that "pre-analytic psychology . . . was more psychological than psychoanalysis" (1929–31, 42).

Two papers that signal Rank's emergence as an avowed foe of psychoanalysis are "Beyond Psychoanalysis," the first chapter of the (untranslated) second volume of *Genetic Psychology,* and "The Psychological Approach to Personal Problems," a talk given at Yale University. Expanding the attack on Freud's biological conception of anxiety in his review of *Inhibitions, Symptoms and Anxiety,* Rank begins "Beyond Psychoanalysis" by observing: "Still less can the problem of *love* be thus purely biologically explained, although Freud attempted to trace it as well as anxiety back to the sexual impulse" (1929a, 1). That Freud misguidedly reduced *affects* to *drives* is a recurrent indictment by both his object relations critics and his humanistic critics. As Erich Fromm writes in *The Art of Loving:* "My criticism of Freud's theory is not that he overemphasized sex, but his failure to understand sex deeply enough" (1956, 37). "Tenderness is by no means, as Freud believed, a sublimation of the sexual instinct" (55).

In "Beyond Psychoanalysis," Rank embraces a radical philosophical relativism as an alternative to Freud's biologism. Recalling his early admiration for Nietzsche, he writes: "The psychical itself is only to be understood phenomenologically. One might say that in the psychical sphere there are no facts, but only interpretations of them" (1929a, 3). This claim aligns Rank with the extreme version of hermeneutics advocated by Donald Spence, who holds that interpretations in psychoanalysis depend for their validity not on their "evidential value" but solely on their "rhetorical appeal" (1976, 32). Similarly, in "The Psychological Approach to Personal Problems," Rank defines psychology as a "science of relations or interrelations, or, if you prefer a more modern term, a science of relativity" (1929b, 20). In chapter 1, I cited the phrase "science of relations" as a distillation of the synthesis of natural science and hermeneutics that is attainable within the framework of object relations theory. Taken in context, however, it is clear that Rank's relativism is stubbornly *anti*scientific and that he seeks not to marry but to divorce subjective and objective modes of knowledge.

The paramount contribution of Rank's mature thought lies in its attention to art, play, and creativity, domains of experience largely neglected by psychoanalysis prior to object relations theory. When he observes in *Art and Artist* that "psychology could not explain how from the sex-impulse there was produced, not the sex-act, but the art-work" (1932a, 26), he trenchantly exposes the difficulty with the concept of sublimation. In the Yale paper he differentiates himself from Freud by virtue of his own belief in "something in the individual himself which is creative, which is impelling, which is not taken in from without, but which grows within" (1929b, 15). Similarly, Winnicott champions the idea of innate creativity when he writes that "our theory includes a belief that living creatively is a healthy state, and that compliance is a sick basis for life" (1971a, 65). Drawing on Schiller's concept of a "play instinct" (as he had drawn on Kant for his understanding of what it means to "use" another person), Rank speaks of the "intermediate quality of the work of art, which links the world of subjective unreality with that of objective reality—harmoniously fusing the edges of each without confusing them" (1932a, 104). This passage foreshadows Winnicott's (1953) seminal concept of the transitional object—the primordial cultural artifact, located in the "intermediate" realm between the child's "subjective unreality" and "objective reality." Although Winnicott never notes his affinity with Rank, Marion Milner cites this sentence from *Art and Artist* in support of her own explanation of how "art provides a method, in adult life, for producing states that are part of everyday experience in healthy infancy" (1952, 98).

But even where the later Rank comes closest to Winnicott, the differences outweigh the similarities. For example, because not all children who play become artists, Rank holds play to be "as useless for the explanation of creative art as the other infantile experiences which all children share in common" (1932a, 324). Winnicott, of course, would disagree, although in linking art and culture to children's play he never claims to banish the mystery of creative genius. Even more decisive is their parting of ways on the subject of illusion. Like Winnicott, Rank defines illusion in the most inclusive terms: "We refer in general to religion, art, play, sport, . . . which not only lift man out of his everydayness, but out of himself" (1929–31, 173). Rank affirms that a capacity for illusion is indispensable if one is to live. But where Rank diverges from Winnicott is in looking upon illusion not as a means of gaining access to truth but as an alternative to it.

In Rank's defense, Esther Menaker contends that he does not offer "a cynical plea for falseness or self-deception" (1982, 125), but this is in fact what "reality"—opposed in his terminology to "truth"—amounts to. He warns: "With the truth, one cannot live. . . . At the moment we begin to search after truth we begin to destroy reality and our relation to it" (1929c, 42).[12] And in *Will Therapy* he goes so far as to aver that a "falsification of the past is necessary" (1929–31, 172) to bring about therapeutic change. Such views are indeed cynical, and with them Rank paradoxically endorses Freud's tendency to equate various forms of illusion with delusion, except that the value sign has been reversed.

Rank's renunciation of truth seeking forms part of the global anti-intellectualism in his final period. The following excerpts from *Psychology and the Soul* are characteristic. "But knowledge of self is not necessary to the understanding of others. . . . I do not believe that psychology began as self-observation or introspection with self-knowledge as its goal" (1930b, 7). "On the whole, psychoanalysis failed therapeutically because it aggravated man's psychologizing rather than healed him of his introspection" (10). Already in the Yale paper Rank had announced that his approach to therapy "does not aim at the individual's complete understanding of himself as the Freudian theory does" (1929b, 17), and he was well on the way "beyond psychology" toward the mysticism of his last books. Rank's abjuring of introspection carries to an indefensible extreme his legitimate accentuation of emotional experience as a therapeutic agent in *The Development of Psycho-Analysis* and *The Trauma of Birth*. As Ferenczi remarks, Rank tends "to exaggerate what are in themselves (in part, at least) interesting views and not infrequently to press the exaggeration *ad absurdum*" (1927, 93).

12. In consonance with my remarks in chapter 2, one expression of this attitude is Rank's untenable claim that the "authentic wisdom" of the Oedipus myth is that the hero "would live happily in his displaced world of appearances" if only he could be induced to abandon his investigation into the death of Laius (1929c, 42).

Set against the backdrop of Rank's career as a whole, the anti-intellectualism of his final period conforms to the pattern of devaluation of his past. In the first entry to his adolescent diary (*Tagebuch*), dated January 1, 1903, Rank wrote: "Before everything, I want to make progress in psychology. By that I understand . . . the comprehensive knowledge of mankind that explains the riddles of our thinking, acting, and speaking, and leads back to certain basic characteristics. For an approach to this idealistic goal, which only a few souls have tried to reach, self-observation is a prime essential and to that end I am making these notes" (Taft 1958, 4). Rank's craving for self-knowledge, whetted by his omnivorous reading in literature and philosophy, made possible the shock of recognition he experienced when he came upon Freud's (as yet unheralded) early masterpieces. Rank, as we know, was inspired to write *The Artist*, which in turn led to his introduction to Freud and to the beginning of what appeared to be a lifelong commitment. But when, more than two decades later, Freud had become the god that failed, Rank could not abide his former ideology; he no longer revered self-knowledge as humanity's loftiest ideal but deprecated it as its greatest bane.

Rank's deconversion from psychoanalysis led him not merely to repudiate but even to misrepresent his past. In his later years Rank (like his followers) looked back to *The Artist* as a harbinger of his mature interest in creativity and hence as only superficially a Freudian work. Nevertheless, although Rank takes art as his theme there, he *devalues* it in favor of science and consciousness. He concludes by proclaiming (in Nietzschean tones) that "as the 'founder of religion' was overcome, so the artistic person must be overcome also; the 'artist' becomes an actor, and the actor must become the physician." This apotheosis of the analyst as an "unartistic, asexual superman, light and strong as a 'god'" (1907, 56), heralds Rank's renunciation of his youthful ambitions to be a creative writer in favor of a career as the first Freudian literary critic. After 1927, Rank reverses himself and privileges art at the expense of consciousness, but he nowhere acknowledges the contradiction between his earlier and later attitudes.

In my judgment, the irrationalism of Rank's final period must be deplored as a retreat from the quest for self-knowledge that prompted him to become a disciple of Freud. That such anti-intellectualism pervades the writings of Rank's last decade attests to their underlying unity, notwithstanding the two phases that may be demarcated within those years. And because it surfaces in his books on creativity and religion no less than in those on will psychology, the former as well as the latter do not evade Progoff's charge of being "fundamentally negative in inspiration."

The reactive quality of Rank's late work is confirmed by his pronouncements on analytic technique. In contrast to what he stigmatizes as Freud's "ideological" therapy, Rank advocates a "dynamic" therapy, which "in every single case, yes in every individual hour of the same case is different. . . . My technique," Rank adds, "consists essentially in having no technique" (1929–31, 105). On the surface, Rank's outlook parallels that of Winnicott, who in Clare Winnicott's words, strove in his clinical work "to enter into every situation undefended by his knowledge, so that he could be as exposed as possible to the impact of the situation itself" (1989, 2). But again, as in their views on illusion, an ostensible concord belies a deeper dissonance. Rank's therapeutic nominalism—his assumption that no two cases or even two moments in the same case have anything in common—arises from an *antagonism* to theory, whereas Winnicott's openness presupposes the necessity and value of a complex theory of emotional development but seeks to hold that theory in abeyance so that the analyst can respond spontaneously to the exigencies of every clinical encounter.

The poverty of Rank's own theorizing is illustrated by the distinction between artistic, neurotic, and average types that forms a mainstay of his mature thought. Although cherished by Rankians, this tripartite schema appears hopelessly wooden when set beside the rich and supple nosology of Freud. As Rank notes of Jung's polarity between "introverted" and "extroverted" characters, "these static types, the products of abstraction, are of little practical use" (1941, 30); and the same might be said of his own set of categories. Having banished both the unconscious and the formative influence of childhood from his conceptual repertoire, Rank was left to espouse a fuzzy brand of existentialism, in which the fear of death and the urge for immortality were seen as the master motives of all human activity, but no effort was made to ground the confrontation with death in a sequence of experiences of separation and loss extending throughout the life cycle.

In sum, the work of Rank's last decade is indeed a retreat—from Freud, from his own earlier psychoanalytic self, and above all from his breakthrough into the territory of object relations theory during the years 1924–27. In the broader perspective of intellectual history, Rank epitomizes what Hegel attacks as the fundamental error of romanticism, namely, the belief that "the only way of being reconciled and restored to peace is to surrender all claims to think and know," instead of recognizing—with Freud—that "the step into opposition, the awakening of consciousness, follows from the very nature of man" (1817, 42).[13] This repudiation of self-consciousness, even more than his rejection of specific tenets, such as the dynamic unconscious and genetic explanation, accounts for the flaccidity of Rank's antipsychoanalytic final period.

Although Rank's theoretical odyssey came to a dead end, his life abides as a human triumph. It may not be possible to accept his post-1927 answers, but Rank never ceased to pose the essential questions. The ghost of Freud returned to haunt Rank's writings, but Rank remained remarkably free of rancor and resentment in his personal dealings. In Anaïs Nin's eloquent tribute: "He did have sorrows, profound depressions, disappointments, frustrations, but he never became bitter or cynical. His faith never died, nor his capacity to feel, to respond" (1939–44, 20–21). If in its explorations of the role of the mother and the unthought known, psychoanalysis has begun to catch up with Rank's anni mirabiles, perhaps Rank may yet be reclaimed for the fold from which he ought never to have departed.

13. I have discussed the relevance of Hegel's concept of an "odyssey of consciousness" to psychoanalysis in *Freud and Oedipus* (1987), 150–74.

5 ♦ WINNICOTT, LACAN, AND KOHUT

In all these fundamental matters, both of theory and
practice, my plea would be essentially for moderation
and balance, rejecting nothing that experience has
shown to be useful, while ever expectant of further
increases in our knowledge and power.—Ernest
Jones, "Introduction to the Congress Symposium"

To undertake a comparative study of D. W. Winnicott, Jacques
Lacan, and Heinz Kohut seems fitting on a number of counts.
Not only are they by widespread consensus the most éminent
and influential analysts of their generation, but each represents a
different nationality—Winnicott being English, Lacan French, and the
Viennese Kohut a naturalized American—and by extension a different
tradition of psychoanalysis. Since all three have died—Winnicott in
1971, Lacan and Kohut in 1981—their lifework has been completed
and can (at least in principle) be surveyed in its entirety. Each embodies
a unique personal and intellectual style, as well as a distinctive relationship with Freud. Finally, the question of the self or subject lies in highly
idiosyncratic ways at the heart of all three analysts' thought.[1]

Although I shall weigh these three theorists on their intellectual
merits, it would be untrue to the subjective spirit in which this book has
been conceived were I to deny that emotional considerations will also

1. The other leading analysts of their generation are Heinz Hartmann and
W. R. Bion. Hartmann does not venture beyond traditional ego psychology,
and I have yet to be inspired by Bion's algebraic "grid." See, however, Eigen
1981a and, for a perceptive critique of Bion that contrasts him with Winnicott,
Hamilton 1982, 238–72. In a comparison of Winnicott and Lacan, Jane Flax
(1990, 89–132) reaches many of the same conclusions I do here but curiously
favors Winnicott from a postmodern standpoint.

play a part in my argument. As I maintained in chapter 1, any attempt to come to terms with Freud must take the measure of him both as a human being and as a thinker. By the same token, when I now ask where psychoanalysis can go after Freud—and unless it can go forward, it must lapse into idolatry and renounce all claims to be a science—I am in one respect announcing my search for a figure to whom I can have a transference as intense and satisfying as that aroused by Freud.

I have found that figure in Winnicott. To acknowledge this bias, however, is by no means to surrender my capacity for critical thought. On the contrary, one reason that Winnicott deserves our admiration is precisely because of his insistence that psychoanalysis not be a matter of blind faith. Responding to the disparagements of psychoanalysis by the organic psychiatrist William W. Sargant, he writes in a letter of June 24, 1969: "I of course know analysts who are dogmatic and indoctrinating types and from my point of view they are all bad analysts. . . . I had my early loyalties to Freud, to Melanie Klein, and to others, but eventually the loyalty is to oneself, and this must be true of most of my colleagues" (Rodman 1987, 193–94). Paradoxically, Winnicott's very recognition of the dangers of discipleship makes him a man we can "believe in," as he expounds this term in "Morals and Education" (1963e), though such belief is best expressed by being ultimately loyal not to him but to ourselves.[2]

In presenting the case for Winnicott, I shall expose what I take to be the stylistic and substantive defects of Lacan and Kohut. It is always hazardous to embark on a polemic, especially against such renowned thinkers, given the danger of demonstrating thereby only the limits of one's own understanding. In taking this risk, I hope to proceed with due respect for the contributions to psychoanalysis that make Lacan and Kohut worthy of such intensive scrutiny.

Because Lacan imports the challenge of postmodernism into psychoanalysis, I shall dedicate most of my discussion to the overriding

2. Compare the warning that Nietzsche issues through his persona Zarathustra to his overly deferential followers: "One repays a teacher badly if one always remains nothing but a pupil. . . . You had not sought yourselves; and you found me. . . . Now I bid you lose me and find yourselves; and only when you have denied me will I return to you" (1883–85, 190). Jung quotes this passage from *Thus Spoke Zarathustra* as a reproach to Freud in a letter of March 3, 1912, immediately before their rupture (McGuire 1978, 218).

choice between him and Winnicott. The views of Kohut are in many ways similar to those of Winnicott, and having declined to go down the Lacanian path, I shall contend that Kohut (despite his own protestations to the contrary) is, in essence, an object relations thinker with little to offer that cannot be better obtained within the framework of the Independent tradition. At the conclusion of this chapter, I shall return to the issue—already broached in my examination of the dispute between Freud and Rank—of the theoretical status of the Oedipus complex and of castration anxiety in relation to preoedipal experience.

Lacan and Winnicott diverge sharply in both their theoretical formulations and their attitudes to the clinical practice of psychoanalysis. These divergences accurately reflect the underlying personal character of the two men. The essential difference in their temperaments is that Lacan invariably fostered divisions, whereas Winnicott strove to mend them. Even Stuart Schneiderman, in his partisan memoir of his experiences as an American in Paris undergoing a training analysis with Lacan, concedes that "accusations of imbecility and the like flowed from Lacan as naturally as water flows downstream" (1983, 19). Not only did Lacan precipitate a schism within the Paris Psychoanalytic Society in 1953 and within his own French Psychoanalytic Society in 1963—the latter schism made irrevocable his expulsion from the International Psychoanalytical Association—but even the Freudian School of Paris he founded in 1964 split five years later over issues of personal loyalty and psychoanalytic training.[3] Finally, during the last years of Lacan's life, a virulent succession struggle erupted between his son-in-law, Jacques-Alain Miller, and Charles Melman, Miller's analyst and a devoted student of Lacan's. Intimating that such internecine strife reflects "an intrinsic or basic flaw in psychoanalysis itself," Schneiderman nonetheless admits that "the cause of psychoanalysis could never have been served by the torrents of hatred that flowed from the pens of Parisian analysts" (46, 45).

3. For the fullest account of these events, see Turkle 1978 and Roudinesco 1986. Some documents pertaining to Lacan's struggles with the International Psychoanalytical Association are gathered in Copjec 1987, 51–80. Winnicott was one of five members of the special committee appointed in 1953 by the International Psychoanalytical Association to investigate the crisis in the Paris Psychoanalytic Society: it recommended in 1955 that Lacan's dissident group be expelled because of its training procedures.

Lacan may not have been the only one to blame for the ruptures that marked his career. During the 1953 disputes he aroused the enmity of powerful figures in the International Psychoanalytical Association— most notably Princess Marie Bonaparte (initially his Parisian ally) and Anna Freud—and he became the victim of a scapegoating process that culminated in his ostracism in 1963. To allow for institutional pressures and the likelihood that others behaved punitively does not, however, remove the onus for his own fate neurosis from Lacan's shoulders, especially since the schismatic cancer continued to metastasize after he left the official movement. As Freud contends (and as we saw in chapter 3 to be true of his own life), such compulsive patterns of repetition are "for the most part arranged by [the individuals] themselves and determined by early infantile influences" (1920, 21).

Nor is it incidental that the focal point of the 1953 controversy should have been Lacan's notorious short sessions. In the context of the history of psychoanalysis, Lacan's idea of dispensing with sessions of fixed length in favor of ones to be ended at the discretion of the analyst is by no means inherently absurd. Indeed, it has venerable precedents in the experiments in termination setting conducted by Freud himself, most notably in the case of the Wolf Man, and by Ferenczi and Rank in the early phase of their active technique. (This active technique originally meant adopting an unusually stern attitude toward the patient and only gradually took on the antithetical connotation of cultivating a more empathic stance than that fostered in classical analysis.) To construe matters in the most favorable light, Lacan sought to promote a distinctively psychoanalytic mode of temporality within treatment by rejecting the criterion of mere duration in favor of a rhythm more attuned to the pulsations of the unconscious.

The problem, however, was that Lacan's sessions regularly turned out to be *shorter* than the prescribed forty-five to fifty minutes, and this inevitably aroused suspicions that the real purpose of his innovation was to serve the convenience of the analyst. As one French colleague cynically remarked: "If sessions of variable length only mean shorter and shorter sessions—and this was the case with Lacan—three minutes, four minutes, five minutes, then the whole idea of punctuating analyses by time as well as by speech is really just letting an analyst be as sadistic as he wants" (Turkle 1978, 114). But even more serious, because it does not depend on impugning Lacan's motives, is the consideration that the deliberate effect of these short sessions is to prevent the patient from feeling relaxed or comfortable in the analytic setting. As

Schneiderman attests from experience, Lacan sought to ensure that the patient "not establish an existence within the space and time of his sessions" (1983, 37). We move here from questions of character to issues of analytic technique. It is evident that Lacan's disruption of the patient's equilibrium would be anathema to Winnicott, who defines playing as "an experience in the space-time continuum, a basic form of living" (1971c, 50) and for whom the analyst's primary responsibility is to provide an atmosphere of reliability and trust so that the patient may begin to "establish an existence" if he or she has not been able to do so earlier in life.[4]

A positive alternative to Lacan's incapacity for compromise is provided by the mediations of Winnicott. Although he could be sharp-tongued, Winnicott always strove to present his criticisms, as he did in writing to Willi Hoffer on April 4, 1952, "within the framework of friendship" (Rodman 1987, 30; see also 33, 94). Winnicott's best-known effort as a peacemaker was his attempt in 1954 to heal the rift between Anna Freud and Melanie Klein and their contentious followers within the British Psycho-Analytical Society. To be sure, Winnicott did not succeed in ending these hostilities and indeed came to be regarded with suspicion in both camps; but if psychoanalysis has the "intrinsic flaw" Schneiderman discerns, which may be traced to the less attractive features of Freud's personality, this impulse to "dire mastery"

---

4. The most devastating account of Lacan's therapeutic technique is offered by Didier Anzieu. As Anzieu reports, after the first two years of treatment Lacan reduced the length of their forty-five-minute sessions to thirty and then to twenty minutes. Lacan's waiting room, moreover, was filled with patients uncertain whether they would be seen; he "would open the door and point to the chosen one, who would cross the room again ten or fifteen minutes later to leave." During his sessions with Anzieu, Lacan would pace the room, read, summon the maid to bring him tea and sandwiches, and accept telephone calls. On one occasion, Lacan disappeared from the consulting room, telling Anzieu, "Don't let that stop you from continuing your session in my absence" (1986, 28)! When, shortly before the termination of the analysis, the number of weekly sessions was reduced from three to two and then to one, Lacan insisted that Anzieu continue to pay the same amount as he did when he had three sessions. In 1953, Anzieu went to be interviewed by the Training Committee of the Paris Psychoanalytic Society, whose members included Marie Bonaparte, to have his training analysis validated. Lacan asked him to conceal the fact that he had been given short sessions (30). Anzieu told the truth and was accepted as a candidate.

(Roustang 1976) is exacerbated by Lacan, whereas it is mitigated by Winnicott. The position of a moderate is no less precarious in psychoanalytic politics than in any other politics, but its inherent nobility shines forth in a letter written (in nonnative English) in 1966 to Winnicott by a South American analyst after she learned that he would not be able to undertake her reanalysis.

> During my analytical formation in Buenos Aires, and, after that, during all the subsequent years of practice and of training activities in Rio, I have seen a strenuous and senseless fighting between analysts who are told "Freudian ones" and analysts *soi-disant* "Kleinian ones." In the psychoanalytic literature, too, I met rarely with analysts who were alien to the spirit of that "sacred war." . . .
>
> Perhaps you consider I wish a "made to measure" analyst, someone idealized, and if so, perhaps you'll be right. But I must try to give to you an idea of my difficulties to meet with the skillful and at the same time available analyst. To express it in your own language: I am looking for a "good-enough" analyst to pay attention both to the environmental factors and to the individual fantasy, one who can accept the equally great contributions both of Freud and Melanie Klein, and Hartmann and others. In a few words, someone with a minimum of onesidedness.
>
> If you know some analyst, in London, with these requisites and the prospect of vacancy, I'll be very grateful to you by suggesting his name. And may be, after this new analysis, I begin "to be alone" with my own ideas and views.

This moving testimonial perfectly captures the inseparability of Winnicott's intellectual and personal qualities: the "minimum of onesidedness" that made him a leader of the Middle Group, the respect for others that caused him to look on them not as prospective converts but as individuals who should be encouraged "to be alone" with their own ideas.

It is disheartening to turn from the civility of Winnicott to the shrill invective that mars the rhetoric of Lacan. Throughout the *Ecrits* one encounters such phrases as "the degradation of psychoanalysis consequent on its American transplantation" (1958b, 283) and, in a mockery of the idea of the autonomous function of the ego, "the latest fetish introduced into the holy of holies . . . that derives its authority from the superiority of the superiors" (1955, 132). Having broken from the Paris Psychoanalytic Society and lost favor with the International Psychoanalytical Association, Lacan evidently felt free to express his scorn for the American tradition of ego psychology—epitomized by the

triumvirate of Heinz Hartmann, Ernst Kris, and Rudolph Loewenstein—in increasingly harsh and uncompromising terms.

What Lacan's disillusioned follower Catherine Clément calls his "familiarity with paranoid inspiration" (1981, 59) cannot predispose readers in favor of his theoretical claims. One measure of Lacan's "paranoid
inspiration" is the way that his citations of analytic authorities often
fluctuate according to an emotional barometer. In "The Mirror Stage
as Formative of the Function of the I," a paper originally delivered in
1936, for example, Anna Freud's *Ego and the Mechanisms of Defense*
(1936) is hailed as a "great work" (1949, 5), whereas in "The Freudian
Thing," which Lacan wrote after she had sided with Lacan's opponents
in the Paris Psychoanalytic Society, Anna Freud's contributions to ego
psychology are derided as "a marriage whose social credit has been on
the up and up . . . to the point where I am assured that it will soon
request the blessing of the church" (1955, 131).[5] There could be no
more telling indictment of Lacan's arrogance than what Jane Gallop
has justly branded the "outrageous fact" that in *Scilicet*, the journal of
the Freudian School founded in 1968, "all articles were published
anonymously except Lacan's, which bore his signature" (1985, 42–43).

Lacan's stylistic excesses, moreover, are replicated in the writings of
his adherents, to the point where they become traits of a recognizable
school. Thus, Maud Mannoni begins *The Child, His "Illness," and the
Others* by casting herself in the role of disciple: "I owe everything in the
field of theory to my master, Jacques Lacan" (1967, x). Although her
emphasis on the linguistic roots of symptoms is frequently illuminat-
ing, her work, like that of her "master," is vitiated by its assumption of a
privileged access to truth and its proclivity to rigid dichotomizing.
Insisting that "all developmental theories" must be "discarded" if psychosis is to be "approached correctly" (x), Mannoni avers that Freud's
discoveries "do not refer back to a real childhood or to the history of an
individual development, but to the language of the unconscious" (6).
She thus misguidedly assumes that a psychoanalytic emphasis on the
unconscious entails a turning away from the external world. As the
foregoing quotation attests, Mannoni is partial to the locution *not . . .
but. . . .* Elsewhere she writes: "The importance to be accorded in treat-

5. Schneiderman conjectures that part of Lacan's hostility to ego psychology
may derive from a sense of betrayal because his analyst, Rudolph Loewenstein,
departed for America without having properly terminated the analysis (1983,
157–58).

ment to *fantasy* . . . should be understood not as the image or trace of an experience lived through, but rather as a word lost" (44). In Mannoni's own parlance, these *not . . . but . . .* antitheses may be regarded as symptoms of an unhealthy tendency toward splitting, stemming from the Lacanian premise that the skeleton key of language permits its holder to dispense with all reference to the environment in the etiology of mental illness.

Lacan's belligerence is exacerbated by the conviction that he is the sole bearer of authentic Freudian revelation. In "The Freudian Thing" he delivers a lengthy harangue in the form of a sermon that announces itself as "the truth in Freud's mouth" (1955, 121). But the inevitable consequence of such ventriloquism is that Lacan smuggles in his own gospel under Freud's name. As one French analyst puts it: "Lacan was constantly exhorting a return to Freud, but most people found it more comfortable to accept his interpretation once and for all, and the book that became dog-eared was not Freud's *Interpretation of Dreams* but Lacan's *Ecrits*" (Turkle 1978, 126). A perennial attender of Lacan's seminars, Clément conveys just how pathetic he became at the end of his life, when his absorption in Borromean knots and abstruse mathematical formulae reduced him to complete incomprehensibility.

> Lacan, facing the blackboard, contemplated his knots. It was deadly. He spoke even less than before and in a muffled voice, as if unwilling to make himself understood. At the same time I began an analysis of my own. . . . I then had a strange experience: Lacan's writings, by themselves, without the support of the oral teaching, turned opaque and resisted all my efforts to penetrate them. . . . As I found my own voice in analysis, droning on day after day, it gradually took the place occupied for so long by the voice of the schools. One day it was inevitable that I should cease to be a schoolgirl. (1981, 187)

The opacity Clément begins to notice in Lacan's writings cannot fail to strike any impartial reader, and the dissolution of transference she undergoes after initiating her own analysis is doubtless a sign of emotional growth. Unlike the freedom the South American analyst received from Winnicott, however, the independence Clément achieved comes about as a reaction against the intellectual servitude demanded by Lacan. As Clément notes: "If Lacan's disciples stuck to him like glue, they were perhaps merely returning affection born of a dangerous proximity that was not their fault but Lacan's" (78). Clément's testimony, like Schneiderman's, comes to us at first hand; and the portrait they draw of Lacan is all the more incriminating because they are such honest and even sympathetic witnesses. In contrast to the dogmatism of Lacan's "return to Freud," Winnicott's spirit of tolerance enables a less oppressive Freud to return to us.

Having impugned Lacan on personal grounds, I turn now to an assessment of his ideas, without, I trust, losing sight of the productive stimulus that Lacan's reading of Freud has afforded to many of the most gifted analysts and humanists of the present generation. To meet Lacan's postmodern challenge, I shall probe two of his most cherished tenets—the mirror stage and the linguistic structure of the unconscious. Only at the close of this chapter, after anatomizing Kohut, will I take up Lacan's obsession with the phallus and the question of the proper balance between oedipal and preoedipal levels of interpretation.

A point of entry into Lacan's theory of the mirror stage is provided by Maud Mannoni's disdain for those analysts who would pay attention to "real childhood" or "individual development." As I have already argued, the consequence of this view is to suppress the role of the environment as an etiological factor in mental illness. What is more, in holding this extreme position the Lacanian outlook overlaps to a surprising degree with that of Melanie Klein and her followers, who likewise leave out the real mother in their attempt to account for infantile psychology solely in terms of fantasy. To be sure, Lacan (1954) differentiates himself sharply from Klein, criticizing her paper on symbol formation (1930) for treating projection and introjection as equivalent processes, whereas in his conceptual scheme projection is a function of the Imaginary register and introjection of the Symbolic register. Notwithstanding these important differences, which reflect Klein's concentration on preverbal, and Lacan's on verbal, experience, they both exhibit what is from a Winnicottian standpoint the idealistic fallacy of constructing theories about infants apart from the caretakers on whom the infants depend for their survival and growth.

That Lacan's hypothesis of the mirror stage in fact ignores the external world is clear from his statement that the "jubilant assumption of his specular image" on the part of a child between six and eighteen months "situates the agency of the ego, before its social determination, in a fictional direction" (1949, 2). Since environmental factors begin to impinge even in the womb, it is preposterous for Lacan to suppose that the ego of a *toddler* precedes any "social determination." At no point in his paper does Lacan acknowledge that adults must be taking care of the child.

Although Winnicott presents his alternative in characteristically modest fashion, simply saying that "Lacan does not think of the mirror in terms of the mother's face in the way that I do here," he summarily refutes Lacan's concept of the mirror stage with his dictum that "*the precursor of the mirror is the mother's face*" (1967e, 111).[6] At a stroke, Winnicott restores to psychoanalysis a theory of the environment that is not provided by either Lacan or Klein. According to Lacan, the ego must not be regarded "as centered on the *perception-consciousness system,* or as organized by the 'reality principle'"; "we should start instead from the *function of méconnaissance* that characterizes the ego in all its structures" (1949, 6). In Winnicott's rejoinder, however, the idea that the ego originates in misrecognition—assumed by Lacan to be a universal truth—is shown to be rather a *breakdown phenomenon* that comes to pass only when the mother does not perform her mirroring function adequately. Winnicott writes: "A mother must fail in satisfying instinctual demands, but she may completely succeed in not 'letting the infant down,' *in catering for ego needs*" (1956a, 312). In upholding the possibility of achieving an integrated sense of self, Winnicott is fundamentally in agreement with the ego psychologists derided by Lacan.

The divergence between the models of mirroring proposed by Lacan and Winnicott epitomizes the contrast between a solipsistic and a relational conception of human experience. Like the pool of Narcissus, Lacan's mirror is inanimate and gives back to the infant only an estranged reflection of his or her image. Because Winnicott's mirror is the face of the living mother, however, she "sees her infant as human at a time when the infant is incapable of feeling integrated" (1964a, 183). Lacan's rejection of "the idea of an environment that is preformed" for its inhabitants as "unthinkable," moreover, leads him to define human relationships—in a psychoanalytic recasting of Hegel's master-slave

---

6. In an important qualification of both Lacan's and Winnicott's emphasis on visual signals, Didier Anzieu points out that "the first communication between the baby and the maternal and familial environment is a mirror, which is both tactile and acoustic" (1985, 52). Anzieu likewise criticizes Klein for her omission of the "body's surface" from her theory of part objects and for the "interpretative bombardment" that tends to follow from this overlooking of the ego's function as a "protective envelope" (37).

dialectic—as based on "an aggressivity linked to the narcissistic relation and to the structures of systematic *méconnaissance* and objectification that characterize the formation of the ego" (1948, 21). According to Winnicott, the ambience of maternal care under good-enough conditions indeed provides a "preformed" environment for the infant and instills a sense of genuine relatedness that can abide throughout life.

Winnicott's vision of the mother-child bond finds consummate poetic anticipation in Wordsworth's meditation on the "infant Babe" in book 2 of *The Prelude*.

> blest the Babe,
> Nursed in his Mother's arms, who sinks to sleep
> Rocked on his Mother's breast; who with his soul
> Drinks in the feelings of his Mother's eye!
> For him, in one dear Presence, there exists
> A virtue which irradiates and exalts
> Objects through widest intercourse of sense.
> No outcast he, bewildered and depressed:
> Along his infant veins are interfused
> The gravitation and the filial bond
> Of nature that connect him with the world.

(1850, ll. 234–44)

In keeping with Winnicott's formulations, Wordsworth's baby discovers the precursor of the mirror when he "drinks in the feelings of his Mother's eye." (The oral imagery fuses gazing on the mother's face with breast-feeding.) Wordsworth's baby is manifestly a real baby, with a real mother and with an innate tendency to form attachments. Unlike Lacan's captive of the mirror stage, moreover, Wordsworth's fondled infant is "no outcast" and does not find himself "bewildered and depressed" by méconnaissance. Indeed, Wordsworth presciently invokes a power that "irradiates and exalts / Objects," and his affirmation that the "filial bond" between mother and child constitutes "one dear Presence" contrasts with the currently fashionable doctrine that the human condition is a perpetual aporia of Absence.

The Winnicottian resonances in this passage from *The Prelude* are augmented when Wordsworth ascribes "the first / Poetic spirit of our human life" to the mother's ability to respond to the infant's spontaneous gestures—such as reaching for a flower—so that he becomes a "creator and receiver both" of what he encounters in the world (ll. 258–61). This illustration of a preformed environment leads Wordsworth, like Winnicott (1953, 1967d), to recognize transitional objects and to locate creativity in the intermediate space between reality and fantasy that has its prototype in childhood play. Although Wordsworth shares Winnicott's incurable optimism, neither the poet nor the psychoanalyst is blind to the tragic dimensions of human life. When Wordsworth was eight years old, his mother died, and he "was left alone, / Seeking the visible world, nor knowing why" (ll. 278–79). Even this loss, however, did not permanently cripple him emotionally.

> The props of my affection were removed,
> And yet the building stood, as if sustained
> By its own spirit!
>
> (ll. 280–82)

To reformulate in psychoanalytic terms, Wordsworth was able to internalize his mother as a good object because she had nurtured his capacity for illusion in infancy, and his psyche did not collapse under the shock of disillusionment when he was forever separated from her by death.

If Wordsworth's *Prelude* exemplifies Winnicott's theory of mirroring, a no less formidable literary counterpart to Lacan's mirror stage is provided by Shakespeare's *Troilus and Cressida.* In act 3, scene 3, Ulysses comes to the tent of Achilles to goad the sulking hero into action by comparing him unfavorably to Ajax. The wily orator begins by extolling a book he has been reading.

> A strange fellow here
> Writes me that man, how dearly ever parted,
> How much in having, or without or in,
> Cannot make boast to have that which he hath,
> Nor feels not what he owes, but by reflection.
>
> (1601, ll. 95–99)

When Achilles protests that such views are commonplace, Ulysses parries by drawing out their most subversive implications.

> I do not strain at the position—
> It is familiar—but at the author's drift,
> Who in his circumstance expressly proves
> That no man is the lord of anything,
> Though in and of him there be much consisting,
> Till he communicate his parts to others.
>
> (ll. 111–15)

Although the identity of the author cited by Ulysses remains a scholarly enigma, I would propose that he has been reading Lacan's *Ecrits*.

For Ulysses' radical extension of the principle of reflection to prove
that "no man is the lord of anything" apart from the "applause" of
others (l. 119) foreshadows Rimbaud's ungrammatical apothegm "Je
est un autre" (I is an other), invoked by Lacan to buttress his hypothesis
of the permanently alienated ego (1954–55, 17), which has since become a veritable mantra of postmodernism. In keeping with Lacan's
theory of "an aggressivity linked to the narcissistic relation," moreover,
Ulysses torments Achilles with a specter of a world of ubiquitous rivalry
in which the honor of one warrior can only be purchased at the
expense of another.

> Take the instant way:
> For honour travels in a strait so narrow
> Where one but goes abreast. Keep then the path,
> For emulation hath a thousand sons
> That one by one pursue.

(ll. 153–57)

The culminating symbol for this universe of specular externality in
Troilus and Cressida is the "putrified core" of the anonymous Greek
warrior slain by Hector for his armor just before he himself is slaugh-
tered in a disarmed state by the vengeful Achilles (5.8.1).

As *Troilus and Cressida* attests, the Lacanian view of the world is
compelling and coherent. Once again, however, I would argue that this
is by no means a normative portrait of the human condition; it is rather
a theoretical codification of the pathological distortions that can take
place when environmental care has been seriously deficient in the
earliest stages of life. Even *Troilus and Cressida*, after all, has an anoma-
lous place in Shakespeare's canon—it falls outside the generic classi-
fications of comedy, history, and tragedy in the First Folio—and is
likewise unsurpassed in the ferocity of its nihilism. The aggressivity
that Lacan exposes is indubitably a blight on human existence, but its
origin lies in a reactive process of disintegration for which his own
theory conspicuously fails to account.

Even more than for his early "Mirror Stage," Lacan is renowned for
his insistence that "the unconscious is structured in the most radical
way like a language" (1958a, 234). This assertion is complemented by
Lacan's definition of the unconscious as "the discourse of the other"
(1953, 55). Just as the hypothesis of the mirror stage is vitiated by its
neglect of the environment, so is Lacan's linguistic bias flawed by his
disregard of the realm of preverbal experience.

To begin with, it is not clear how Lacan's concept of the mirror stage, which is preverbal, can be squared with his linguistic paradigm; together they suggest that the Imaginary does not belong to the unconscious. Whatever the solution to this conundrum, Lacan loses no opportunity to deprecate nonverbal experience. In "Intervention on Transference" he boasts that "a dialectical conception of psychoanalysis" is "an orientation peculiar to my thinking" and that it is a "self-evident fact" that psychoanalysis "deals solely with words." Any attention paid to "the mute aspects of behavior," he continues, "merely demonstrates a preference on the part of the analyst for a point of view from which the subject is no more than an object" (1966, 63). Elsewhere Lacan opines that "there is nothing in the unconscious which accords with the body" (1975, 165).

In spite of its initial seductiveness, however, the poverty of this orientation may be seen in its inability to account for what Wordsworth calls the "mute dialogues" that he as a baby held "by intercourse of touch" with his "mother's heart" (1850, 2.267–68) and which Bollas has dubbed the "unthought known." Far from stripping the analysand of his or her status as a subject, as Lacan supposes, the technical consequence of this attention to nonverbal self-states—beginning with the papers of Paula Heimann (1950, 1956)—has been to sensitize analysts to the heuristic importance of countertransference and hence (as I argued in chapter 1) to render the analytic situation not less but more dialectical. To follow Bollas's (1987, 280) exegesis of Freud's terminology, Lacan confounds *secondary* repression, which involves "mental representations" and may therefore indeed be said to be structured like a language, with *primary* repression, which arises from the interplay between "operational processes" and inherited endowment—Winnicott's True Self—and constitutes the unthought known.

Once allowance has been made for the foundation laid by preverbal experience, however, it is possible to emend Lacan's proposition to read: the unconscious is also structured like a language. There is nothing disconcerting to an object relations theorist in the idea that the unconscious is the "discourse of the other" once the definition of *discourse* has been expanded to include holding and handling as well as speaking. As Ulysses might put it, "I do not strain" at Lacan's "position," which is "familiar," but only at his "drift," at the overstatements that stretch his argument beyond the bounds of credibility.

In sum, by reaffirming the role of the environment and of preverbal experience, it may be possible to synthesize Lacan's view with object relations psychoanalysis. Such a project, for example, might juxtapose Winnicott's transitional object with Lacan's *objet a*, which, as André Green has explained, "becomes effective only when the break between the subject and maternal object separates irremediably the two entities" (1966, 167). One could then rethink fetishism as a response at once to the agony of maternal abandonment and to the shock of discovering maternal castration.[7] At moments, Lacan himself seems to glimpse such a reconciliation, as when he writes to Winnicott on August 5, 1960: "Does not the 'transitional object,' all of whose merits I have shown to those close to me, indicate the site at which, precociously, that distinction of desire in relation to need is marked?" (Copjec 1987, 78).

Unfortunately, however, this note of compromise is all too rarely sounded in Lacan's published writings, where he prides himself rather on his intransigence. In "The Signification of the Phallus," for example, Lacan berates those "analyst-nurses" with their "psychology of child-rearing," who display an "ever-present obscurantism that is still more boring" when they seek to effect a "theoretical and practical reduction of desire to need." The child's "insatiable demand," Lacan assures us, has nothing to do with "the effect of his real dependence" (1958b, 286). Especially when read against the 1960 letter, this passage seems to be a veiled attack on Winnicott, whose critique of the mirror stage is precisely its neglect of "real dependence" and who might well be satirized as an "analyst-nurse" who reduces desire to need.

In one of his diatribes against ego psychology, Lacan warns: "If this point of view is true, we must abandon the notion that I claim to be in the essence of the Freudian discovery, the decentering of the subject with regard to the ego. . . . If it is true, everything I say is false" (Richardson 1983, 64–65). This ultimatum typifies Lacan's predilection for either-or thinking, a cast of mind that Victoria Hamilton—in a trenchant critique of Kleinianism—has labeled the *tragic vision* (1982, 239). (That both Lacan and Klein regularly resort to all-or-nothing formulations is a defect of their intellectual styles that corresponds to their emphases on language or fantasy as all-embracing explanatory principles.) Like the ego psychologists, Winnicott rejects "the decentering of the subject" and hence by Lacan's criterion must be oblivious to "the essence of the Freudian discovery." But it is Lacan's own suppres-

---

7. Susan Deri proposes that the fetish, in addition to its familiar phallic meanings, could be "born of early distress due to abandonment" (1984, 258–59).

sion of the third area of experience—his refusal to emulate Winnicott's double vision—that makes integrating his thought and Winnicott's so difficult. If I prefer Winnicott *to* Lacan, my reasons include the paradoxical hope that it may yet be possible to have Winnicott *with* Lacan.

In contrast with the far-reaching issues at stake in the confrontation between Winnicott and Lacan, the choice between Winnicott with Kohut is circumscribed in its implications. To be sure, the controversy generated by self psychology has engulfed the psychoanalytic world, but the quarrel remains a parochial one, and its impact has not extended to contemporary philosophy and literary criticism. What is more, since Winnicott and Kohut agree on most matters of principle, both being representatives of the broad shift in psychoanalytic thinking away from Freud's drive model, the grounds for distinguishing between them are largely stylistic and temperamental. Nonetheless, an appraisal of Kohut's work remains indispensable to any mapping of the post-Freudian psychoanalytic domain, and I shall explain why I find his work far less compelling than Winnicott's.

Kohut's first and most obvious liability is rhetorical. Whereas Winnicott writes masterly prose, pellucid yet profound, Kohut's is hopelessly turgid. He routinely presents even straightforward ideas in the most convoluted manner.

> The point of view, for example, taken with regard to such seemingly esoteric questions as whether it is correct to say that man is born helpless because he is not born with a significantly functioning ego apparatus—rather than that he is born powerful because a milieu of empathic self-objects *is* indeed his self—or whether man's untamed drives are the primary units in the world of complex mental states with which introspective-empathic depth psychology deals—rather than that the primary units are *ab initio* the complex experiences and action patterns of a self/self-object unit—is closely connected with the attitude (manifested in concrete behavior) that the depth-psychologist chooses to adopt as the most appropriate one for the therapeutic setting. (1977, 249–50)

This tortuous sentence insinuates that changes in analytic thinking about drives and dependence lead to subtle shifts in behavior with patients. But when, as Morris Eagle has complained, psychoanalytic writing "includes formulations so vague and jargon-filled that there is serious question whether they have any empirical meaning" (1984, 180), there is little incentive to wade through the text at all.

Kohut's most serious drawback as a thinker is his persistent refusal to confront the relations between his own ideas and those of other analysts. In the preface to *The Restoration of the Self*, Kohut lists ten major figures—including Lacan and Winnicott—whose areas of research "overlap" with his own but defends his "continuing lack of integration of their contributions," saying his book is a personal one and not "a technical or theoretical monograph written detachedly by an author who has achieved mastery in a stable or established field of knowledge" (1977, xx). This line of reasoning is at best disingenuous. It assumes that engagement with the work of others must be "detached," rather than a vehicle for highly committed and subjective thought, and that a body of knowledge can be "stable." Kohut thereby seeks to avoid acknowledging that others have preceded him into the territory that he regards as his private intellectual preserve.

The charge of slighting the contributions of colleagues is one to which Winnicott is also vulnerable. He begins one paper by declaring: "I shall not first give an historical survey and show the development of my ideas from the theories of others, because my mind does not work that way. What happens is that I gather this and that, here and there, settle down to clinical experience, form my own theories and then, last of all, interest myself in looking to see where I stole what" (1945, 145). Such a lighthearted confession could not endear Winnicott to those who found their ideas thus unconsciously plagiarized. Indeed, in a letter of December 14, 1966, Michael Balint—Winnicott's most distinguished ally in the Middle Group of the British Psycho-Analytical Society—protests that the way Winnicott posed a question (about whether Balint had grasped the implications of Winnicott's newly minted term *the location of cultural experience*) "is really unfair because it does not allow any freedom to one who wishes to reply sincerely." Balint goes on to frame a more sweeping indictment.

> Perhaps I ought to say here that this has happened several times during our friendship. You emphasized on more than one occasion that "though—(I quote from memory)—Ferenczi and Dr. Balint have said all these many years ago, here I am not concerned with what they said," or "I have not had time to read that but I shall ask the Honorary Librarian to fill this gap," etc. Of course, in this way you always have the audience laughing and on your side—no-one among us likes to read boring scientific literature and if somebody of your stature admits it in public, he can be certain of his success.
>
> ... Your way of expressing your ideas forces one into the position of either saying "this is splendid and entirely new" or of remaining silent.

Balint's rebuke attests to the human toll exacted by Winnicott's commitment to following his own inner development and suggests that the evasions of Kohut are to some degree simply the self-protective measures of any original thinker against the anxiety of influence (Bloom 1973).

In spite of this resemblance, however, Winnicott and Kohut differ in one crucial respect in their attitudes toward other people: Winnicott, unlike Kohut, was capable of genuine contrition for his lapses. In January 1967, only a few weeks after receiving the letter from Balint, Winnicott began an informal autobiographical talk to the 1952 Club (a society of senior British analysts) with the following words: "I've realized more and more as time went on what a tremendous lot I've lost from not properly correlating my work with the work of others. It's not only annoying to other people but it's rude and it has meant that what I've said has been isolated and people have to do a lot of work to get at it. It happens to be my temperament, and it's a big fault" (1967b, 573). In contrast, Kohut, in a retrospective paper published the year before his death, attempts to rebut the hypothesis that "vanity is the culprit" responsible for his lack of scholarly scruples: "I have done everything in my power to avoid succumbing to the petty desire to have the stage to myself" (1980, 476). In view of Kohut's failure even to acknowledge his fault, let alone atone for it, we must conclude that his negation is a Freudian one and that the theorist of narcissism was himself afflicted with more than a touch of grandiosity.

From the beginning to the end of his career, Kohut betrays acute uneasiness with respect to the claims of object relations theory. In his first major paper, "Introspection, Empathy, and Psychoanalysis," in which he adopts an implicitly hermeneutic perspective, Kohut asserts that the hypothesis that childhood sexuality and the Oedipus complex are "related to, or part of, the prolonged, biologically necessitated dependence of the human infant" is "not based on psychoanalytic observation," and he attacks the "unreliability" of efforts to establish links between "repressed dependence strivings in an adult analysand" and an infant's dependence on its mother (1959, 473–74). Kohut thereby seeks to eviscerate the principle of genetic explanation, which, as I argued in chapter 4, is a cornerstone of the psychoanalytic edifice that must be retained even after Freud's drive theory has been abandoned.

Similarly, in his retrospective 1980 paper, Kohut returns to the possibility of a synthesis between self psychology and the work of other theorists, particularly Mahler and Winnicott. Kohut's polemic is compounded of intellectual confusion and a distortion of the views of those from whom he wishes to dissociate himself. He reproaches Mahler and Winnicott because their "focus on circumscribed periods of individual development" prevents them from furnishing the "broad concept of man" purportedly provided by both classical analysis and self psychology (474). Kohut does not specify what these "circumscribed periods" are, but he clearly means infancy and childhood. No less than in 1959, Kohut treats the earliest years of life as merely one phase of life on a par with the rest and supposes that a "broader" version of psychoanalysis may be obtained by jettisoning a developmental perspective.

In his apologia, Kohut classifies Winnicott, Mahler, and René Spitz together as "psychoanalytic child observers" (1980, 478). Now, it is true that Winnicott is famous for having seen over sixty thousand children and their parents in his pediatric clinics over the course of his career and that his account of the spatula game in "The Observation of Infants in a Set Situation" (1941) is a masterpiece of psychodynamically informed experimental research. In addition to being unfair to Mahler and Spitz, who were major theorists as well as pioneers in direct observation, Kohut overlooks two facts: Winnicott was above all a practicing analyst of both adults and children, and (whether rightly or wrongly) he repeatedly affirmed that "it is not from direct observation of infants as much as from the study of the transference in the analytic setting that it is possible to gain a clear view of what takes place in infancy itself" (1960b, 54). Winnicott was equally at home in empirical and clinical modes of psychoanalytic inquiry, and Kohut's one-sided summary in no sense does justice to the complexity of his genius.

This misrepresentation of Winnicott is heightened by an egregious distortion of object relations theory. Kohut stresses that according to self psychology, "man lives in a matrix of selfobjects from birth to death" and that violent emotions are seen "not as primary givens but as secondary phenomena due to disturbances in the self-selfobject unit" (1980, 478, 479). Thus, self psychologists will not focus on the baby's "clutching of substitutes for the unresponsive or unavailable mother" as though this were a "primary" psychological configuration. Kohut fails to realize that what he depicts as the unique insight of self psychology forms a mainstay of object relations thinking. That transitional objects come into play, not when the mother is "unavailable or unresponsive" but in the normal course of a child's development, is a further telling distortion of Winnicott's ideas. When Kohut adds that, as part of their study of the abiding need for self-objects, self psychologists "will ask how in tune with the small baby's specific needs the responses of the selfobject were at the beginning of extrauterine life," he awkwardly reframes the central question posed by Winnicott in his investigations into what makes a good-enough mother.

The apogee of Kohut's blundering comes when he pronounces it to be "the unquestioned—and even unmentioned because it is taken for granted—assumption of all the schools of child observation that are not guided by the self psychological point of view that man's life from childhood to adulthood is a move forward from a position of helplessness, dependence, and shameful clinging to a position of power, independence, and proud autonomy" (1980, 480). Persisting in his misleading equation of object relations theory with "schools of child observation," Kohut goes astray on two major counts: in imputing to this school the belief that a baby's attachment to its mother is somehow "shameful" and the belief that complete independence in life can be achieved, let alone "proud autonomy." On the contrary, Fairbairn expressly defines human development in terms of an evolution from infantile dependence to mature dependence, adding that he terms the final goal "'mature dependence' rather than 'independence,' since a capacity for relationships necessarily implies dependence of some sort" (1946, 145).

A more fatally skewed assessment of the British school than Kohut's could scarcely be imagined. Ironically, however, his inaccuracies and defensive evasions of influence only serve to call attention to the essential truth about self psychology: that it is a hybrid offshoot of object relations theory, notable chiefly for its metapsychological focus on issues of narcissism.[8] Because he fails to recognize this kinship—and, indeed, actively represses it from awareness—Kohut does not exploit the parallels between his ideas and those of British psychoanalysts to any constructive purpose. Nonetheless, the parallels confront his readers at every turn, especially in *The Restoration of the Self,* where Kohut finally emancipates himself from Freud's economic model, upon which he had continued to rely in *The Analysis of the Self* (1971).

I have already cited Kohut's statement that human beings spend

8. Similar conclusions are reached by Jay Greenberg and Stephen Mitchell (1983, 352) and by Morris Eagle (1984, 74). Extended discussions of Kohut's links to the British school are offered by Bernard Brandschaft (1989) and Howard Bacal (1987, 1989).

their lives "in a matrix of selfobjects" as one instance when he unwittingly echoes object relations theory. He likewise merely recapitulates the revision of Freud's libido theory already effected by Fairbairn and others in Britain in the 1940s and 1950s when he writes: "The infantile sexual drive in isolation is not the primary psychological configuration. . . . [This configuration] is the experience of the relation between the self and the empathic self-object" (1977, 122). What is more, Kohut's central idea of the self-object is far more cogently expressed in terms of Winnicott's distinction between "the subjective object and the object objectively perceived" (1971c, 38).

On numerous other occasions, Kohut wraps himself in robes borrowed from Winnicott. Without acknowledging Winnicott's aphorism "The precursor of the mirror is the mother's face," Kohut posits that behind the threat of castration posed by the female genitals there "lies the cold, unresponding, nonmirroring face of the mother" (1977, 189). Even more famous than Winnicott's remark about the mother's face is his concept of the good-enough mother. Paradoxically, to be "good enough" is also to be "bad enough," that is, able through gradual and phase-appropriate failures of adaptation to permit the infant to undergo the process of separation. "The mother's main task," Winnicott observes profoundly, "(next to providing opportunity for illusion) is disillusionment" (1953, 13). Kohut reinvents this Winnicottian wheel when he alludes to the "principle of optimal frustration" or to "optimally frustrating parents," who have accepted their place in the transient sequence of generations (1977, 78, 237). Winnicott coins the term *primary maternal preoccupation* to describe the state of undivided care that the mother gives to her baby after birth (1963d, 85–86). Kohut likewise refers to one adoptive mother's failure to develop "that total intimacy which normally establishes itself between a mother and her baby" (1977, 27).

Nor is it only Winnicott whom Kohut seems inadvertently to circumlocute. He compares the oxygen needed for physical survival to the "empathic-responsive human milieu" required by the growing child (1977, 85) but neglects to mention that Balint had used the same analogy to describe the "harmonious 'mix-up'" between the individual and the environment beginning even before birth (1968, 66). Kohut's evocation of the "crumbling, decomposing, fragmenting, enfeebled" modern self (1977, 286) dovetails more generally with R. D. Laing's anatomy of ontological insecurity in *The Divided Self* (1959). In discussing how artists anticipate shifts in the psychological temper of an era,

Kohut singles out Kafka's protagonist K. as "the Everyman of our time" (1977, 287). Nearly two decades earlier, Laing had named Kafka and Beckett, in contrast to Shakespeare and Keats, as writers who have imagined a world "in which there is no contradictory sense of the self in its 'health and validity' to mitigate the despair, terror, and boredom of existence" (1959, 40–41). Kohut enlists Kafka to support his distinction between Tragic Man and Guilty Man, that is, between the complementary aspects of human nature as seen through the lenses of conflict psychology and self psychology. But, as Steven Marcus has noticed, this polarity is "foredoomed from the outset" (1986, 324) since Kafka—Kohut's paradigmatic Tragic Man—is one of the most guilt-ridden authors in modern literature.

It is, of course, not suspect or surprising for two prominent researchers in the same field to find themselves working independently toward a common goal. If anything, such parallel investigations serve to corroborate the timeliness of a line of inquiry. In this instance, Winnicott in London and Kohut in Chicago came to very similar conclusions about the reforms that were needed in the theory and practice of psychoanalysis. Kohut's "Two Analyses of Mr. Z" (1979)—to my mind his most impressive paper—is an exemplary demonstration of the therapeutic consequences of the paradigm shift brought about by both self psychology and object relations theory.

Although Kohut deserves a place of honor in the pantheon of contemporary psychoanalysis, and he has unquestionably exerted a great influence on the clinical work of analysts in the United States, he falls short when measured against the supreme standard set by Winnicott. Not just his belatedness but his rebarbative style, his neglect of childhood and genetic explanation, and his deliberate ignoring of the contributions of colleagues all tell heavily against him. Symptomatically, in *The Restoration of the Self*, Kohut's scattered references to Klein and his single mention of Rank—who is faulted for "narrowing" the focus of analysis to issues of separation anxiety (1977, 101)—are wholly negative. Both Rank and Klein can be criticized on various counts, but their work is of inestimable importance, and any fair-minded assessment requires that some attention be paid to their strengths as well as to their weaknesses.

Kohut's dismissal of Rank and Klein, along with his rigidly defensive posture toward Winnicott and Mahler, sustains the judgment that self psychology is a historically deracinated species of object relations theory stunted by transferential jealousies. The most positive feature of self psychology is its focus on the self as a superordinate category of experience. But the first two references in *The Analysis of the Self* are to Heinz Hartmann, and Kohut emancipates himself from his background of ego psychology only with the utmost difficulty. If, as I argued (following Guntrip) in chapter 1, the decisive question for contemporary psychoanalysis is whether to adhere to a notion of the system ego or the person ego, on this score, too, I conclude that one should eschew the Viennese-American tradition of Hartmann and Kohut in favor of the British tradition of Fairbairn and Winnicott.

As Leo Rangell has observed, "recurrent controversies over psychoanalytic theory have continuously centered on the role played by the Oedipus complex in psychological life," and since the time of Jung, "alternative systems have been aimed at effacing its role alternately from above and below, first by emphasizing environmental factors and then by turning with equal force to pregenital determinants as preceding and replacing the centrality of the oedipal." The history of psychoanalysis, Rangell adds, exhibits the melancholy spectacle of "a repression of the Oedipus complex in theory, and an acting out of it in group life" (1982, 39, 38).

Rangell sets the debate in its proper historical context, and his defense of the continued centrality of the Oedipus complex is spirited. Nonetheless, his championing of neo-Freudian orthodoxy contains several troubling features. Although it is doubtless true, as he contends, that analysts' intellectual loyalties are often shaped by transferential motives, which take root during their experiences in training, Rangell calls these dynamics "pathological" and seems to think that they apply only to those tendencies that he regards as "deviations in theory" (30). Rangell thus commits the psychoanalytic sin of believing that he himself is exempted from the neurotic failings that he complacently diagnoses in others. Such a denial of his own transferential investment makes Rangell's paper not a working through but a perpetuation of the tragic phenomenon of oedipal blindness in psychoanalysis.

Rangell exhibits this authoritarian attitude throughout his paper. In his view, "indefensible arguments . . . are invariably the glue which binds a new group together" (31). By this standard, all psychoanalytic dissidents must be irrational and all their arguments invalid! He again brands self psychology and allied movements as "pathological developments" (33) and deplores that the seeds of "a negative transference to psychoanalysis itself" are sown in the training analysis (35). (That the candidate might justifiably resent the flaws of his or her analyst is inconceivable to Rangell.) At the same time, a "positive transference" to the psychoanalytic cause is accepted as unproblematic. Rangell thereby perpetuates the worst excesses of Ernest Jones's attacks on Ferenczi and Rank in his biography of Freud, and his dogmatism masquerading as intellectual objectivity must be reprehended by all those who value an independent tradition in psychoanalysis.

The extremism of Rangell's formulations prepares us for what might otherwise be a surprising fact—the congruence between his views on the Oedipus complex and castration anxiety and those of Lacan. Rangell protests: "In common to all of the alternative theories is a down-playing of the castration danger and an attempt to eliminate this nuclear anxiety from the reservoir of neurosogenic factors" (1982, 40). In the same vein, Lacan laments that "no one is any longer concerned, with certain rare exceptions found among my pupils, with the ternary structure of the Oedipus complex or with the castration complex" (1973, 11). To a query from Françoise Dolto about whether it might not be necessary to retain the idea of developmental stages in theories about childhood, Lacan replies: "The fear of castration is like a thread that perforates all the stages of development. It orientates the relations that are anterior to its actual appearance—weaning, toilet training, etc. It crystallizes each of these moments in a dialectic that has as its centre a bad encounter" (64).

I cited Rangell's comments on the "down-playing of the castration danger" in chapter 4, and in point of fact, the "alternative theories" he impugns frequently do conform to his description of them. There is, as I have argued, a continuity between Rank's declaration that "the Oedipus complex is only a transient phase of development and that its success or failure has been decisively determined beforehand by the original relation to the mother" (app. A) and Fairbairn's conclusion that "the role of ultimate cause, which Freud allotted to the Oedipus situation, should properly be allotted to the phenomenon of infantile dependence" (1944, 120). Indeed, Fairbairn claims to have "dispensed with" it as an "explanatory concept" (120). To the revisionist stock, which also includes Harry Stack Sullivan, we must now graft Kohut, for he rejects the "universal applicability" of the Oedipus complex and ascribes its "conflict-ridden" quality not to any "maturational necessity" but merely to empathic failures on the part of "narcissistically disturbed parents" (1977, 223, 247). He reiterates in the posthumously published *How Does Analysis Cure?* that self psychology "will not view castration anxiety as a feature of the oedipal phase of the healthy child of healthy parents" (1984, 14).

To correct the astigmatisms blurring vision on both sides of this dispute—the orthodox reducing everything to the Oedipus complex, the revisionists denying it any explanatory power—a more dialectical sensibility is clearly required. Like the tension between the poles of inner fantasy and external environment, that between a preoedipal (or developmental) and an oedipal (or structural) perspective is inherent in psychoanalytic theory. Didier Anzieu strikes exactly the right note when he remarks: "The two positions are, in my opinion, complementary, and the antagonism between them must be preserved so long as it remains fruitful for psychoanalytic research" (1985, 4).

Of the three figures in contemporary psychoanalysis scrutinized in this chapter, Winnicott's outlook is far and away the most flexible and comprehensive. In contrast to those Lacanians and Rangellians for whom the whole of infantile sexuality is determined by the "signification of the phallus," Winnicott is prepared to grant that there is a phallic *stage* at which "there is plenty of room for unhappiness and distress in small girls who simply feel inferior when their brothers swank," but he suggests that there is also a "corresponding male envy of female" nurturing and reproductive functions that must be taken into account (1988, 45). In this, he follows Melanie Klein against Freud. Yet he also dissents when Klein traces the origins of the Oedipus complex to the infant's relation to the mother's breast. Winnicott writes: "I think something is lost if the term 'Oedipus Complex' is applied to the earlier stages, in which there are only two persons involved and the third person or part object is internalized, a phenomenon of inner reality. I cannot see the value of the term Oedipus Complex where one or more of the trio is a part object. In the Oedipus Complex, for me at least, each of the three of the triangle is a whole person, not only for the observer but also and especially for the child" (49).

This reasoning likewise addresses the later objections of André Green, who remains true to his Lacanian heritage when he maintains that there is no properly dyadic relation of mother and child, since "between them we find the father who is somewhere in the mother's unconscious" (1975, 50). Green's structural brief for the ubiquity of the phallus possesses considerable force—it returns us to the possible conjunction between Lacan's *objet a* and Winnicott's transitional object—but like the speculations of Klein, it becomes unbalanced when used to deny that there is such a thing as dyadic or preoedipal experience from the standpoint of the child.

Just as Winnicott parts company with those apostles of orthodoxy who talismanically invoke the name of Oedipus, he also abjures the apostates who refuse to pronounce Freud's shibboleth. According to Winnicott, Klein's depressive position—the sense of guilt experienced by the infant when it recognizes that the formerly split images of the good and bad breast belong to the same person and hence that it has tried in fantasy to destroy the mother whom it also loves—"ranks with Freud's concept of the Oedipus complex" as a contribution to psychoanalysis (1962b, 176), but this takes it for granted that Winnicott esteems the Oedipus complex as Freud's greatest discovery. Precisely because Winnicott holds arrival at the Oedipus complex to be a developmental achievement, which is not vouchsafed to psychotic individuals, he affirms that "it is the simple triangle that presents the difficulties, and the full richness of human experience" (1988, 39). Thus, unlike either Lacan or Kohut, Winnicott balances an awareness of the continuity of the Oedipus complex against an appreciation of its unique status as the portal of entry into human culture.[9]

9. See also Mahler, who asserts that the Oedipus complex "forms the core of both normal development and the 'normal' infantile neurosis," although it is shaped by the "ubiquitous phenomenon" of the earlier dyadic rapprochement crisis (1988, 149).

6 ♦ WINNICOTT AND FREUD

Psycho-analytic theory is all the time developing, and it must
develop by a natural process rather like the emotional
condition of the human being that is under study.—D. W.
Winnicott, *Human Nature*

As André Green has observed, "Winnicott's originality of thought and his originality as a person were inseparable" (Clancier and Kalmanovitch 1984, 139); in this chapter, I approach Winnicott and Freud in both biographical and intellectual terms. I take their contrasting attitudes toward religion as a point of departure for a selective comparison of their personal histories, then I turn to the domain of ideas and show how Winnicott's meditation on the mother-child bond leads not only to a recasting of psychoanalytic theory but also to an account of culture as a whole. A brief conclusion uses the dichotomy between Winnicott's optimism and Freud's pessimism to tie together the biographical and the theoretical threads of the discussion.

Clare Winnicott tells of a Sunday when the young Donald, walking home with his father from church, asked him about religion. The reply: "Listen, my boy. You read the Bible—what you find there. And you decide for yourself what you want, you know. It's free. You don't have to believe what I think. Make up your own mind about it. Just read the Bible" (app. B). In fusing liberal Christian values with free-thinking, this parable of Winnicott and religion poses the paradox of his posture as a *believing skeptic*.[1]

1. Unless otherwise noted, all quotations from Clare Winnicott in this chapter are from the interview transcribed in the appendix. Michael Neve interviewed her in June 1983, less than a year before her death. Anne Clancier and Jeannine Kalmanovitch (1984) use the concept of paradox as a guiding thread in their assessment of Winnicott. The only other comprehensive studies of Winnicott available to date are those of Davis and Wallbridge (1981), A. Phillips

On the one hand, as Clare Winnicott insists, he "was never anti-religion" and "he was only too thankful if anybody could believe in anything." Winnicott himself asserts that "what is commonly called religion arises out of human nature" (1968a, 143), though for him religion has nothing to do with miracles or the afterlife. This argument extends that in "Morals and Education," where he explains that by religion he means that capacity for "such things as trust and 'belief in', and ideas of right and wrong" (1963e, 94), which evolves spontaneously in the child who is reared in an atmosphere of security and love.

On the other hand, in several late letters (to H. J. Howe, April 25, 1966; to Ian Rodger, June 3, 1969) Winnicott proudly identified himself as a modern-day Lollard, who would once have been burned for his heretical views; and he wrote to the *London Times* on December 22, 1969, "I would not describe myself as a practicing Christian, having reached a degree of maturity appropriate to age." Clare Winnicott says her husband's discovery of Darwin "changed his attitude toward religion" and prompted his allegiance to "a scientific way of working." In "Psychoanalysis and Science: Friends or Relations?" Winnicott stresses that "when a gap in knowledge turns up, the scientist does not flee to a supernatural explanation," although he gives this positivistic tenet a characteristically paradoxical twist when he adds that this ability to tolerate uncertainty entails "a capacity for faith," a faith "perhaps in nothing" or else in "the inexorable laws that govern phenomena" (1961, 14).

His benevolent attitude toward religion contrasts markedly with the militant atheism of Freud. How is this tension to be accommodated within a psychoanalytic weltanschauung? In part, the tension is healthy, for surely every person oscillates between doubt and faith of some kind. In my judgment, however, Winnicott does not always draw a sufficiently clear distinction between his theses about the constructive role of illusion in human experience and children's "innate tendencies toward morality" (1964a, 96)—both of which are highly compelling—and his assertions about the existence of a transcendental God. When he declares, "It is certainly helpful when the reigning monarch quite

---

(1988), and Grolnick (1990). A collection of papers concerning Winnicott's idea of the transitional object has been edited by Grolnick, Barkin, and Muensterberger (1979) and another on the clinical applications of his theories by Fromm and Smith (1989). For a further discussion of Winnicott's relationship to Freud, see Davis 1985.

easily and sincerely . . . proclaims a belief in God" (1950, 255), he seems to go beyond upholding the capacity for "belief in" to invest belief with a positive supernatural content.[2]

To readers of Freud, Winnicott's youthful conversation with his father will inevitably recall a similar walk taken by Freud with *his* father. I refer to the story recounted in *The Interpretation of Dreams* (1900) of how Sigmund's father told the boy, then ten or twelve years old, of the anti-Semitic abuse he had endured in his youth: his cap had been knocked off, and he had been ordered off the pavement. Disillusioned to learn of his father's "unheroic" conduct on that occasion, Freud consolidated his identification with the warlike Semitic general Hannibal.

Both these incidents show the future psychoanalysts coming to terms simultaneously with their filial legacies and religious identities. Clare Winnicott notes that accompanying his father home from church was Donald's "privilege," and Freud writes with evident feeling of what it meant to him "when my father began to take me with him on his walks and reveal to me in his talk his views upon things in the world we live in" (1900, 197). But the psychological impact of the episodes on the two boys could not have been more antithetical. Whereas Winnicott's walk had the positive effects of facilitating his maturation and deepening his respect for his father, Freud's walk was to a like degree traumatic. Freud's long-standing inhibition against visiting Rome, which provides the context for his discussion of this childhood memory, bears out his rueful statement that its shattering impact "was still being shown in all these emotions and dreams" (1900, 197). Indeed, Freud's repetition compulsion and his ambivalent struggles with male figures throughout his life confirm the arrest in his emotional development due to his unresolved sense of disappointment in his father. The contrast between these parallel events in the childhoods of Winnicott and Freud exemplifies Clare Winnicott's generalization that "there aren't disasters in the Winnicott home; there are just funny episodes." Whereas Winnicott's ready assimilation of his father's Protestantism left him a believing skeptic, Freud's coming to terms with his religious patrimony

2. See W. W. Meissner, who, in discussing faith as a transitional experience, sidesteps the question of "the truth value of the believer's faith" and terms the clash between supernatural and natural perspectives "perhaps the most significant and least resolvable" point of divergence between religion and psychoanalysis (1984, 178, 216).

made him into that more fiercely paradoxical being—a godless Jew, who very actively fought anti-Semitism.

Just as both boys had the privilege of walking with their fathers, so too did they occupy advantageous positions within their family constellations. Winnicott was the youngest of three children; his two sisters were six and seven years older than he. Freud, conversely, was the oldest of seven surviving children of his parents' marriage (the eighth, Julius, died in infancy), the next five of whom were girls. As the typically spoiled youngest child, Winnicott never had to undergo displacement by a rival, whereas Freud, more precariously situated, suffered the loss of his mother to his successors. Since, however, Freud was the offspring of his father's second (or third) marriage, for a brief period he was also the youngest in the extended family unit that included his two grown half brothers, Emmanuel and Philipp.

Freud writes memorably that if a son "has been his mother's undisputed darling he retains throughout his life the triumphant feeling, the confidence in success, which not seldom brings actual success along with it" (1917, 156). Alluding to the special problems posed by twins, Winnicott observes that the mother's task "is not to treat each child alike, but to treat each child as if that one were the only one" (1964a, 139). Both men, it is fair to assume, must have received during their infancy that special feeling of having been an "undisputed darling," which gave rise to their indomitable self-confidence. Freud, as is well known, viewed his life in heroic terms and identified with Hannibal and numerous other figures from history, literature, and myth. As Clare Winnicott told Michael Neve, Winnicott did not resemble Freud in this respect, but in a quieter way he did share something of Freud's sense of destiny. We can discern this conviction at the outset of his career when he writes to his sister Violet on November 15, 1919: "I am now practicing so that one day I shall be able to help introduce the subject [psychoanalysis] to the English people so that he who runs may read" (Rodman 1987, 2). In a letter of September 23, 1966, to Inês Besouchet, a Brazilian analyst, Winnicott retrospectively explains that he found himself drawn to "that part of paediatrics which my colleagues were not so much interested in, namely the area covered by the words the emotional development of the child."

Like Freud, Winnicott was reared in an extended family household: the family of his father's elder brother, Richard, including five children, lived just across the road in Plymouth. In Freud's case, as I have argued elsewhere (1987, 3–17), the involutions of kinship structure resulting from the disparity between the ages of his father and mother and from the existence of two grown sons from his father's first marriage predisposed Freud from birth to solve riddles and led to his eventual discovery of the Oedipus complex. The family of Frederick Winnicott, a merchant who twice became mayor of Plymouth, in addition to being much better off materially than Jakob Freud's, was much less complicated. Clare Winnicott writes in her memoir that the large household left "plenty of chances for many kinds of relationships, and there was scope for the inevitable tensions to be isolated and resolved within the total framework" (1978, 21). Both Freud and Winnicott could play multiple roles within their family units, but as in the walks with their fathers, Winnicott's opportunities to do so came in a more benign fashion.

One further difference in their upbringing is that Winnicott was reared in a far more female-dominated environment; his father was rarely at home. Clare Winnicott lists all the women—mother, sisters, aunts, governess, and nanny—by whom Donald was surrounded and reports his comment: "I was left too much to all my mothers. Thank goodness I was sent away at thirteen." He was dispatched to the Leys School in Cambridge by his father after he met a new friend at the age of twelve and one day said "drat" at the dinner table. Thus, despite his remoteness from the family, Frederick Winnicott also played the necessary role of an oedipal antagonist to his son. Clare Winnicott quotes from Winnicott's notebook, which she read only after his death; he says that it meant a great deal to him to discover that his father "was there to kill and be killed" (1978, 24).

Although Winnicott's rearing in a feminine ambience doubtless sensitized him to the importance of the mother, it did not lead him to sentimentalize her task. On the contrary, it is Freud who even in his final years naïvely claims that a mother's relation to her son "is altogether the most perfect, the most free from ambivalence of all human relationships" (1933, 133). With far greater realism, Winnicott writes that "it may easily happen" that a woman "resents" the "terrible interference" with her life that comes with being pregnant and that "babies are a lot of trouble, and a positive nuisance unless they are wanted" (1964a, 19). Since Amalie Freud, unlike Elizabeth Winnicott, did in fact have more children after Sigmund, the next one (Julius) less than a year and a half later, it is plausible to infer that Freud idealized the mother-son relationship partly in order to deny his resentment at having been so soon displaced from his mother's lap and attentions. In two crucial letters to Fliess (October 3 and 15, 1897), Freud relates the well-known incident in which either he or his nanny stole coins from his mother. Winnicott addresses the causes of stealing in children: "A two-year-old child who is stealing pennies from his mother's handbag is playing at being a hungry infant who thought he created his mother, and who assumed that he had rights over her contents. Disillusionment can come only too quickly. The birth of a new baby, for instance, can be a terrible shock in just this particular way" (1964a, 164). Although Winnicott does not refer to Freud, he reconstructs with uncanny accuracy the disillusionment that the infant Sigmund must have experienced at the birth of his first sibling rival.

Undoubtedly, Winnicott did have a happy childhood.[3] But this good fortune was fraught with its own developmental perils. In his introduction to Winnicott's selected letters, F. Robert Rodman says that "probably a study of his life would reveal the conditions under which 'being himself' had become a continuing issue" (1987, xxix). Winnicott himself remarks, in two autobiographically resonant passages, that "children find in security a sort of challenge, a challenge to them to prove that they can break out," and that what is needed for the healthy development of the individual is "a well-graduated series of defiant iconoclastic actions, each of the series being compatible with the retention of an unconscious bond with the central figures or figure, the parents or the mother" (1965a, 30, 92).

Clare Winnicott mentions two such "iconoclastic actions" in her interview. In one instance Donald smacked a doll belonging to his sister with a croquet mallet because his father had teased him about it. Although he was "frightfully pleased" at this expression of defiance, he was likewise "quite glad when his father melted the wax of the doll's face and put it together again." Clare quotes Donald's interpretation of this event: "This early demonstration of the restitutive and reparative act certainly made an impression on me, and perhaps made me able to accept the fact that I myself, dear innocent child, had actually become violent directly with a doll, but indirectly with my good-tempered father, who was just then entering my conscious life" (1978, 23). He seems to glance at this experience when he theorizes about a child's impulsive actions: "A strong father enables the child to take the risk

3. See, however, the qualifications of this statement offered in chapter 7.

because the father stands in the way or is there to mend matters or to prevent [destructiveness] by his fierceness" (1968b, 237).

The closest equivalent in Freud's life to this incident is found in his analysis of the "botanical monograph" dream: "It had once amused my father to hand over a book with *coloured plates* . . . for me and my eldest sister to destroy. . . . I had been five years old at the time and my sister not yet three; and the picture of us blissfully pulling the book to pieces (leaf by leaf, like an *artichoke*, I found myself saying) was almost the only plastic memory I retained from that period of my life" (1900, 172).

Both Freud and Winnicott take pleasure in engaging in destructive acts. But Freud's pulling apart of the book with his sister has been shown to be primarily a veiled allusion to childhood sexual play and masturbation (Swales 1982, 9), whereas Winnicott's smashing of the doll's face and its repair by his father illustrates Melanie Klein's (1937) themes of love, guilt, and reparation, as well as his own (1969) concept of the "use" of an object.

Winnicott's second iconoclastic action came when he looked at himself in the mirror, decided he was "too nice," then starting blotting his copybook, doing poorly in school, torturing flies, and so forth. As Clare Winnicott puts it, the universally liked child needed to find the "other dimension" of "nastiness" in himself. In Winnicott's (1960a) own terms, it is not difficult to understand this compulsion to misbehave as the protest of his suppressed True Self, including its destructive urges, against an outwardly compliant, but inauthentic, False Self. Winnicott (1956a; 1967c) repeatedly makes the point that expressions of "the antisocial tendency"—from bed-wetting in early childhood to stealing and more violent criminal behavior in adolescence and beyond—actually represent signs of hope in a deprived individual. (Delinquency for Winnicott is the antisocial tendency compounded by secondary gains.) He writes: "The child knows in his bones that it is *hope* that is locked up in wicked behaviour, and that *despair* is linked with compliance and false socialization" (1963e, 104).

A crucial moment in Winnicott's ongoing struggle to be himself came with his decision to become a doctor at fifteen after he broke his collarbone during sports at school and chafed under the need to be treated in the infirmary (Clancier and Kalmanovitch 1984, 100). (This decision entailed the disappointment of his father's hopes that Donald would succeed him in the family's wholesale hardware business.)[4] Clare

4. Adam Phillips curiously asserts that the Winnicott family business specialized in "women's corsetry" (1988, 23).

Winnicott quotes him as saying: "I could see that for the rest of my life I should have to depend on doctors if I became ill, and the only way out of this position was to become a doctor myself" (1978, 25).

In December 1968 Winnicott suffered a grievous heart attack—one of a series during his later years—while on a lecture tour in New York. After returning to London, he wrote on January 31, 1969, to Dr. Richard Crampton, the physician who had treated him in the cardiac care unit at Lenox Hill Hospital: "I recognise that I was in a rather peculiar state of mind during that illness and I am sure that you and your colleagues found me at times rather trying as a patient. As you did say to my wife, and this was helpful, you knew that the dependence of a patient who is very ill is a difficult thing, especially for a doctor who has at any rate some knowledge of what is going on." More than any other analyst, Winnicott stressed the primacy of dependence both in human development and in the analytic process. But this extraordinary sensitivity was undergirded by Winnicott's own difficulties in acknowledging his dependence on others.

In *On the History of the Psycho-Analytic Movement,* Freud relates a series of anecdotes designed to explain the "bad reception" accorded to his views on the "sexual aetiology of the neuroses" (1914, 12). From his early encounters with three eminent senior physicians—Josef Breuer, Jean-Martin Charcot, and the Viennese gynecologist Rudolf Chrobak—he took away a single lesson condensed in the memorable maxim of Charcot: "*C'est toujours la chose génitale*" (14). Freud's epiphanies on sexuality find a counterpart in the way that Winnicott during his medical training learned—both by precept and example—from his mentor Dr. Thomas Horder the importance of practicing a nondirective technique with patients. According to Clare Winnicott, Horder exhorted: "Listen to your patient. Don't you go in with your wonderful knowledge and apply it all. Just listen. They'll tell you quite a lot of things. You'll learn a lot if you listen."

Winnicott looked upon psychoanalysis as "a vast extension of history-taking, with therapeutics as a by-product" (1963h, 199); and in "Psychoanalysis and Science" he notes that the discovery of the free association technique enabled Freud to shift his attention from the removal of symptoms to a "more important" task: "to enable the patient to reveal himself to himself" (1961, 13). As he grew older Winnicott strove increasingly to hold in check what in "The Use of an Object" he calls his "personal need to interpret." In the same paper he distills a lifetime of clinical wisdom: "I think I interpret mainly to let the patient know the limits of my understanding" (1969, 86–87).

Freud, it must be admitted, did not always restrain his own "personal need to interpret" and, during his discovery of transference in the Dora case, even exemplifies Winnicott's general description of "a bad analyst making good interpretations" (1963b, 252). Nonetheless, as Clare Winnicott puts it, Winnicott "admired tremendously" not only Freud's "clear thinking" but above all his ability to "change his mind." Winnicott himself avers that Freud "was easy to criticize because he was always critical of himself" (1962b, 177). Clare Winnicott adduces Winnicott's conviction that "once you're defending your position, you've lost sight of science." Characteristically, he traces the capacity for "a scientific approach to phenomena" back to the baby at the breast, to the mother's successful introduction of the external world "in small doses, accurately graded to the infant's or child's understanding" (1965a, 28; see also 1945, 153). Although, as he admits, "most of us, alas, have put at least some of human nature outside the realm of scientific inquiry," by his own lack of defensiveness he holds up an ideal not only for psychoanalytic work but also for the conduct of our daily life.

That Winnicott should ground the capacity for a scientific weltanschauung in the baby's experience at the breast is scarcely surprising. As Clare Winnicott remarks, Winnicott's writings span a wide range of topics, including delinquency and adolescence, but "his main contribution is likely to be in the study of the earliest relationships, and its application to the etiology of psychosis and the psychotic mechanisms in all of us" (1978, 18). Whereas for Freud, in the sweeping peroration to *Totem and Taboo,* "the beginnings of religion, morals, society and art converge in the Oedipus complex" (1913b, 156), for Winnicott these beginnings lie even earlier, in the child's bond with the "ordinary devoted mother."

Deservedly Winnicott's most famous concept, and that by which he elaborated his theoretical understanding of the mother-child relationship, is the transitional object, which, as Anna Freud wrote to him on October 30, 1968, "has conquered the analytic world." As he explains in his seminal paper, two essential features of this "first 'not-me' possession" are that it exists on the boundary between internal and external reality—in what he will term "potential space"—and that "it must survive instinctual loving, and also hating and, if it be a feature, pure aggression" (1953, 1, 5).

The liminal status of the transitional object—the doll, blanket, or teddy bear to which the young child clings as he or she begins to

separate from the mother—is integral to Winnicott's (1967d) contention that art and cultural experience as a whole are located in this same
intermediate realm of play, between fantasy and reality. What is unique
about Winnicott's approach to creativity is that he avoids treating works
of art merely as products of instinctual sublimation, as in classical
Freudian theory, while yet insisting that their roots lie in infancy. The
second aspect of the transitional object—its capacity to withstand instinctual loving and hating—gets to Winnicott's assumptions about
human nature. Although he rejects Freud's hypothesis of the death
instinct, which was championed by Melanie Klein, Winnicott takes over
from Klein his conviction that "the primitive love impulse has an
aggressive aim; being ruthless, it carries with it a variable quantity of
destructive ideas unaffected by concern" (1958a, 22). Because the infant's aggression—in Winnicott's view, initially a diffused expression of
the life force—comes to be focused on the mother's breast, the first
external object and in fantasy an *object of attack*, both it and its surro-
gates must continue to exist if the infant is to achieve the sense of guilt
that heralds the stage of concern, as Winnicott (1963c) renames Klein's
depressive position.

Winnicott's most important later development of the idea of the
transitional object is to be found in "The Use of an Object." This paper
has a tragic aura, because when first read to the New York Psychoanalytic Society, on November 12, 1968, it was sharply criticized by its three
discussants—Edith Jacobson, Samuel Ritvo, and Bernard D. Fine—
and Winnicott suffered his heart attack shortly thereafter. None of
these individuals, of course, is responsible for what ensued, and the
record shows that the tone of the meeting was one of spirited intellectual exchange untainted by any personal rancor.[5] But Winnicott, who
is quoted as having responded "in a charming and whimsical fashion"
that "his concept was torn to pieces and that he would be happy to give
it up," regarded the evening as a failure; and it is impossible to separate
the theme of the paper—the survival of the analyst—from the circumstances of its presentation.

The U.S. analysts were troubled in part by Winnicott's terminol-

5. The library of the New York Psychoanalytic Institute contains, in addition
to the original version of Winnicott's paper, which differs slightly from that
eventually published, a summary of the entire proceedings prepared by David
Milrod, as well as the complete texts of the responses by Jacobson and Fine.
The following quotations are from Milrod's (1968) summary.

ogy—his definition of "relating" to an object as a purely subjective phenomenon that precedes its objective "use." Above all, however, they took issue with what I have identified as the Kleinian component of Winnicott's paper, namely, the thesis that all object relationships have a destructive root and that for an object to survive its fantasied destruction is thus the precondition for its assuming an independent existence. "Essentially Dr. Jacobson could not understand Dr. Winnicott's meaning of 'destructive attack' and 'survival'; and she described as an extreme statement his summary comment—that 'the object is always being destroyed,' a destruction which becomes the unconscious back-cloth for love of a real object." Again, "Dr. Ritvo could not understand the statement that acceptance of the object outside the subject's omnipotent control meant the destruction of the object." And again, "Dr. Fine found it unclear and not at all proven that in the process of developing from what Dr. Winnicott calls object-relating to object use that the subject destroys the object."

The proposition that the primitive love impulse contains an irreducible core of aggressivity is admittedly not subject to empirical verification. A compelling argument in its favor is offered by Marion Milner, who points to the "double fact that what one loves most, because one needs it most, is necessarily separate from oneself; and yet the primitive urge of loving is to make what one loves part of oneself. So that in loving it one has, in one's primitive wish, destroyed it as something separate and outside and having an identity of its own" (1950, 66). She appositely adds: "The cannibal may be prompted to eat his enemy by love for his courage and strength and the wish to preserve these, but it is a love which certainly does not preserve the loved enemy in his original form" (58).

As the responses of the New York analysts show, "The Use of an Object" is incomprehensible without some appreciation of this line of reasoning; and this paper, which Winnicott says belongs to "the direct line of development that is particularly mine" (1969, 86), is important precisely because it discloses the connection between his twin themes of ruthlessness and the shift from a subjective to an objective mode of experiencing reality. When the mother has failed to do so, the analyst of the borderline patient must be placed "outside the area of omnipotent control" by bearing the brunt of the "maximum destructiveness" of which the patient is capable; this "capacity to survive" means specifically to "not retaliate" (91).

An extension of Winnicott's ideas concerning transitional objects to the political sphere may be seen in "The Place of the Monarchy."

(Indeed, the title of this paper in manuscript is "Applied Theory"; it begins with the following words, omitted from the posthumously published version: "An application of theory provides a test, a test of its validity and its usefulness. As an exercise in the application of the theory of what I call 'transitional phenomena' . . .") Winnicott builds on his view of what it means to use an object to argue that "*what is good is always being destroyed*" and that the continued survival of the monarchy despite the unconscious popular desire for its destruction therefore helps to make England "a place to live in," not merely a place "to fear or be complied with or to be lost in" (1970b, 262, 264). Whatever "sentimental or scandalous" stories may be invented, he observes, the monarch retains a collective "dream-significance" by refusing to divulge the details of his or her personal life. "In the centre of it all is a woman (or man) who has or has not the capacity to survive, to exist without reacting to provocation or to seduction, until at death a successor determined by heredity takes over this tremendous responsibility" (266–67).

As this characterization makes clear, Winnicott envisions, as it were, a metonymic chain, in which the nonretaliating monarch takes the place of the analyst, who in turn substitutes for the transitional object of infancy. But the transitional object itself is a surrogate for the breast of the mother, as well as a "symbol of the union" between the infant and the "environment-mother" who knows when to minister to the infant's needs (1967d, 96). Winnicott describes breast-feeding in wonderfully evocative detail. The mother holds her baby lovingly and without anxiety, and in some unpredictable way her breast comes into contact with the baby's mouth and saliva begins to flow. The saliva is a sign of ideas in the baby's mind, and "gradually the mother enables the baby to build up in imagination the very thing she has to offer." After nursing for a time, the baby turns away, having "finished with the idea" of the breast, and the nipple disappears. A few minutes later, the process recommences. The baby turns again toward the nipple, which the mother willingly offers, and "a new contact is made, just at the right moment." As Winnicott emphasizes, it is especially in the second phase of the experience, "where she takes the nipple away from the baby as the baby ceases to want it or to believe in it, that she establishes herself as the mother" (1964a, 45–49).[6]

6. For a theoretical elaboration of the issues underlying the dynamic of the feeding situation, see "The Observation of Infants in a Set Situation" (1941). Clare Winnicott singles out this paper as one of the best examples of Win-

This prototypical encounter of the infant with the breast, which is repeated until it becomes part of a regular and reliable feeding schedule, is pivotal to Winnicott's thought because it suggests the possibility of discovering in the external world what one has imagined, thus preparing the way for the ontological paradox of the transitional object—its simultaneous existence in fantasy and reality—and making creativity in general possible.[7] Of course, the breast will not always be available, and Winnicott (1953) insists that a gradual process of disillusionment must follow the infant's acquisition of the capacity for illusion. But unlike Lacan (1949), who, as we saw in chapter 5, views the ego's relation to the world as constituted by an ineradicable méconnaissance, Winnicott offers a far more benign vision of the power of language and other vehicles of the imagination to give access to a reality that they themselves help to create.

This progression from "Transitional Objects and Transitional Phenomena" through "The Use of an Object" to "The Place of the Monarchy" illuminates not only how Winnicott enriches psychoanalytic theory by complementing Freud's paradigm of the Oedipus complex with a powerful model of the relationship between mother and child but also how this model gives him a tool with which to investigate apparently remote cultural problems. Indeed, whereas Lacan elevates the Oedipus complex into a linguistic Name-of-the-Father, Winnicott may be said to speak of an equally universal Name-of-the-Mother: "There is a separated-out phenomenon that we can call WOMAN which dominates the whole scene, and affects all our arguments. WOMAN is the unacknowledged mother of the first stages of life of every man and woman" (1964b, 192).[8] In a moment of candor, he points to the auto-

---

nicott's scientific technique. A forerunner to the full developed theory of the transitional object (1953), it includes a commentary on the fort-da episode in *Beyond the Pleasure Principle* (1920), which has attracted so much attention in French psychoanalytic circles.

7. "Ought we not to say that by fitting in with the infant's impulse the mother allows the baby the *illusion* that what is there is the thing created by the baby; as a result there is not only the physical experience of instinctual satisfaction, but also an emotional union, and the belief in reality as something about which one can have illusions" (Winnicott 1948, 163).

8. The Lacanian Name-of-the-Father contains a play on the French words Nom-du-Père (name of the father) and Non-du-Père (no of the father), which is lost in English translation and for which what I call Winnicott's Name-of-the-Mother possesses no equivalent.

biographical roots of his work on devotion: "to make a fully informed and fully felt acknowledgement to my own mother" (1957, 126).

Although Winnicott differs from Freud in emphasizing not the father but the mother as the prototype for later transference relationships, the two analysts agree in approaching political questions from the standpoint of individual development. As Winnicott writes: "Cultural influences are of course important, vitally important; but these cultural influences can themselves be studied as an overlap of innumerable personal patterns. In other words, the clue to social and group psychology is in the psychology of the individual" (1958a, 15). Although it may well be advisable at times to adopt a more global perspective, this reliance on individual experience as the touchstone of truth stands in direct antithesis to Fredric Jameson's Althusserian Marxist contention that "the need to transcend individualistic categories of interpretation is in many ways the fundamental issue for any doctrine of the political unconscious" (1981, 68), and remains at the heart of psychoanalysis.

Even those who disagree with Winnicott must admire him for recognizing that his allegiance to psychoanalysis has political implications and for seeking to make these explicit. In "Some Thoughts on the Meaning of the Word 'Democracy,'" he unabashedly argues that democracy is the most "mature" form of social organization. Maturity in individual terms Winnicott defines as "an appropriate degree of emotional development" for a person's "chronological age and social setting" (1950, 241). This conviction coexists with his reverence for the monarch as a collective transitional object; as he is a believing skeptic in matters of religion, so in the political sphere he can be labeled no less paradoxically a *democratic monarchist*.

Indeed, the paper on democracy highlights some questionable features of Winnicott's outlook by virtue of being his boldest venture into "applied theory." For example, Winnicott ascribes the importance of the secret ballot to the fact that "it ensures the freedom of the people to express deep feelings, *apart from conscious thoughts*" (1950, 241). Although this analysis sheds unexpected light on the democratic process, it overlooks the objection that the secret ballot is intended to secure freedom from political oppression. Similarly, when Winnicott explains the phenomenon of dictatorship in terms of a collective need to seek domination at the hands of a leader who takes on "the magical qualities of the all-powerful woman of fantasy" (253), giving an insight at once constructive and compelling, he prefaces his explanation by saying that "there is no relation to the father which has such a quality" of absolute dependence as that to the mother, "and for this reason a man who in a political sense is at the top can be appreciated much more objectively by the group than a woman can be if she is in a similar position" (253). With this remark, he at once minimizes the degree of ambivalence that disturbs people's perceptions of fathers and disparages people's ability to recognize the authority of a woman.

Just as it is possible to uphold Winnicott's concept of "belief in" without using it to justify the existence of God—another dubious twist of the democracy paper—so I would maintain that his assertion of a link between biological and social processes remains valid despite occasional lapses into sexist stereotypes.[9] Winnicott's differentiation between the "female elements" and "male elements" in individuals of both sexes in terms of a distinction between *being* and *doing* (1971a, 72–85), for instance, is a clinical contribution of the utmost importance that should not be discarded simply because it can mistakenly be given a prescriptive connotation. If one happens to be disconcerted by this or any other of Winnicott's pronouncements—on theoretical no less than on social or religious issues—it suffices to call to mind his liberating advice in a letter of June 18, 1968 to L. Joseph Stone concerning the application of his famous squiggle technique: "Essential is the absolute freedom so that any modification may be accepted if appropriate" (Rodman 1987, 178). As Winnicott counsels, if the student "must read instead of making observations let him read descriptions by many different authors, not looking to one or another as the purveyor of the truth" (1964a, 147).

Prompted by a question from Michael Neve, Clare Winnicott agrees that there was an "enormous difference" between the optimism of Winnicott and the pessimism of Freud. Citing the statistic that Winnicott saw sixty thousand children and their parents during nearly forty years of practice at his Paddington Green and other clinics, she observes that because of his training in pediatrics and his extensive "experience of normal family working," his outlook "comes with something positive. It comes at psychoanalysis from health, rather than

9. For an integration of feminism and object relations theory that does justice to the complexities of both modes of inquiry, see Chodorow 1978, 1989. Nancy Chodorow's later essays move beyond the sociological determinism that limits her influential first book.

from illness." Winnicott himself goes even further: "It is of first importance for us to acknowledge openly that absence of psychoneurotic illness may be health, but it is not life" (1967d, 100).

This opposition between Winnicott's optimism and Freud's pessimism inheres in their religious attitudes, and if Freud's preoccupation with the sense of guilt identifies him as an heir of St. Augustine, the playfulness and paradoxicality of Winnicott make him akin rather to Erasmus. Between them, Freud and Winnicott reincarnate a perennial dichotomy in the history of ideas. On one side are those thinkers who emphasize the innate depravity of human nature; on the other, those who see people as basically good and emphasize the influence of the environment in shaping them for better or worse.

Winnicott, who affirms that "religions have made much of original sin, but have not all come round to the idea of original goodness" (1963e, 94), is well aware of the theological resonances of his recasting of psychoanalytic theory. Indeed, he expressly rejects the concept of the death instinct because it "could be described as a reassertion of the principle of original sin. I have tried to develop the theme that what both Freud and Klein avoided in so doing was the full implication of dependence and therefore of the environmental factor" (1971a, 70–71). Yet, as we have seen, Winnicott concurs in part with Klein; he writes to Barbara Lantos on November 8, 1956, that "it is necessary to retain the idea of the attack on the mother's body which is ruthless and which only gradually gathers to itself guilt feeling" (Rodman 1987, 109). Adam Phillips has aptly characterized Winnicott's idiosyncratic theory of human nature as one of "Original Ruthless Virtue" (1988, 107). Thus, Winnicott's temperament is in no sense utopian, and his comic vision is one that has transmuted—without betraying—the tragic wisdom of Freud.

Winnicott's revision of Freud's libido theory provides a case in point. Whereas in Freud's (1905) scheme, development is seen as passing through a series of foreordained psychosexual stages, any one of which might become a fixation point for later regressions, Winnicott is concerned "not merely with regression to good and bad points in the instinct experiences of the individual, but also to good and bad points in the environmental adaptation to ego needs and id needs in the individual's history" (1954, 283). He speaks not of "regression" but of *"regression to dependence,"* which communicates the deprived individual's hope that "certain aspects of the environment which failed originally may be relived, with the environment this time succeeding instead of failing in its function of facilitating the inherited tendency in the individual to develop and to mature" (1959–64, 128).

Winnicott's revision of the libido theory in turn has a direct bearing on the practice of psychoanalytic therapy. Within a traditional Freudian perspective, therapeutic action is attributed to the "breaking up and reorganizing of existing pathological structures" (Atwood and Stolorow 1984, 61). If the past exerts a determining influence on a person's behavior and is itself unalterable, then all that can be hoped for is that by becoming aware of one's compulsions to repeat, a feedback loop of consciousness, as it were, can somewhat diminish their tyrannical sway. This heightening of awareness is a limited aim at best, especially since psychoanalysis sees the intellect as quite ineffectual against the power of unconscious forces. Freud, as is well known, espoused an attitude of therapeutic pessimism by the time he wrote "Analysis Terminable and Interminable" (1937).

From a Winnicottian standpoint, however, the objective of psychoanalytic therapy with the borderline patient is not so much to undo the past or even to understand it intellectually—though this has its place— as to facilitate "growth of psychical structure that is missing or deficient as a consequence of developmental voids and interferences" (Atwood and Stolorow 1984, 61). In other words, an arrested maturational process is brought to completion. As Winnicott writes: *"The patient needs to reach back through the transference trauma to the state of affairs before the original trauma. . . .* Reproduction in the treatment of examples as they arise of the original environmental failure, along with the patient's experience of anger that is appropriate, frees the patient's maturational processes; . . . and the next phase needs to be a period of emotional growth in which the character builds up positively and loses its distortions" (1963g, 209). Like his modification of the libido theory to account for the role of the environment, Winnicott's reconceptualization of the dynamics of treatment provides a more hopeful version of psychoanalysis yet remains true to Freud's fundamental principles.

It is a fitting testament to Winnicott's comic spirit that his last words, spoken to his wife after watching a televised film about old cars, were "What a happy-making film!" His wife reports that he died on the floor in his sleep and that the two of them "always sat on the floor—him on the one side, me on the other." This detail takes on symbolic significance in light of Winnicott's challenge to the "armchair philosopher" to "come out of his chair and sit on the floor with his patient" to discover what it means for someone to *use* an object (1969, 90). No armchair

psychoanalyst himself, Winnicott was not afraid to meet his patients—
young and old—on even ground.

Many who knew Winnicott have mentioned how deeply they were
impressed by his physical presence. Masud Khan writes that "what
stands out vividly is his relaxed physicality and a lambent concentration
in his person" (1975, xi). Marion Milner compares him to a clown in a
troop of acrobats, who occasionally "made a fruitless attempt to jump
up and reach the bar. Then, suddenly, he made a great leap and there
he was, whirling around on the bar, all his clothes flying out, like a huge
Catherine wheel, to roars of delight from the crowd" (1978, 37). Clare
Winnicott vividly recalls Donald's bodily energy in the images of him
climbing a tree to chop down a branch in the last year of his life, riding
a bicycle down Haverstock Hill with his feet on the handlebars, and
driving a car with his head through the roof and his walking stick on
the accelerator. This vitality is integral to his genius as a therapist and
helps to make him truly, in his wife's words, "the most spontaneous
thing that ever lived."

Nor can his exceptional talents in the fields of art and music be
overlooked. Clare Winnicott reports that he would "rush up and play
the piano between patients" and end the day with "a musical outburst
fortissimo." He often played Brahms and Bach and near the end of his
life "was permanently listening to late Beethoven quartets." As a visual
artist, Winnicott profited analytically through his use of the squiggle
technique with children. Freud, in marked contrast, was notoriously
insensible to music and gave no evidence of artistic endowment. It is
perhaps for this reason that Freud wrote brilliant criticism of both
literature and plastic art, whereas Winnicott—whose theory that art
inhabits the same potential space as childhood play is the most satisfactory psychoanalytic account of art—has virtually nothing to say about
specific works of any kind. Almost alone among psychoanalysts, however, Winnicott approaches Freud as a master of expository prose.

For Winnicott the moment at which the infant begins to feel a sense
of integration is one of extreme vulnerability. "Only if someone has her
arms round the infant at this time can the I AM moment be endured, or
rather, perhaps, risked" (1965a, 148). Elsewhere, Winnicott appeals to
the memory of having been held by "everlasting arms" as an experiential basis for religious belief: "We may use that word 'God,' we can make
a specific link with the Christian church and doctrine, but it is a series of
steps" (1968a, 149). But this invocation of a mother's love may be
contrasted with Freud's stoical resignation in the final sentence of "The

Theme of the Three Caskets": "It is in vain that an old man yearns for the love of woman as he had it first from his mother; the third of the Fates alone, the silent Goddess of Death, will take him into her arms" (1913a, 301). Between these antipodes of faith and doubt, the psychoanalytic thinker must continue to steer.

7 ◆ THE TWO ANALYSES

OF HARRY GUNTRIP

It would appear to follow from general psychoanalytic principles that the choice of psycho-analysis
as a career is as much determined by unconscious
motivation as resort to psycho-analytical treatment
for the alleviation of symptoms.—W. R. D.
Fairbairn, "On the Nature and Aims of Psycho-
Analytic Treatment"

Harry Guntrip's record of his analytic experiences with W. R. D.
Fairbairn and D. W. Winnicott is at once a moving autobiographical memoir, an invaluable historical document for
the study of the British school, and an important theoretical discussion
of the nature of therapeutic action in psychoanalysis. In my discussion,
I shall attempt to do justice to all three of these dimensions of Guntrip's
paper and to show how they are inextricably interconnected.

Central to Guntrip's paper and his motivation for seeking analysis in
the first place is "a complete amnesia for a severe trauma at the age of
three and a half years, over the death of a younger brother," Percy
(1975, 447). Recognizing that this trauma led him to become a psychotherapist, Guntrip quotes Fairbairn as having said to him, "I can't think
what could motivate any of us to become psychotherapists, if we hadn't
got problems of our own," and concurs: "It seems that our theory must
be rooted in our psychopathology" (448, 467). As proof of this interplay between personal suffering and scientific insight, Guntrip instances "Freud's courageous self-analysis at a time when all was ob-
scure" (467).

As Guntrip's comparison to Freud indicates, the self-analytic component of his paper lifts it from its immediate context in the ideas and
personalities of the British school to situate it within a set of problems

inherent in the very origins of psychoanalysis. The culmination of a lifelong process, Guntrip's introspection has, moreover, a luminous quality. In the psychoanalytic autobiography he wrote before his death in 1975, it emerges that in 1936, at the age of thirty-five, Guntrip started to record and analyze his own dreams and that he continued to do so throughout his prolonged treatments with Fairbairn in the 1950s and Winnicott in the 1960s. What is more, Guntrip wrote up each of his thousand-plus sessions with Fairbairn and 150-plus with Winnicott as they took place. These contemporaneous notes of his dreams and his analyses, which he had not previously reread, provided the raw material for the autobiography he resolved to write in the early 1970s, in response to a climactic sequence of dreams, using himself as a specimen with which to investigate the theoretical claims of psychoanalysis.[1]

In the introduction to his autobiography, Guntrip cites the examples of Marion Milner's *Hands of the Living God* (1968) and Hannah Green's autobiographical novel, *I Never Promised You a Rose Garden* (1964), for their presentations of case material, but what Guntrip has done is unprecedented in the annals of psychoanalysis, only excepting what Freud himself has done. Milner's work is an account of a treatment from the analyst's point of view, and Green's from the patient's, but Guntrip—like Freud—fuses in himself the roles of both analyst and patient. Guntrip writes: "I have come to see, in light of this study, that my intellectual theoretical research, as summed up in . . . *Personality Structure and Human Interaction* and *Schizoid Phenomena, Object Relations and the Self,* and presented in condensed form in *Psychoanalytic Theory, Therapy and the Self,* was in fact all a part of my search into the psychic depths, the conscious and intellectual aspects of that search, in quest of a solution to my own personal problem. I believe that this is true of us all." He continues, "I have come to regard this work as my final contribution to psychoanalytic research," and again links himself to Freud: "Freud's own 'psychoanalytic autobiography,' at least so far as his Oedipus complex is concerned, will be a classic of all time" (1:3–4). Although Guntrip's *Psycho-Analytical Autobiography* is as yet almost unknown, I am convinced that upon publication it will take its place beside *The Interpretation of Dreams* as a work of systematic self-scrutiny that advances the frontiers of psychoanalytic knowledge.

1. Guntrip's two-volume *Psycho-Analytical Autobiography* is currently being edited for publication by John D. Sutherland. I shall give volume and page numbers from the manuscript.

As an autobiography, moreover, Freud's *Interpretation of Dreams* is itself in the tradition of St. Augustine's *Confessions*. In keeping with Guntrip's background as a Congregational minister, his narrative exhibits the religious underpinnings of autobiography with exceptional clarity. His life is organized around a series of paradigmatic moments. First, there is the moment of *trauma*—the death of his brother in infancy. With some exaggeration, Guntrip declares that "nothing particularly unusual has happened to me, except for one thing" (1:1), that being his discovery at the age of three and a half of the two-year-old Percy naked and dead on their mother's lap. Next, there is the moment of *conversion*—Guntrip's retirement from the active ministry in 1946 at the age of forty-five (precipitated by events that had taken place three years earlier) in favor of a full-time career as a psychotherapist. Guntrip calls this decision "the critical turning point of my life" and likewise refers to the discovery of psychology as his "vocation" (1:322–23). Finally, there is the moment of *breakthrough*—the extraordinary sequence of dreams, commencing when Guntrip was seventy years of age, in which he overcame the amnesia that had disoriented him throughout his life. These dreams brought about "a final and decisive change in my inner world" (1:202), he writes, as a result of which he felt himself fundamentally integrated for the first time.

Both the *Psycho-Analytical Autobiography* and the paper distilled from it are written from the retrospective vantage point of Guntrip's double discovery, first, of his calling to practice psychotherapy and, second, of his solution to the mystery of his "personal problem." Guntrip died without completing the section of his autobiography on his analysis with Winnicott. Nonetheless, like Augustine, who structures the *Confessions* around his conversion to Christianity, Guntrip imparts to his life a remarkable sense of closure, which even the missing ending does not seriously impair. Indeed, that he could condense his whole story into "My Experience of Analysis with Fairbairn and Winnicott" is a fitting testimony to the resolved nature of his life's journey.

I cannot contemplate Guntrip, Freud, and self-analysis without recalling also the original psychoanalytic hero—Oedipus. Although Guntrip repressed all memory of his brother's death, it "remained alive in me, to be triggered off unrecognizably by widely scattered events" (1975, 455). At the ages of both twenty-six and thirty-seven, separation from a friend who was a brother-substitute gave rise to a mysterious exhaustion illness, similar to the illness causing his nearly fatal collapse immediately after Percy's death. By the second of these separations, in 1938, having studied classical analytic theory and begun his self-analysis, Guntrip realized that he lived, as it were, atop the long-lost memory of his early childhood. He reports a dream: "I went down into a tomb and saw a man buried alive. He tried to get out but I threatened him with illness, locked him in and got away quick" (456). This search for a hidden traumatic scene evokes Oedipus's assembling of the clues to his past in *Oedipus the King*. In the autobiography, Guntrip quotes himself as saying in an early session with Fairbairn: "I've serious fears of what's going to happen in analysis. My realistic self says 'I knew this and want it and am going through with it.' But another part of me is twisting, turning, dodging, evading, anything to escape seeing something" (2:20). Guntrip's ambivalence toward the psychoanalytic process replicates the tension between courage and fear that sunders Oedipus during his investigation into the murder of Laius.

Although Guntrip, like Freud, goes on the oedipal quest, the two self-seekers are different in one crucial respect. Whereas Freud in his unconscious psychic life had arrived at what Melanie Klein (1935) terms the depressive position, which entails the capacity to deal with people as whole objects, Guntrip had not. As Winnicott remarks: "Freud's own early personal history was of such a kind that he came to the Oedipus or prelatency period in his life as a whole human being, ready to meet whole human beings, and ready to deal in interpersonal relationships. His own infancy experiences had been good enough, so that in his self-analysis he could take the mothering of the infant for granted" (1954, 284). Just such good-enough mothering, however, is what Guntrip could *not* take for granted, and its lack impelled him to undergo two arduous analyses. If Freud incarnates the classic oedipal reading of the Oedipus drama, Guntrip, who quotes Winnicott as having twice said to him, "You show no signs of ever having had an Oedipus complex" (1975, 453), embodies the revisionist interpretation of *Oedipus the King* that I offered in chapter 2, in which Oedipus is a hero afflicted not with the Oedipus complex but with Balint's "basic fault."

Furthermore, as we have seen, repressed memories from the oedipal period can be recovered in analysis through *recollection*, but earlier memories, which are preverbal and constitute the unthought known, can be recaptured only through *repetition*. In chapter 2, I drew upon Winnicott's paper "Fear of Breakdown" for its exegesis of the way the catastrophe that is dreaded in the analysis is one that *has already taken place* but, because of the immaturity of the infant ego, *has not yet been experienced* and hence is sought for in the future. Guntrip remarks in one of his analytic sessions with Fairbairn: "If I gave up resistance what would emerge would be intolerably painful, a fear of experiencing what I've experienced once before and have a deep dread of encountering. There's some deep fear in me of being overwhelmed by something utterly frightful that I've no means of coping with" (2:254). Guntrip carries within him a "deep dread of encountering" those "intolerably painful" infantile traumas that, as Robert Michels has written of Oedipus, "took place before he was able to remember or register them" (1986, 614).

Also like Oedipus, Guntrip relives and hence experiences his dissociated breakdown through a regression to the womb that is simultaneously a rebirth. Early in his analysis with Fairbairn, Guntrip read Marion Milner's *On Not Being Able to Paint* (1950), and he embarked on a series of "free drawings" to release his unconscious emotions. A number of drawings depicted embryos in glass jars, and Guntrip interprets these as returns to the womb that "expressed the inner core of my withdrawn schizoid reactions" when he collapsed and nearly expired on his mother's lap after Percy's death (2:99). He describes his most extraordinary drawing as follows. "An embryo in the womb, but not a safe enclosed bottle, but like that large 'vagina with teeth,' only it wasn't a mouth but a closed oval with sharp teeth all round the inside. . . . There was a sharp spike coming up from the bottom of the oval and penetrating the embryo in the centre, so that it looked speared" (2:100). Guntrip imagines not merely the conventional fantasy of a *vagina dentata* but also an even more ominous toothed womb and connects it to the knowledge that his mother had miscarried during her first pregnancy and his conviction that she had hated him even before his birth.

No less than Oedipus, Guntrip had a profound birth trauma, which he both feared and longed to reexperience in his analysis. During a 1954 session he told Fairbairn, "I'm beginning to feel breathless, labouring with a suffocated feeling of its being an effort to carry on as an active adult," and he comments in the autobiography that these words seemed to "express exactly that kind of feeling of struggling to get born out of mother, to become a separate individual person" (2:288). In a 1955 session, Guntrip alluded to Franz Alexander's idea that "as analysis draws to an end, patients begin to produce birth symbolism" (2:340). But, as we know, the presence of birth symbolism in the end phases of an analysis was first pointed out by Rank in *The Trauma of*

Birth, and Guntrip's personal experience of this phenomenon doubtless lies behind his respectful criticism of Rank's ideas, pointed out in chapter 4. According to Guntrip, the analyst "must see the patient through into the ultimate acceptance of a therapeutic regression from which he must be mentally nursed to a rebirth and regrowth of a real self" (1968, 362). This regression to the womb is not to be explained by a physical birth trauma, as Rank originally maintained, but is rather "the profoundest expression of infantile dependence, when a weak infantile ego cannot cope with an inadequate or traumatic environment" (54).

As we shall see, Guntrip finally achieved his own "regrowth of a real self" in the liberating series of dreams precipitated by the death of Winnicott. Puzzled as to what gave him the strength to face the basic trauma of his mother's failure, Guntrip realizes: "It must have been because Winnicott was not, and could not be, dead for me, nor certainly for many others" (1975, 464). According to Hans Loewald, "The extended leave taking of the end phase of analysis is a replica of the process of mourning" (1962, 259). When Winnicott died, Guntrip, like Oedipus, answered Nicodemus's query to Jesus about the mystery of rebirth by imaginatively returning to his mother's womb for a second time as an old man in order to be reborn and to lay to rest the infantile memories by which he had been haunted for a lifetime.

The analogies between the self-analyses of Guntrip and Freud are reinforced by some remarkable parallels in their personal histories. Chief among these is the accident of sibling loss.[2] As is well known, Freud was profoundly affected by the death in infancy of his younger brother, Julius, when he himself was just under two years of age. Although mentioned in the memory-laden letter to Fliess of October 3, 1897, and later recalled in a 1912 letter to Ferenczi, the death of Julius is nowhere alluded to in any of Freud's published writings. Max Schur has elucidated the importance of the "non vixit" dream in terms of Freud's recurring experience of the "guilt of the survivor" (1972, 153–71); and Ernest Jones has drawn upon Freud's paper "Some Character Types Met With in Psycho-Analytic Work" (1916) to depict Freud as

---

2. I have addressed this issue in an earlier paper (1988b). The only other discussions of Guntrip's analysis with Fairbairn and Winnicott to my knowledge are in Pontalis, Anzieu, and Rosolato 1977, Glatzer and Evans 1977, Eigen 1981b, Landis 1981, and Hughes 1989, 105–17.

one who was himself "wrecked by success" through the fulfillment of his unconscious death wishes against Julius (1955, 146).

Given Freud's oedipal neurosis and Guntrip's borderline condition of fractured selfhood, their respective experiences of sibling loss take place, appropriately enough, in different psychic registers. Whereas in Freud the death of Julius gives rise to the conflict between ambivalent feelings of love and hatred that leads to guilt, Guntrip's inability to recall, and hence to mourn, the death of Percy indicates his arrest at a more primitive stage of emotional development. The disparity between Freud's unresolved ambivalence and Guntrip's "absence of grief" (Deutsch 1937) is all the more striking in that Guntrip was more than eighteen months older when his brother died than Freud was when his brother died.

The responses of Freud and Guntrip to the loss of their brothers were conditioned by their underlying relationships to their mothers. Freud, as we saw in the previous chapter, despite his panoply of complexes, shared with Winnicott the feeling of having been his mother's favorite. In a marginal annotation to *The Interpretation of Dreams,* Guntrip admits: "I did not have that" (1:226). On the contrary, although locked in a defensive conflict with his mother, at bottom he did not even receive from her a secure sense of his own existence.

To summarize the salient biographical details, Guntrip's mother was the eldest daughter of eleven children, who had already played the part of "little mother" to her younger siblings and did not want any children of her own when she married Guntrip's father, an eloquent and protective Methodist preacher, in 1898. In Guntrip's teenage years, he was told by his mother that she had breast-fed him because she believed it would prevent another pregnancy; when she refused to breast-feed Percy, her husband blamed her for Percy's death. After Percy died, she refused further sexual relations with her husband. Upon seeing his brother dead on his mother's lap, the three-and-a-half-year-old Harry rushed up and called out, "Don't let him go. You'll never get him back!" (1975, 455). He then succumbed to his exhaustion illness and would certainly have died had he not been sent to the home of a maternal aunt.[3]

The Kleinian aspects of Guntrip's experience of breast-feeding—the

3. For a perceptive study of the connections between a mother's own sibling experience and her attitude toward her firstborn child during a second pregnancy, see Abarbanel 1983.

breast became consolidated as a bad object, so no good loved object could be installed within his ego—are evident. Because no good object was introjected, his ego remained frozen at the schizoid position and, in Helene Deutsch's words, was "not sufficiently developed to bear the strain of the work of mourning" (1937, 13). Guntrip exhibits both the regressive anxiety and the mobilization of defenses—above all, the blocking of affect—that are the responses of an immature ego to the threat posed by object loss.

But a Kleinian analysis purely in terms of internal objects needs to be supplemented by an awareness of the importance of environmental provision. As Winnicott has shown, the infant's attainment of the depressive position "is not so much dependent on the mother's simple ability to hold a baby, which was her characteristic at the earlier stages, as on her ability to hold the infant-care situation over a period of time during which the infant may go through complex experiences" (1958a, 23). The failure of Guntrip's mother to "hold the infant-care situation" is the crux of his difficulties; the struggles over breast-feeding are but their most striking metaphor.

Because his mother was not good enough, Guntrip sought to find in other family members the love that he could not obtain from her. Rather than a rival, as Julius primarily was for Freud, Percy was both a "love-object" and a "buffer state" shielding Guntrip from his mother (2:50). When Percy died, Guntrip was abandoned to the care of a mother who could not emotionally nourish her children. To some degree, Guntrip's father provided a positive alternative to and a protective barrier against the mother's hostility and depression. Guntrip's childhood shows how ego needs can override sexual attraction in choosing a parental object: "My love was for my father, but that did not make me homosexual in an inverted Oedipus Complex sense. It left me free to love a feminine woman and make a happy marriage" (1:225). This personal experience underlies Guntrip's theoretical critique of the universality of the Oedipus complex (1978, 218).

Guntrip's inability to triumph over, and hence to mourn, his brother's death allows us to reconceptualize Freud's persistent struggle with the revenants of his unconsciously murdered rivals. Since guilt heralds the arrival at the depressive position, it may be viewed not as a curse or burden but rather as a positive achievement. As Winnicott explains, the sense of guilt, "even when unconscious and even when apparently irrational, implies a certain degree of emotional growth, ego health, and hope" (1958a, 19). In spite of its neurotic quality, Freud's guilt of the survivor is thus paradoxically a sign of his comparative psychological health and maturity.

Although Guntrip strives to maintain an impartial attitude toward both his eminent analysts, characterizing Fairbairn as more innovative in theory and Winnicott as more spontaneous in practice and expressing gratitude to each, in point of fact his autobiography and his paper mount a telling indictment of Fairbairn's limitations as a therapist while paying a corresponding tribute to Winnicott's genius. Guntrip acknowledges that he saw Fairbairn after he had passed the peak of his creative powers and when his health was already in decline, but his first analysis remains a story of ultimate failure.

Fairbairn's interpretations were excessively intellectualized, his manner rigid. Characteristically, he placed the patient's couch in front of a large desk and seated himself on the other side, an arrangement that induced in Guntrip the fantasy that Fairbairn might lean over and hit him on the head.[4] In frustration, Guntrip knocked over Fairbairn's pedestal ashtray, kicked his glass doorstopper, and strewed some of the books from a huge bookcase over the floor—this last being a particularly vivid protest against the "textbookish" nature of Fairbairn's interpretations (Anzieu in Pontalis, Anzieu, and Rosolato 1977, 34). Guntrip's analysis was stymied by the experiences that took place when he was between three and a half and seven years old, after he returned from his aunt's to his parents' home and tried to force his mother to love him, first demanding attention with various psychosomatic ailments and then, after the age of five, with a more active defiance. But the traumas of his brother's death and his mother's failure of empathy remained inaccessible. As Guntrip remarks in his autobiography, "I felt I had had an Oedipal rather than an object-relations analysis with Fairbairn" (2:141–42), and it did not reach down to the breakdown of the primary love relationship that defines the area of the basic fault.

4. In his final paper, "On the Nature and Aims of Psycho-Analytical Treatment" (1958), Fairbairn discloses that he has ceased to use the couch because it prevents the establishment of a genuine human relationship with his patients. This evolution—doubtless influenced in part by his experience with Guntrip—is complemented by Guntrip's surprised realization that there was "a small settee" beside Fairbairn's desk at which he could (and eventually did) sit (1975, 452). Nevertheless, Guntrip had ample reason to regard Fairbairn's technique as insufficiently flexible.

Guntrip shares with Freud the accident of sibling loss, but his life and Fairbairn's correspond in other ways. In a recent biography, John D. Sutherland has in an exemplary fashion documented the way that Fairbairn's theory is a creative outgrowth of his personal pathology. From posthumously preserved self-analytic notes, Sutherland learned that in middle age Fairbairn became afflicted with a severe phobia of public urination, which interfered with his social life and freedom of movement. This symptom condensed Fairbairn's identification with his father, who also suffered from a urinary inhibition, and Fairbairn's relationship with his forbiddingly aggressive mother. On one occasion, when Fairbairn as a boy asked his mother about some blood-stained diapers he had seen in a pail, suspecting that they had something to do with her sexuality, she retaliated by getting "into a frenzy of rage, gave him a beating and then locked him in the parents' bedroom for hours" (1989, 72).

In light of this history, it is scarcely surprising that Fairbairn's revolutionary contribution to psychoanalysis focuses on the exciting and frustrating hold of bad objects over the internal world or that he conducted his analyses principally on that level. Because Guntrip's mother was no less sadistic than Fairbairn's, moreover, he provided ample grist for Fairbairn's analytic mill. Not only did she cane Harry for his transgressions between the ages of five and seven—sending him to buy a new cane when the old one broke—but her violent behavior extended even to animals. As she admitted to him in her old age, "I tried keeping a dog but I had to give it up. I couldn't stop beating it" (1975, 457). In her most monstrous action—suppressed in the published paper but divulged in the autobiography (1:43)—when Guntrip was five, she, having tired of washing under his foreskin, put him on a table (in the same parlor where he had seen Percy dead on her lap) and without warning had a doctor anesthetize and circumcise him. This episode marked a turning point: afterward Guntrip ceased to use psychosomatic illness to try to manipulate his mother and began in a deliberate way to grow more independent of her.

As a result of these early experiences, Guntrip developed a far milder case of urinary retention than Fairbairn's, an illness he ascribed to the way that "mother both excited and inhibited me" (2:118). What is more, during the decadelong analysis both Guntrip's mother and Fairbairn's wife died, and the daughters of both men married. But these parallels between Fairbairn's personal history and Guntrip's proved to be a mixed blessing. As Guntrip surmises, "My real life situation . . . was too close to the emotional pattern of his own life, . . . and he felt some unconscious need to get away from me to other patients" (2:272).

Although Guntrip derived considerable benefit from Fairbairn's dissection of his "world of internalized libidinally excited bad-object relations" (1975, 457), he also found it to be stultifyingly *re-created* in the analysis. Fairbairn's obsessively precise style helped to cast him in the role of a "dominating bad mother" (450), and his insistence on framing his interpretations in conventional Freudian terms of castration anxiety—instead of addressing the existential issues of loss of self—compounded Guntrip's negative transference. The analysis took on the quality of a battle of wills, such as Guntrip had waged in childhood with his punitive preoedipal mother.

Guntrip calls this destructive pattern "one up and the other down" (2:6) and said in one session to Fairbairn: "The struggle is battle to the death. I must have felt she'd kill me. She wouldn't, couldn't give up unless killed" (2:176). As a child, Guntrip was fascinated by a story his mother had read to him of the hunter Nimrod spearing a lion, which, as Winnicott later pointed out to him, "could be read in two ways, mother attacking me, and me retaliating on mother" (2:26). Early in his analysis with Fairbairn, Guntrip described himself in a fantasy as "at one with both the attacker and the victim, both the bad breast and the angry baby destroying each other" (2:70). Guntrip's "battle to the death" with his mother, transferentially restaged in the analysis with Fairbairn, thus enacts the fight for recognition that inaugurates Hegel's master-slave dialectic. In spite of being thoroughly *social*, however, Hegel's paradigm (in addition to assuming that both its protagonists are male) is not sufficiently *environmental*. From the perspective of object relations theory, as I argued against Lacan in chapter 5, the quest for recognition need not lead to a life-and-death struggle; it does so only as a breakdown phenomenon if a mother fails to infuse with love the intercourse with her infant, which is truly the first dialectic of human life.

In his late paper "Observations on the Nature of Hysterical States," Fairbairn proposes that the erotogenic zones of Freud's libido theory can best be understood, not as irreducible biological givens, but as the sites for hysterical "conversion-symptoms" of disturbed personal relationships. He interprets to one patient that he "was trying to escape from the clash of personalities [with his mother] by imaginatively localizing the drama in the penis itself" (1954, 121).[5] But in his analysis with Guntrip, Fairbairn failed to follow through on the implications of this radical recasting of theory. As Guntrip complains, Fairbairn could not get beyond linking Guntrip's anxiety with the fear of castration, "for that was symbolic, although a real involved element, in a much larger fear of 'personality-castration,' the crushing of my whole Ego, my independent vitality and activity and spontaneity as a small growing person" (2:22).

The frustration that Guntrip came increasingly to feel in the later years of his analysis with Fairbairn was mitigated by conversations that took place after their formal analytic hours; there he and Fairbairn discussed theoretical problems in an atmosphere of mutual respect and equality. During the sessions Fairbairn played the role of the transferential "bad mother," but afterward he assumed the more realistic characteristics of Guntrip's "understanding good father" (1975, 450). During these extra-analytic chats, furthermore, Fairbairn confided details of his personal life, disclosing, for instance, tensions in his marriage and his childhood memory of seeing the bloody diapers that were the evidence of his mother's menstruation (2:170).

To many orthodox practitioners, Fairbairn's relaxation of the parameters of the analytic setting will doubtless seem a grievous error of technique. Although Fairbairn's flexibility may indeed have been excessive, the underlying problem is that his attitude during the analysis itself remained (in the terms I employed in chapter 1) fundamentally *authoritarian*, rather than *dialectical*. As Guntrip puts it: "His interpretations were always categorical. I now hold the view that they should be hypothetical, to be tested by the patient's reaction, not based on the assumption that the analyst must be right" (2:352).

From his own therapeutic practice, Guntrip learned many years later how he should have replied to Fairbairn's reproach that "you don't let me know anything." Guntrip quotes two patients as saying to him, "I

5. Sutherland reports that Guntrip told him that he was the patient called Jack in Fairbairn's paper (1989, 140). It is striking that a different patient, named Morris, to whom Fairbairn addresses his comment about localizing a personality clash with his mother in his penis, was—like Guntrip—circumcised at the age of five. But it does not appear that Morris, like Jack, is therefore really Guntrip.

can't get to you. If you can't get in touch with me, I'm lost," and continues: "I was not keeping myself from Fairbairn. I was telling him that behind the frightened small child who had no means of standing up to a mother who could be so ferocious, I was hiding my real self . . . and needing help by being recognized and given a relationship to grow in. *That was what I was not hiding but letting him know*" (2:153). It is fitting that Guntrip's patients should have taught him a crucial lesson about his analysis with Fairbairn. Like Ferenczi, who was both the analysand of Freud and a master analyst of others, Guntrip cultivated the capacity to see analysis from the patient's point of view, which is integral to a dialectical outlook. Guntrip's addendum that his reticence was "what I was not hiding but letting him know" highlights Fairbairn's inability, in Bollas's words, to "relive elements of [the analysand's] infantile history through his countertransference" or to tolerate the suspension in an "unknowable region" that goes along with a truly Socratic way of working (1987, 200).

Because of his personal and theoretical investment in bad objects, Fairbairn was not prepared to follow Guntrip into the sphere of the "faceless depersonalized mother" of the period before Percy's death (1975, 464). His hammering on the oedipal issues overlaid on this schizoid core had the effect, as Guntrip writes in the autobiography, of serving to "keep them going as a defence against falling into that deep experience of isolation where he failed to find me" (2:357). His patients' longing to regress became increasingly threatening to Fairbairn as he grew older. On one occasion in 1956, when Guntrip moved from a chair to lie down on the couch and informed him, "I need to regress to get at something," Fairbairn "became very agitated and said, 'Regression is terrible.'" Not surprisingly, Guntrip returned to his chair, having concluded that "whatever was involved I knew I would never solve it with him" (2:360).

To compound matters, Leslie Tizard, the friend whose departure thirty years earlier had caused the first adult eruption of Guntrip's exhaustion illness, died in December 1957. Then, in July 1958, Fairbairn fell gravely ill, and Guntrip's analysis was interrupted until January 1959. Prompted by Fairbairn's own recognition that since his illness, he had taken the place of Guntrip's deceased brother, Guntrip reached a crucial insight, though he could not bring himself to impart it directly to Fairbairn: either remaining in analysis and awaiting Fairbairn's death or losing him by ending the analysis would cause a repetition of the trauma of Percy's death, with no one to help him through it. In view of Fairbairn's declining health, Guntrip phased out his analysis during 1959.

Part of the courage needed to terminate his treatment with Fairbairn came from Guntrip's decision to seek analysis with Winnicott, with whom he had begun corresponding at Fairbairn's instigation in 1954. Guntrip writes: "By 1962 I had no doubt that he was the only man I could turn to for further help" (1975, 459). In this well-placed confidence in Winnicott's healing powers, the sixty-one-year-old Guntrip echoes the distressed plea of the Piggle, two years and four months old, before her first consultation: "Mummy take me to Dr. Winnicott" (Winnicott 1977, 7). Even though Winnicott did not bring Guntrip to his journey's end, Guntrip could not have achieved his final self-analytic breakthrough without Winnicott's intervention. As he acknowledges, Winnicott's "uncanny accuracy of intuition gave me the profoundest clue to my personality problem that I ever had" and "enabled me to find my way in the final 1970 dream-sequence" (2:142).

In spite of his ultimately negative verdict on his analysis with Fairbairn, however, Guntrip never calls Fairbairn's brilliance into question. More importantly, he allows the reader to glimpse the kindness beneath Fairbairn's reserved exterior. At their final meeting, when Guntrip reached out to shake hands with Fairbairn—something they had never done during the long years of their association—"at once he took it, and I suddenly saw a few tears trickle down his face. *I saw the warm heart of this man with a fine mind and a shy nature*" (1975, 454).

Fittingly, Guntrip and Fairbairn ended their relationship on excellent terms. Fairbairn shed tears at their final parting, and when Guntrip published his paper on ego weakness a year later, Fairbairn wrote to him to say that this concept "yields better therapeutic results than interpretation in terms of libidinal and anti-libidinal tensions" and that "if I could write now, that is what I would write about" (452). Although he could not hold Guntrip's regressed ego in the analytic setting, Fairbairn had the grace and honesty to recognize that Guntrip had moved beyond him theoretically. In showing himself ready to learn from his patient, Fairbairn evinced his spiritual nobility and likewise released Guntrip to minister unto himself.

In "The Two Analyses of Mr. Z," Heinz Kohut says that in his first analysis his theoretical convictions "had become for the patient a replica of the mother's hidden psychosis, of a distorted outlook on the world to which he had adjusted in childhood, which he had accepted as reality" (1979, 16). In the second analysis, however, undertaken after he had begun his metamorphosis from classical drive psychology to self psychology, Kohut explores—with vastly improved therapeutic success—the patient's use of masturbatory self-stimulation "to obtain temporarily the reassurance of being alive, of existing" and suggests that Mr. Z's mother "may not have lost her penis but her face" (17, 20).

Kohut's two analyses with Mr. Z are strikingly similar to Guntrip's two analyses with Fairbairn and Winnicott. The comparison holds not simply in the intellectual evolution that permitted Kohut, like Winnicott, to move beyond a preoccupation with bad objects and threats of castration to his patient's sense of lifelessness and depersonalization but also in the way that his conversion to self psychology (which, as I argued in chapter 5, is an offshoot of object relations theory) brought with it a radical transformation in the dynamics of the clinical encounter.

Unlike the "categorical" Fairbairn, Winnicott was genuinely "hypothetical" in treating Guntrip. A hallmark of Winnicott's style is his readiness to admit his own uncertainty as part of the analytic discourse while remaining exceptionally attuned to the anxieties of his patient. Winnicott told Guntrip near the end of their first session: "I've nothing particular to say yet, but if I don't say something, you may begin to feel I'm not here" (1975, 460). He soon divined the root of Guntrip's discomfort at silence and his need to talk hard: "You feel silence is abandonment. The gap is not you forgetting mother, but mother forgetting you, and now you've relived it with me. You're finding an earlier trauma which you might never recover without the help of the Percy trauma repeating it. You have to remember mother abandoning you by transference on to me" (461). Winnicott guided Guntrip not only to the trauma of Percy's death but even beyond it to the dreaded underlying catastrophe of maternal abandonment, which could only be reconstructed by their reenacting it in the transference.

A useful gloss on Guntrip's ordeal is provided by André Green's concept of the "dead mother." Contrasting this notion with castration anxiety, which has to do with the fear of a bodily wound, Green proposes that a second paradigm of anxiety, whose context is "never bloody," is needed to subsume threats of abandonment and object loss (1983, 145). Rather than the red of blood, this form of destructiveness "bears the colours of mourning: black or white [blanc]" (146); and Green maintains that the blackness of depression is in fact secondary to the blankness of anxiety. He stresses his concern, not with the actual death of the mother, but with the effects of maternal depression, which transforms "a living object, which was a source of vitality for the child, into a distant figure, toneless, practically inanimate," and he plumbs the heart of Guntrip's mystery when he alludes to the "psychical holes" that the mother's inner lifelessness bores in her child, observing that "manifestations of hatred and the following process of reparation are manifestations which are secondary to this central decathexis of the maternal primary object" (142, 146). (In Guntrip's terms, the libidinal and antilibidinal egos are secondary to the regressed ego.) No less pertinently, Green remarks that "the dead mother complex is a revelation of the transference" and that the intractable problem she poses is that she "refuses to die a second death" (148, 158).[6]

The value of Guntrip's paper as a historical document stems largely from its portrayal of Fairbairn and Winnicott from the patient's point of view. A second, equally moving account of Winnicott as a clinician has recently been provided by Margaret Little. Even more disturbed than Guntrip, Little courageously describes the psychotic breakdowns with which she was struggling in the course of her analytic training and which her earlier analysts had failed to reach. Little reveals that Winnicott shed tears over losses that she herself was unable to mourn, held her hand during prolonged sessions, and uttered such statements as "I really hate your mother" (1985, 23). Guntrip's injunction that the analyst's interpretations be "tested by the patient's reaction" is exemplified by Little's description of Winnicott's technique: "He gave very few interpretations, and these only when I had reached the point where the matter could become conscious. Then of course the interpretation would ring true. He was not 'infallible,' but spoke tentatively, or speculated: 'I think perhaps . . . ,' or 'It seems as if. . . . ' This let me taste or feel what he said, and be free to accept or reject it" (23–24). As he does with Guntrip, Winnicott builds his own uncertainty into his analytic encounters with Little and leaves her free to "accept or reject" his interventions. Like Guntrip, Little had to contend with Winnicott's coronary episodes in the course of her analysis, and was burdened with the memory of a mother, who, in Winnicott's words, "would not let you die" (31).

The first-person narratives of Guntrip and Little find a counterpart

6. In this 1983 paper Green anatomizes the anxieties aroused by the dead mother without resorting to the superfluous hypothesis of the death instinct, as he often does elsewhere in *On Private Madness*.

from the analyst's standpoint in the case Winnicott first presented to the British Psycho-Analytical Society in 1966 under the title "On the Split-off Male and Female Elements to Be Found in Men and Women" and later published as a section of "Creativity and Its Origins" in *Playing and Reality*. In this paper Winnicott tells of a man afraid he would be called mad for thinking himself a girl, to whom Winnicott responded: "It was not that *you* told this to anyone; it is *I* who see the girl and hear the girl talking, when actually there is a man on my couch. The mad person is myself." By inducing the patient "to see himself as a girl *from my position*," Winnicott achieved a breakthrough. "He and I have been driven to the conclusion (though unable to prove it) that his mother (who is not alive now) saw a girl baby when she saw him as a baby before she came round to thinking of himself as a boy" (1971a, 74).

This clinical vignette is an exemplary demonstration of Winnicott's willingness to include his own sense of uncertainty—even madness—in the analytic dialogue, and of the way in which his encounter with the patient allows the two of them together to *relive* and hence to *reconstruct* the trauma of maternal madness or abandonment. As Winnicott wrote on March 17, 1966, to Herbert Rosenfeld: "I would like to hear it discussed how when a patient's mother was mad, does the patient bring this into the transference? It is not true that at some moment or other the patient must find that the analyst is mad?" (Rodman 1987, 153–54).

Beyond its heuristic value as a specimen of Winnicott's technique, this case is germane in the present context because it dovetails with Guntrip's personal history. As we learn from the autobiography, he, too, possessed split-off female elements.[7] Guntrip writes of his mother that "the only baby she could have accepted would have been a girl baby" and adds that she "dressed me as a girl so long that at last even customers in the shop protested to her that it was not right" (1:23). Although the conjecture is an alluring one, it does not appear that Guntrip is the patient that Winnicott describes. (Winnicott mentions the same individual in "Nothing at the Centre" [1959], written before Guntrip had begun to see him, and the discrepancies between the details of their lives exceed even the distortions that one would expect to safeguard confidentiality in a published case history.)

7. In my previous paper on Guntrip, I incorrectly asserted the contrary (1988b, 427). Before reading Guntrip's autobiography, I had no idea how uncanny the parallels between these two cases would be.

Ultimately, however, the interconnections between Guntrip and the patient in Winnicott's case do not depend on their literal identity. Winnicott writes: "The pure female split-off element found a primary unity with me as analyst, and this gave the man a feeling of having started to live" (1971a, 77). In his autobiography, Guntrip cites a January 1, 1921, diary entry, recorded when he was active in the Salvation Army: "I must be Being as well as Doing." Rereading this youthful exhortation, Guntrip retrospectively comments: "There are far larger implications in these few words than I could have realized at the time. Many years later the problem of 'Being as well as Doing' was to occupy an important part in the exposition of the psychodynamic concepts of D. W. Winnicott. As he pointed out, I could not take for granted my own 'ongoing Being' and was torn by trying to maintain it by 'Doing,' against the undermining powerful pull away from 'this earthly life'" (1:112).

In view of Guntrip's own engagement with "the problem of 'Being as well as Doing'" in his treatment with Winnicott, he and the patient in "Split-off Male and Female Elements" are unquestionably kindred spirits, even if not the same person. In *Schizoid Phenomena, Object Relations and the Self*, Guntrip quotes the sentence from Winnicott's paper that I cited in the preceding paragraph, and he emphasizes that "clinically *it is always the female element that we find dissociated, in both men and women, and that the fundamental dissociation is of the female element*" (1968, 253). Guntrip's theoretical amalgamation of his own concept of the regressed ego with Winnicott's female element fuses his reading of Winnicott's paper, his personal analysis with Winnicott, and his own extensive therapeutic practice. Such a dialectical conflation of roles—analyst and patient, teacher and pupil—is integral to psychoanalytic experience, especially as transmitted by the Independent tradition. Fittingly, Winnicott remarks in his paper about his patient's female element finding a "primary unity" with him as a therapist: "I have been affected by this detail, as will appear in my application to theory of what I have found in this case" (1971a, 77).

From these converging examples of Winnicott's technique—the testimonials of Guntrip and Little and "Split-off Male and Female Elements"—we may formulate in more general terms the contrast between Guntrip's experiences with Fairbairn and Winnicott. Insofar as Fairbairn opened himself up to Guntrip in their conversations after the formal consultation, their relationship did contain an element of what Ferenczi would call "mutual analysis." But the crucial point is that this dynamic was split into discrete phases, one inside, one outside, the analytic session. The genius of Winnicott, by contrast, was to have *permitted this role reversal to unfold within the analysis itself*. In so doing, therapy became truly a dialectical process, in which each person could learn from, and be changed by, the other.

The transformation proved efficacious. Winnicott not only enabled Guntrip in an extremely limited number of sessions "to reach right back to *an ultimate good mother, and to find her recreated in him in the transference*" (Guntrip 1975, 460) but also led Guntrip to cultivate his own nurturing powers. Acknowledging his vulnerability, Winnicott went so far as to say: "You too have a good breast. You've always been able to give more than you take. Doing your analysis is almost the most reassuring thing that happens to me. The chap before you makes me feel I'm no good at all. You don't have to be good for me. I don't need it and can cope without it, but in fact you are good for me" (462). As Guntrip writes in his autobiography, despite the calamities of his upbringing, he did not abandon hope that "it was possible to make good that early let down," and in becoming first a minister and later a psychotherapist he was expressing "this faith in the possibility of making good what mother had failed to do for me and Percy" (2:284). By providing a holding environment for the emergence of Guntrip's True Self, and in a way that would only become clear in the fullness of time, Winnicott transformed the meaning of Percy's death and afforded Guntrip access to the inner strength needed to face his double traumas of sibling loss and maternal deprivation.

In true psychoanalytic fashion, the most enduring results of Winnicott's interventions only manifested themselves after the event, through deferred action. Guntrip saw Winnicott for the last time in July 1969, and in February 1970 Guntrip was warned by a physician that he was seriously overworked. Rather than accept retirement, he continued to write feverishly, until in October he contracted pneumonia and spent five weeks in the hospital. Even then Guntrip did not fully appreciate that his hyperactivity was a result of his struggle to assert himself as a living being in the face of his mother's apathy. Early in 1971, Guntrip heard that Winnicott had had flu, and dropped him a line. Winnicott called soon afterward to thank him for his note. Two weeks later Winnicott's secretary called with the news that he had died.[8]

---

8. Henriette Glatzer and William Evans mistakenly give the year of Winnicott's death as 1968 (1977, 83). They likewise brand Guntrip a "narcissistic

For Guntrip, Winnicott's death precipitated an extraordinary series of dreams. In the first dream "*I saw my mother*, black, immobilized, staring fixedly into space, *totally ignoring me* as I stood at one side staring at her and feeling myself frozen into immobility" (1975, 463). In previous dreams, his mother had always attacked him. Although he initially assumed that Winnicott's death repeated his brother's, Guntrip soon recognized that he had not dreamed of his mother in this way on the two earlier occasions when he had been separated from someone who had reminded him of Percy. Now, moreover, he did not fall ill, as he had in 1927 and 1938. Dreaming of his mother's indifference was thus a sign that Guntrip was beginning, for the first time, to remember the events of the period before his brother's death. In "Dreaming, Fantasying, and Living," Winnicott makes the profound observation that "dreaming and living have been seen to be of the same order, daydreaming being of another order" (1971b, 26). In dreaming of what he had previously forgotten, Guntrip was making contact with his dissociated past and, as a result, learning to live.

The next two months led Guntrip through a "compelling dream-sequence which went on night after night, taking me back in chronological order through every house I had ever lived in" (1975, 463). Like Oedipus, Guntrip had to undo the knots of his past in the reverse order from that in which they were tied. The climax came in two dreams in which Guntrip clearly saw himself as he was during his brother's life and death. In the first, he was three and holding onto a pram which contained his one-year-old brother; their mother was staring vacantly into the distance. The second dream is even more startling: "I was standing with another man, the double of myself, both reaching out to get hold of a dead object. Suddenly the other man collapsed in a heap. Immediately the dream changed to a lighted room, where I saw Percy again. I knew it was him, sitting on the lap of a woman who had no face, arms, breasts. She was merely a lap to sit on, not a person. He looked deeply depressed, with the corners of his mouth turned down, and I was trying to make him smile" (464). In this dream, Guntrip actually recaptures the memory of trying to reach out to his brother when he beheld him dead on his mother's lap; and in both dreams he also breaks

---

patient," who extorted "concession after concession" from his hapless analysts, both of whom "did his bidding" and failed to recognize that keeping detailed records of his sessions was "part of his resistance" (84–87). A more complete misconception of the truth would be difficult to imagine.

through to the earlier period before Percy's death "to see the faceless depersonalized mother, and the black depressed mother, who totally failed to relate to both of us" (464).

Through his death, Winnicott thus enabled Guntrip to summon his emotionally absent mother and prematurely deceased brother back to life in his mind. As Guntrip writes, "*He has taken her place and made it possible and safe to remember her in an actual dream-reliving of her paralysing schizoid aloofness*" (464–65). In Kleinian terms, Guntrip negotiates the transition from the paranoid-schizoid to the depressive position. Because of his mother's failure, Guntrip harbored within him the "*threat of annihilation,*" which Winnicott defines as a "very real primitive anxiety, long antedating any anxiety that includes the word death in its description" (1956b, 303). Only by reexperiencing the trauma of maternal abandonment first in his analysis and then in reality could Guntrip discover a "self that can afford to die" (304). Through his belated internalization of Winnicott as a good-enough mother, Guntrip in old age achieved what Freud, likewise confronted by sibling loss but sustained from infancy by his mother's love, struggled with for a lifetime—the ambivalence accompanying the guilt of the survivor.

In his second climactic dream Guntrip refers to standing with "a double of myself." This double is evidently a recollected image of himself as a child. But this "other man collapsed in a heap" could represent the deceased Percy no less than Guntrip's own regressed ego. Indeed, the effect of a double is precisely to break down the distinctions between self and other or between interpersonal and intrapsychic realms. When, in the "non vixit" dream, Freud declares, "My emotional life has always insisted that I should have an intimate friend and hated enemy" (1900, 483), he defines his life as a series of encounters with revenants of his nephew John, beneath whom lies the shadowy figure of the dead Julius. As I have argued elsewhere, the constant ambivalence in Freud's dealings with male counterparts is an externalization of the oscillation between "delusions of inferiority" and "megalomania" in his own self-esteem (1987, 44–49).

The intertwined motifs of doubling and sibling loss in Freud and Guntrip receive a fascinating gloss in an autobiographical paper by George L. Engel on his experience of being an identical twin. Engel's paper is relevant here both because it is a venture in self-analysis, displaying courage comparable to that of Guntrip and Freud, and because it turns on the death of a brother. Unlike the brothers of

Guntrip and Freud, however, Frank Engel, George's elder by five minutes, died not in early childhood but at forty-nine years of age. This difference is of only secondary importance. The Engels' father, like Frank, died unexpectedly of a heart attack, at the age of fifty-eight. Freud, as I have documented, although forty years old when his father died, was inordinately afflicted by the death because it reawakened the feelings of self-reproach implanted by the premature death of Julius (1987, 18–23). George Engel's father died before his brother, as one would expect in the normal course of events, and George's reaction likewise lacks the infantile factor. But the psychological dynamics of his survivor guilt are otherwise comparable to those found in Guntrip and Freud.

In his paper George Engel describes his mourning process, including anniversary reactions and parapraxes. He includes some astonishing photographs taken of himself in April 1972 and of his father in April 1928, when each man was fifty-eight years old, as well as a photograph of his brother, Frank, taken on the same day in April 1928, when the twins were fourteen. The poses of the three men reading are truly uncanny in their likeness. Engel ponders the question: "Had I unconsciously begun to fuse the images of my father and my twin? Indeed, had he in my unconscious become my twin?" (1975, 29).

One example of a parapraxis committed by Engel must stand for many. When lecturing at the University of Rochester, Engel misspoke and said, "December 10th, 1971, was my ninety-eighth birthday," instead of his fifty-eighth birthday. After being convulsed with "uncontrollable laughter," in which his audience joined wholeheartedly, he interpreted his slip to express "my wish to live to a ripe old age, or better still, forever." Engel's fifty-eighth birthday was, of course, a milestone, because that was the age at which his father had died. But as a perceptive medical student in the audience pointed out, his slip was overdetermined because ninety-eight represents twice forty-nine, the age at which his brother had died. Engel sardonically comments, "By doubling his life span I shall live his life for him and enjoy the twinship for both of us. What a triumph! What a marvellous joke! No wonder the uncontrollable laughter and tears" (29).

Very few people have an identical (or even a fraternal) twin, but the exceptional individuals to whom such a lot falls can—like heroes— throw more ordinary lives into sharper relief. Percy was for Guntrip only an "imaginary twin" (Bion 1950), but the motif of doubling is no less prominent in his psychic life than in that of George Engel. Guntrip's mother used to say regularly of Percy in later years, "He was a fine bouncing baby. He'd have made two of you." As Guntrip comments, "She idealized the dead baby and depreciated the living one presumably to assuage her feelings of guilt" (1:28). This split between idealization and depreciation is reenacted in inverted form by Winnicott in the transference when he tells Guntrip that the preceding patient makes him feel "no good at all," whereas Guntrip's analysis "is almost the most reassuring thing that happens to me."

Guntrip's analytic autobiography contains little in the way of wordplay or, for that matter, any explicit attention to language—an omission likely to strike anyone even remotely influenced by Lacan—but one noteworthy exception bears directly on the themes of doubling and sibling loss. Guntrip reports a dream from early in his self-analysis: "I was going into a cemetery and saw the Messenger of Death who comes for folk. I there saw Arnold Mee (a Salem lad who had become a minister and who had a dead brother). It was dark, and as I passed a tombstone, I saw two letters of a name glowing in the dark,—EE" (1:214). In artistic fashion, this dream parallels Guntrip's condition— as a minister at Salem Congregational Church in Leeds—with that of another minister, the aptly named Arnold Mee, who likewise had a deceased brother. As Guntrip immediately notes, "The missing letter was obviously 'M.' It was the tomb of the dead brother of whom Arnold was very fond." But Guntrip's dream goes beyond equating himself and Percy with Arnold and his brother to fusing the living and the dead siblings in each instance. In his autobiography, Guntrip says he "felt the 'Messenger of Death who comes for folk' must have been coming for ME," and this role reversal stands "for my breakdown into an 'apparently dying state' after Percy died; and . . . mother's often speaking of Percy in a way that made me feel I should have died and not him" (1:299).

Just as Engel seeks to "live the life" of his deceased twin, Guntrip puts himself in the place of the dead Percy, and Guntrip, like Engel, also identifies with his father. In 1938, during his second adult exhaustion illness, brought on by the departure of his ministerial colleague at Salem, Guntrip had one of the few "big dreams" of his life. Like many other dreams we have examined, this one is haunted by death. To sketch only the barest details, Guntrip enters an "ancient tomb" where "a dead man lay clothed on top of a coffin" (1:244). The dream takes place on the tenth anniversary of his father's death, and Guntrip comments that the man in the tomb reminds him of his father. He continues: "But there was more than this to the dream, for as a process in my own mind, this 'man buried alive' was a part of myself, and I certainly had an unconscious identification with my father. I developed his pains when he was dying, and only marriage I am sure saved me from one of my 'exhaustion illnesses' then. For years I thought I would die like him at 63, till I passed that age" (1:245). No less than Engel, who had "unconsciously begun to fuse the images of my father and my twin" and who had condensed in his parapraxis the number of years in their lives, Guntrip imitates his father as well as his brother in his exhaustion illness and carries them both "buried alive" in his mind. The intertwining of filial and fraternal guilt of the survivor inheres in psychoanalysis from Freud's discovery of the Oedipus complex, and this classic configuration is variously replicated in the self-analyses of both Engel and Guntrip.

From identical twins through imaginary twins, we return to the ubiquitous phenomenon of the double. Following Rank (1914), Freud has argued that the idea of the double—including belief in an immortal soul—was "originally an insurance against the destruction of the ego"; but then it "reverses its aspect," and "from having been an assurance of immortality, it becomes an uncanny harbinger of death" (1919b, 235). The same ambiguity attaches in reverse form to the revenant. The ghost of a loved or hated person who haunts us from beyond the grave, it carries the promise that we, too, may be remembered after death.

In his autobiography, as we have seen, Guntrip avers that his theoretical writings form the "conscious and intellectual" aspects of the quest for "a solution to my own personal problem." In addition to paralleling Kohut's two analyses of Mr. Z, Guntrip's two analyses may be correlated also with his major books—*Personality Structure and Human Interaction* and *Schizoid Phenomena, Object Relations and the Self.* (A number of chapters of the latter, including "Ego-Weakness and the Hard Core of the Problem of Psychotherapy," were published before Guntrip's analysis with Winnicott started in 1962, but the correlation remains generally valid.) Indeed, when Guntrip writes near the end of *Personality Structure and Human Interaction* that "it appears to me that long analyses may well end inconclusively because the Regressed Ego is not reached" (1961, 443), it is impossible not to detect a veiled reproach against his own lengthy treatment with Fairbairn. By the same token, Guntrip's exploration of ego weakness and the regressed ego in *Schizoid Phenomena, Object Relations and the Self* addresses the personal issues that he was able to get at in his clinical work with Winnicott. Guntrip's hyperactivity, as we know, was a defense against his underlying feeling of lifelessness, and the axiom that *"a regressed illness is usually a conflict between a struggle to keep going at all costs, and a longing to give up, in which the latter drive is of dire necessity winning over the former"* (1968, 164) is clearly one that Guntrip has proved on his own pulses.

As we have also seen, Fairbairn's mapping of the territory of bad objects has a biographical dimension in his symptom of urinary inhibition and his relationship to his punitively aggressive mother. But because Fairbairn's mother was more nearly good enough than Guntrip's, she did establish in him an adequate sense of his own existence, albeit one that left him too defended to respond to Guntrip's appeal to probe beyond the outerworks of the antilibidinal ego to the citadel of the regressed ego. The progression from Freud to Fairbairn to Guntrip suggests that advances in psychoanalytic theory depend on the courage of analysts to wrestle with their personal pathologies at ever-deeper (or at least different) levels. At the same time, however, this transmutation of subjective distress into objective insight could not be accomplished without the innate drive to health that is an indispensable catalyst of the creative process.

Given the connection between the emotional travails of Fairbairn and Guntrip and their contributions to psychoanalysis, the question arises: What was it in Winnicott's experience that enabled him to go so deep, both as a theorist and a clinician? It seems safe to conclude that what I said in chapter 6 about his having a happy childhood does not tell the full story. Adam Phillips quotes the following lines from a poem, "The Tree," written by Winnicott at the age of sixty-seven.

Mother below is weeping
        weeping
        weeping
Thus I knew her

Once, stretched out on her lap
  as now on dead tree
I learned to make her smile
  to stem her tears
  to undo her guilt
  to cure her inward death
To enliven her was my living.

Although on a conscious level Winnicott identifies himself with Christ and the tree with the cross, Phillips is surely justified in surmising that

"Winnicott was recalling an early experience of his mother's depression, and her consequent inability to hold him" (1988, 29). Indeed, Winnicott's image of being "stretched out on her lap / as now on dead tree" bears a haunting likeness to Guntrip's memory of his mother with the dead Percy on her lap, and both men sought to find ways to ransom their mothers from "inward death." Beneath his vitality and self-confidence, Winnicott must have had a tenaciously regressed ego of his own to tolerate his stressful work with patients. They used him to get at their schizoid core, and Winnicott needed them to make contact with areas of himself he could not revivify in any other way.

In view of Fairbairn's urinary inhibition and Guntrip's traumatic circumcision and the attendant "personality-castration," it bears mentioning that Winnicott is alleged to have suffered for much of life from problems of potency.[9] If proved true, this would not discredit or invalidate his theory, but neither should such a material piece of information be suppressed to protect Winnicott's reputation. Rather, in keeping with Guntrip's dictum "Our theory must be rooted in our psychopathology," I offer this third example of a disturbance in phallic functioning in an analyst of the British Independent tradition to symbolize the inseparability of the wound of neurosis from the bow of insight in the history of psychoanalysis.

The interplay of subjective and objective elements in the theories of Fairbairn, Winnicott, and Guntrip is complemented by the inherently dialectical nature of the analytic enterprise brought out in Guntrip's encounters with Fairbairn and Winnicott. To the previously considered clinical aspects of this reciprocity, it should be added that Guntrip was forthright in his intellectual assessments of his two analysts. In *Schizoid Phenomena, Object Relations and the Self*, Guntrip quotes Winnicott's declaration from "Communicating and Not Communicating Leading to a Study of Certain Opposites" (1963a) that *"each individual is an isolate, permanently non-communicating, permanently unknown, in fact unfound. . . . The question is: how to be isolated without being insulated?"* (1968, 236). Branding this a "dubious proposition," Guntrip rejoins that Winnicott's notion of the True Self as an "incommunicado" core does not reflect an immutable reality but is rather "a primitive fear reaction, such as we could envisage in an infant who is not adequately protected and ego-supported by his mother and thus exposed to a fear of annihilation because of his own extreme weakness" (236–37).

9. This assertion was made to me by Hanna Segal in a personal interview in London on May 13, 1989.

Adam Phillips has representatively hailed "Communicating and Not Communicating" as Winnicott's "greatest paper" (1988, 144), but Guntrip, arguing more rigorously than Winnicott from an object relations position, exposes its essential fallacy. Since "a self can only experience itself in the act of experiencing something else," Winnicott's distinction between "isolation" and "insulation" is untenable, Guntrip points out, and the proper formulation of the problem is "how to have *privacy and self-possession without isolation or insulation*" (1968, 238, 236). In contrast, Phillips, like others, has faulted Winnicott for his omission of "even an implied account of how a person fathers himself," as well as for the "flight from the erotic" in his work (1988, 95, 152). In spite of their superficial plausibility (not diminished by the rumor of Winnicott's impotence), these charges do not withstand careful scrutiny. In *Human Nature*, for example, Winnicott explicitly describes the father as one who "can survive and punish and forgive" and affirms the importance of Freud's having gone "to the full length of tracing the origins of adult or mature genital sexuality to childhood genital sexuality, and of showing the pregenital roots of childhood genitality" (1988, 54, 58). Rather than these canards concerning sexuality and the father, it is Guntrip's deflating of Winnicott's idealization of a "permanently unknown" True Self that pinpoints the most substantive weakness in his thought.

The critique of Winnicott proffered by Guntrip in *Schizoid Phenomena, Object Relations and the Self* has its roots in the beginnings of their association. In 1954, at Fairbairn's request, Winnicott sent Guntrip a copy of his paper "Metapsychological and Clinical Aspects of Regression within the Psycho-Analytical Set-up" (an apt choice given the role that Guntrip's need to regress would play in both his analyses), and a brief correspondence between the two men ensued. The topic of Winnicott's two letters is Guntrip's relationship with Fairbairn and by extension Fairbairn's relationship with Freud and psychoanalysis. Winnicott had broached the larger issue of the validity of Fairbairn's theoretical innovations a year earlier in a review, written jointly with Masud Khan, of *Psychoanalytic Studies of the Personality*, and this review forms a subtext of his letters to Guntrip.

Winnicott's coauthored review of Fairbairn's book is an essential document for assessing the vexing questions of his own attitude toward tradition and innovation in psychoanalysis and his uneasy allegiance to object relations theory. Indeed, the review is deeply confused, bringing to light the contradictions in Winnicott's outlook at the time. On the one hand, Winnicott and Khan pay tribute to Fairbairn as someone who "challenges everything, and who puts clinical evidence before accepted theory, and who is no worshipper at a shrine." On the other hand, they inconsistently rebuke him for claiming that his theory "supplants that of Freud" (1953, 413). "While sharing many of Fairbairn's dissatisfactions," they equivocally conclude, "one is nevertheless left with the feeling that Freud's developing ideas provided and still provide a more fertile soil than the developed theory of Fairbairn" (421).

In retrospect, it is clear that Winnicott and Khan's attack on Fairbairn is wholly unfounded. For one thing, as Sutherland has remarked, "Fairbairn was challenging not Freud, but his libido theory. Towards the person Freud, along with his work, Fairbairn's admiration and respect were reverential" (1989, 174). (In this deference toward Freud, Fairbairn differs drastically from Ian Suttie, who, as I noted in chapter 1, combined a trenchant critique of Freud's metapsychology with a satirical disquisition on his personal limitations.) Furthermore, the upshot of Winnicott's position is to render hypocritical his professed dedication to unfettered thinking, since he places the "accepted theory" of Freud above "clinical evidence" to the contrary. In their authoritative overview of object relations theory, Jay Greenberg and Stephen Mitchell cite Winnicott and Khan's review of Fairbairn's work to support their claim that Winnicott exhibits a Bloomian "anxiety of influence" toward his precursors, most notably Freud and Klein, and that he "recounts the history of psychoanalytic ideas not so much as it developed, but as he would like it to have been" (1983, 189). Winnicott, they continue, seeks to position himself as the heir of Freud and Klein by "a combination of assimilation, distortion, and strategic avoidance" and "takes great pains . . . to proclaim himself at one with Freud in all respects" (202, 205).

Although Greenberg and Mitchell's presentation of Winnicott is unsympathetic, it does contain a measure of truth. Their critique requires qualification on two important counts. First, the inconsistency in Winnicott's point of view was immediately and persistently challenged by Guntrip. Second, Greenberg and Mitchell overlook that Winnicott by the end of his life came to recognize the error of his ways and belatedly acknowledged his affinity with Fairbairn.

Guntrip's readiness to differ with Winnicott is already evident in Winnicott's two letters of 1954. Quoting his review almost verbatim in his letter of July 20, Winnicott chastises Fairbairn for the way he "spoils a very good book" by his preoccupation with "supplanting Freud's theories" and contrasts Fairbairn with himself: "Any theories that I may have which are original are only valuable as a growth of ordinary psycho-analytic theory" (Rodman 1987, 75). In his letter of August 13, Winnicott adds that he finds Guntrip "very much influenced by Fairbairn" and admonishes Guntrip "to have a look into this matter of your relationship to psycho-analysis in general, so that you can have your own relationship and not Fairbairn's" (77).

The note of condescension in Winnicott's advice to Guntrip becomes especially ironic when one considers that both Guntrip and Fairbairn were at this stage considerably more independent in their thinking than he. Winnicott urges Guntrip to have his own relationship to psychoanalysis, but it is he himself who is in danger of idolatry. Winnicott's premise that his ideas are "only valuable as a growth of ordinary psycho-analytic theory" bears out Greenberg and Mitchell's diagnosis of an anxiety of influence. Unlike Fairbairn, who practiced in the relative isolation of Edinburgh, and Guntrip, who had in the early 1950s declined Willi Hoffer's invitation to come to London for psychoanalytic training (2:1–2), Winnicott was caught up in the politics of the British Psycho-Analytical Society, serving as president from 1956 to 1959 and again from 1965 to 1968. These institutional pressures, combined with his naturally irenic disposition, made him look for compromises and continuities wherever possible, but they also initially led him to minimize his own divagations from Freud. Only toward the end of his life, a decade and a half after his initial exchange of letters with Guntrip, could Winnicott face the implications of his discovery of the transitional object in the early 1950s and break definitively with the libido theory.

Following the preliminary contacts of 1954, the second stage in Guntrip's relationship with Winnicott was reached in 1961, shortly before he approached Winnicott about taking him on for personal analysis, and was signaled by an unpublished letter, dated September 13, that accompanies a presentation copy of *Personality Structure and Human Interaction*. Guntrip thanks Winnicott for the "great stimulus" that he has received from his writings but says that he "liked least" the review of Fairbairn's book. "So far as I can judge your theory is more orthodoxly Freudian than your clinical concepts would permit." In the book itself, Guntrip observes that the "real point" of Winnicott and Khan's criticism of Fairbairn "is by no means clear and convincing," adding that "it is a little difficult to see why Winnicott makes it in view of the fact that his own writings imply an unformulated theoretical revision of Freud that is very close to that of Fairbairn" (1961, 297).

Replying on September 15, Winnicott concedes that "our review of Fairbairn's book was not a good review" and expresses the hope that he and Guntrip will have an occasion one day to meet to discuss their differences.

Whereas in the mid-1950s Winnicott upbraided both Fairbairn and Guntrip from an orthodox standpoint, by 1961 he was plainly uncomfortable with his review of Fairbairn, although he had not yet succeeded in articulating the grounds for his change of heart. The third and final stage in Winnicott's relationship with Guntrip, and by extension in his intellectual evolution, may be dated to 1967; it is distilled in "The Location of Cultural Experience," where he acknowledges that "I can see that I am in the territory of Fairbairn's concept of 'object-seeking'" (1967d, 101). In the same year, Winnicott gave the informal talk to the 1952 Club quoted in chapter 5 for its expression of contrition about his tendency to slight the writings of others. Winnicott here recalls a paper Fairbairn had read to the British Psycho-Analytical Society—presumably "Object-Relationships and Dynamic Structure" (1946; Sutherland 1989, 132). He confesses that "at that time I couldn't see anything in Fairbairn" but explains that he later came to realize that Fairbairn had "got an extremely important thing to say which had to do with going beyond instinctual satisfactions and frustrations to the idea of object-seeking" (1967b, 579). In closing, he underscores Fairbairn's "tremendous contribution" in elaborating this area of object seeking and in directing attention to the need that patients in analysis have for "feeling real instead of feeling unreal" (582).

By 1967—when he plunged into writing the papers that went into *Playing and Reality*—Winnicott had cast off the docility that impelled him to find continuities between himself and Freud and Klein at all costs and embraced a radically Fairbairnian object relations outlook. Indeed, in his last years Winnicott seems positively to revel in the iconoclasm that he had kept under wraps for most of a lifetime. He affirms the existence of a quasi-Rankian "creative impulse" (1971a, 69), insists that "the absence of psycho-neurotic illness may be health, but it is not life" (1967d, 100), resolves that it is time for psychoanalysis "to tackle the question of *what life itself is about*" (1967d, 98), and even rails against those of his colleagues with a "rigid analytic morality" who miss what there is to be learned from allowing themselves to touch their patients (1970a, 257).

That Winnicott should have modified his views so drastically at the end of his life is a tribute to his remarkable lack of defensiveness and his resilience of spirit. His final papers also confirm the inadequacy of Greenberg and Mitchell's (1983) assessment of his career, for their negative verdict leaves out of account the breakthrough in which, to use their terminology, Winnicott abandons a "drive/structure" in favor of a "relational/structure" model. His belated conversion is likewise a tribute to Guntrip, for it was he who first confronted Winnicott with the inconsistency between his theory and his practice and exhorted him to permit the former to catch up with the latter. Just as Rank deserves credit not only for having incited Freud to write *Inhibitions, Symptoms and Anxiety* (as a refutation of *The Trauma of Birth*) but also for having in his 1927 review immediately grasped its significance—as a turning point in which Freud abandoned the libido theory—Guntrip, too, set in motion and explicated a similarly momentous shift in Winnicott's thinking.

Since Guntrip was the patient of both Fairbairn and Winnicott, one might have expected him to fall under a transferential spell preventing him from appraising his two great analysts realistically. Such, indeed, was Winnicott's suspicion in 1954, when he castigated Guntrip for adhering to Fairbairn too closely. In the end, however, Guntrip combined a wholly justified idealization of his two masters with an exceptionally just and penetrating assessment of their strengths and weaknesses. That Guntrip should have become, in effect, the analyst of his analysts and the teacher of his teachers seals the greatness of his lifelong psychoanalytic odyssey.

When the Piggle asks about Winnicott's birthday, Winnicott does not hesitate to interpret in terms of opposites: "What about my death day?" (Winnicott 1977, 124). In the analysis of a little girl, as in the analysis of an elderly man, the end of life joins with the beginning. By addressing the hidden anxiety in the Piggle's question, Winnicott was tactfully preparing her for the eventual termination of her treatment and also for his own death, which occurred within five years.

Similarly, Clare Winnicott records in her memoir of her husband that "in conversation he would often refer to his deathday in a light-hearted way, but I knew that he was trying to get me and himself accustomed to the idea that it would come" (1978, 20). She concludes by recounting a dream, which she had over two years after Donald's death, in which the two of them went on a glorious Christmas shopping spree until Donald looked into her eyes and said, "This is a dream," and then, "Yes, I died a year ago." "For me," she writes, "it was through this dream of playing that life and death, his and mine, could be experienced as a reality" (33). Through an equally exquisite playing into reality, Winnicott wrought a miracle in the analysis of Guntrip, bestowing with his death the gift of living.

These themes of mourning and survivor guilt, manifested in Guntrip's relationships with Fairbairn and Winnicott and central also to the life of Freud, acquire a further sad resonance from the posthumous publication of Guntrip's paper: it first appeared in print a few weeks after his death in 1975 (Pontalis in Pontalis, Anzieu, and Rosolato, 1977, 30). The interplay of life and death, begun in Guntrip's infancy by his mother's depression, as well as by the actual death of Percy, and reenacted in his analytic rebirth with the death of Winnicott, continues after Guntrip's death to reverberate in the reader of his paper. But even those of us whose contact with Guntrip and his two analysts must now be mediated through their writings can have our lives changed by theirs. Like Freud, Guntrip, Fairbairn, and Winnicott have become part of our permanent analytic and cultural heritage.

Three years after Guntrip died, in 1978, a second posthumous paper of his appeared, a defense of psychoanalysis against its scientific critics. In its mustering of clinical evidence to show the therapeutic efficacy of psychoanalysis, this paper complements the autobiographical testimonial of "My Experience of Analysis." To support his contention that two indispensable psychoanalytic hypotheses are, first, the shaping influence of the mother-infant relationship on later character development and, second, the *"psychically alive but unconscious"* persistence of these earliest experiences, Guntrip cites "the most dramatic example" of the recovery of infantile memories that he has witnessed (1978, 223). A schizoid young mother who had attempted suicide subsequently began at night to "act out" childhood terrors, supported by her husband and the reliability of her therapist, Guntrip. "Then suddenly her total amnesia for those traumatic events broke up: memories flooded back. Her mother had burned her with a red hot poker, and once with a heated flat iron. . . . The breakdown of her total amnesia and the security gained by reliving it all with me and her husband, initiated an enormous improvement through which she was ultimately able to end the treatment" (223).

The sadism of this young woman's mother exceeds anything inflicted on Guntrip, but amnesia is overcome in both instances, and Guntrip must have seen in this patient's search for lost time a mirror of his own. Indeed, he alludes in passing to his "training analysis" with

Winnicott and to the two dreams he had at the age of seventy in which he saw himself as a small boy of three and a half in a "traumatic situation" (218, 219). The dialectical process that affected Fairbairn and Winnicott in their analysis of Guntrip is extended when this patient becomes a surrogate for Guntrip.

Responding to the charges of Karl Popper and others, Guntrip maintains that psychoanalysis deserves to be considered a science, "not because of any prestige value science may have, but because we need the most accurate sifted knowledge we can formulate, to give genuine help to the tortured 'self' patients bring to us" (216). Accepting Popper's criterion of falsifiability, Guntrip points out that many hypotheses of psychoanalysis—such as Freud's model of psychic energy—have in fact been disproved by object relations theorists. In contrast, however, Guntrip argues that Popper gives too little weight to the provisional confirmation that empirical observations can give to a theory they do not invalidate. Thus: "I have found no observations that would falsify the hypothesis that the 'qualitative pattern of parent-child relations,' whatever it is, is the environment in which the child grows, and which he psychically internalizes as the structure of his personality" (218).

Guntrip combines a respect for scientific principles with an endorsement of what he calls a "hierarchical model of the structure of knowledge" and its corollary: *"we cannot reduce psychology to any lower level science."* Effectively seconding the passage from Aristotle's *Nicomachean Ethics* that I took as my epigraph to chapter 1, Guntrip remarks: "No study can be 'scientific' if it refuses to study its field in terms properly relevant to just those phenomena that are in question" (211). The practical effect of Guntrip's principles is to help therapists accept with equanimity a Socratic state of learned ignorance. "Analytic 'interpretation' is not a 'technique' but an 'intuitive understanding' guided by the best theory we have to date, a 'hypothesis' to be confirmed or falsified by the patient's reaction. In the end every patient knows more about himself than we can ever do, even though he is unconscious of so much of it" (216).

Guntrip places in the forefront of his thought the problem of the self, which, as I have argued throughout this book, is central to contemporary psychoanalysis. Quoting Popper's gibe, "As for Freud's epic of the ego, super-ego and id, no substantially stronger claim for scientific status can be made for it than for Homer's collective stories from Olympus," Guntrip agrees that the notion of an id reflects an "epistemological confusion" of biology and psychology but counters that

"Freud's terms ego and super-ego are not 'theories' but names given to certain recognizable psychic phenomena so that we may identify and discuss them" (217, 219). For Guntrip, "the term super-ego registers the fact that our conscience begins to develop in us as children as a product of the influence of parents, as if the parent were 'super-imposed' on our developing ego." Even more emphatically, Guntrip insists on the indispensability of the concept of an I or ego. Invoking his own dreams at the age of seventy in which he saw himself as a boy of three and a half, Guntrip writes: "I recognized myself as the same 'I' then and now, and know that no one else possesses that memory but me, my ego as an unbroken continuity over 70 years. 'Ego' is not a myth, not even theory, but the naming of an experience we all have of our personal reality and continuity, or rather of one aspect of it, for there are others. It is not even Freud's invention but a common posses-sion of all times and languages." In a familiar but nonetheless effective philosophical gambit, Guntrip seizes on Popper's own use of the pro-noun "I" to refute his dismissal of the ego as merely a myth: "The term ego registers the fact that every one of us recognizes himself as an 'I,' a subject of experience" (219).

To some readers, Guntrip's championing of "personal reality and continuity" will doubtless seem hopelessly old-fashioned, for postmod-ern theorists have devoted a considerable portion of their formidable intellectual energies (and ideological apparatus) to deconstructing the subject and to stigmatizing the self as an unacceptable category of thought. Guntrip died before he could take up the gauntlet thrown down by Jacques Derrida and his followers. But Guntrip never shirked the challenge of trying intellectually to combat, and therapeutically to heal, the "schizoid despair and loss of contact with the verities of emotional reality" (1968, 48) promoted by the nihilists of his day, and he would not likely have been daunted by their contemporary variants. Those for whom "essentialist humanism" will never be an opprobrious epithet could ask for no more stalwart an ally than Harry Guntrip, who found in psychoanalysis a means to implement his belief in "the su-preme value of the individual human person" and who dared to pro-claim the good news that *the meaningfulness of the life of personal relation-ships is the never changing basis for all human living*" (1:196, 241).

8 ♦ THE PSYCHOANALYTIC SELF

Even though we still inhabit a moral and psychological system based upon our legitimate existence as individuals, that existence has come to seem strange as if our idea of nature were itself revealed to be a cunningly wrought artifice, or as if our property rights to ourselves had been called into question.—Stephen Greenblatt, "Fiction and Friction"

An efflorescence of intellectual activity in widely disparate fields began in France in the late 1960s. What used to be known as the humanities and social sciences (lately amalgamated into the human sciences) may now be contemplated collectively under the rubric "postmodernism." Associated with such distinguished names as Jacques Derrida, Michel Foucault, Roland Barthes, Jacques Lacan, and Louis Althusser and giving rise directly or indirectly to the innovative theoretical modes of deconstruction and new historicism, as well as to influential trends in Marxist, psychoanalytic, and feminist thought, this movement is far too complex and heterogeneous to be readily reduced to a unity or to be satisfactorily treated here. Nonetheless, in closing this study of the tradition I believe constitutes the most promising elaboration of Freud's legacy, I want to expand the horizons of my inquiry and address in at least an abbreviated way the issues presented by this dominant constellation in the contemporary intellectual firmament.

To draw together the threads of this book, my focus will be on the problem of the self and on the allied debate over whether there is such a thing as an abiding human nature. Postmodernists may be said to fall into two major camps—the linguistic wing led by Derrida and the political wing led by Foucault. Although these factions are at odds on many points, they present a united front in their implacable enmity to any form of essentialist humanism. In *Radical Tragedy*, Jonathan Dollimore (1984, 252) invokes Althusser's definition of the two "complementary and indissociable postulates" fundamental to humanism: "(i) that there is a universal essence of man; (ii) that this essence is the attribute of '*each single individual*' who is its real subject."

The thoroughly representative nature of Dollimore's critique is confirmed by other prominent advocates of antihumanism. With respect to the individual, for example, Stephen Greenblatt (1986a, 33) endorses Pierre Bourdieu's categorical Marxist declaration: "Since the history of the individual is never anything other than a certain specification of the collective history of the group or class, *each individual system of dispositions* may be seen as a *structural variant* of all the other group or class habitus." Conversely, with respect to human nature, Jean E. Howard notes that "one of the most striking developments of contemporary thought is the widespread attack on the notion that man possesses a transhistorical core of being." Recognizing that this is "a much more radical view" than has obtained in the past, she continues: "It is quite different to argue that man has no essential being and to argue that, while in different periods people display different customs and social arrangements, they nonetheless possess an unchanging core of human traits" (1986, 10).

In what follows I shall seek to rehabilitate the two propositions: "the history of the individual" is *not* reducible to that of his or her "group or class," and "man" *does* have an "essential being." To forestall a possible misunderstanding, however, I should make clear from the outset that my essentialist contention is not that human beings, either as individuals or as a species, exist in a timeless realm of archetypes. Rather, I am defending the more circumspect hypothesis that through hundreds of thousands of years of evolution, human beings have indeed come to possess a "core of being," which has remained virtually unchanged during the few millennia of recorded history. Although a definition is admittedly elusive, it is this common bond that allows members of widely different cultures to beget offspring with, as well as understand, one another. The question is by no means one of *denying* history but rather of setting history itself against a biological backdrop, which can for practical purposes be described as "transhistorical."

One of the postmodernists' most cherished assumptions, in Dollimore's words, is that "essentialism" is tantamount to a defense of "idealist culture," whereas postmodernism alone is committed to a "materialist conception of subjectivity," which engages "the historical, social and political realities of which both literature and criticism are inevitably a part" (1984, 249–50). But, I would ask, where in this supposedly "materialist" outlook is there a place for biology? The proposal that biological "realities" also be taken into account in any consideration of the human condition places postmodernists in a dilemma. On the one hand, if they admit that human beings are constituted as a biological species, they strip the contingent factors of "group or class" from the pride of place to which they are doctrinally obliged to assign them. On the other hand, by excluding biology from their theoretical purview, they themselves prove to be the unwitting champions of "idealist culture."

To speak of biology and the problem of human nature is immediately to be reminded of Darwin, who in *The Expression of the Emotions in Man and Animals* (1872) maintained that each distinctive category of affective experience—happiness, sadness, fear, anger, disgust, surprise, interest, and shame—has, in Daniel Stern's summary words, "an innate discrete facial display and a discrete quality of feeling and that these innate patterns evolved as social signals 'understood' by all members to enhance species survival." As Stern points out, cross-cultural studies confirm that "photographs of the basic facial expressions will be similarly recognized and identified in all cultures tested," and this "universality in the face of wide socio-cultural differences argues for innateness." Anticipating objections from relativists, he concedes that "the subjective quality of feeling associated with any facial expression" will assuredly vary somewhat from culture to culture but affirms that "the same finite set of affective expressions" is shared by human beings in all times and places (1985, 54–55).

Thus, biology plays an indispensable role in vindicating the idea that there is a "universal essence of man" at the species level. But it is no less decisive with respect to the corollary about each individual partaking of that essence. From the ontogenetic rather than the phylogenetic standpoint, how one looks upon the fetus is pivotal to the entire debate. The importance of the prenatal period in the formation of the self has been theoretically expounded by Winnicott: "Certainly before birth it can be said of the psyche . . . that there is a personal going-along, a continuity of experiencing. This continuity, which could be called the beginnings of self, is periodically interrupted by phases of reaction to impingement" (1949, 191). Implicit in this statement is Winnicott's later concept of the True Self and the False Self, fully elaborated in 1960. Central here is the distinction between *existing*, which is the innate human tendency and obtains as long as the environment is sufficiently supportive, and *reacting*, which supervenes in the event of environmental impingement or deprivation. As Winnicott puts it, "The True Self comes from the aliveness of the body tissues and the working of body functions, including the heart's action and breathing. It is . . . essentially not reactive to external stimuli, but primary" (1960a, 148). In another paper from the same year, he writes: "The central self could be said to be the inherited potential which is experiencing a continuity of being, and acquiring in its own way and at its own speed a personal psychic reality and a personal body-scheme" (1960b, 46).

Winnicott (1965b) enables us to see that there are inherent "maturational processes," which begin before birth and continue to unfold in interaction with the "facilitating environment" throughout the life cycle. The same conclusions are reached within the French psychoanalytic tradition by Didier Anzieu. In *The Skin Ego,* Anzieu examines the way that "the skin performs a series of functions that are essential to the living body when looked at as a whole, in its individuality and in its spatial-temporal continuity" (1985, 15). Like Winnicott, Anzieu rejects postmodernism, instead taking the individual as an object of analysis and upholding the principle of a biologically backed "continuity of being." In consonance also with the developmental emphasis of Stern, Anzieu maintains: "At birth and in the days immediately following, the child seems to have the first rudimentary outline of an Ego, by reason of the sensory experiences it has already undergone towards the end of its intra-uterine life, and also no doubt by virtue of the genetic code which predetermines its development in this direction" (55). What Anzieu calls the "bodily pre-Ego" is the "precursor of the feeling of personal identity and the sense of reality which characterize the psychical Ego proper" (58).

Once biology has been granted its due weight, it becomes not just possible but mandatory to rehabilitate the two postulates disdained by postmodernists, that the human species has a transhistorical essence and that this essence is uniquely possessed by each individual. As Winnicott tells mothers, "Even in the womb your baby is a human being, unlike any other human being" (1964a, 20). For the postmodernists, in contrast, especially Foucauldians, everything is collapsed into the intermediate categories of "group or class." To forestall a misunderstanding, let me say again that history and politics are not unreal or unimportant. I am convinced that political issues—of war, poverty, racial prejudice, sexism, pollution of the environment, and so forth—are of immense consequence and demand both local and global action. My quarrel is simply with those who reduce *everything* to politics and who refuse to acknowledge the need to think of human beings in both individual and universal terms.

The point of view I wish to challenge has been eloquently espoused by Stephen Greenblatt in his essay "Psychoanalysis and Renaissance Culture." Citing the most famous instance of mistaken identity in the Renaissance—when the impostor Arnaud du Tilh attempted to usurp the place of the absent Martin Guerre until the real Martin Guerre finally returned to his French village—Greenblatt contends: "The case of Martin Guerre offers, in this context, neither a universal myth nor a perfectly unique and autonomous event; it is a peculiarly *Renaissance* story, the kind of story that the age told itself in a thousand variations over and over again" (1986b, 218).

I agree that this historical fable contains distinctively sixteenth-century features but cannot accept Greenblatt's conclusion, for surely the uniqueness of the case is indisputable, even though there may be others that resemble it in various ways. (The word *autonomous* begs the question, as does the qualification "in this context.") With respect to myth, Greenblatt himself points to themes of "impotence, oedipal transgression, and flight" that connect the life of Martin Guerre to "the classic materials of Freudian speculation" (212). To allow social and political determinants to override both the individual and universal dimensions of the story is thus sheer churlishness on his part.

It is noteworthy that Greenblatt's account of psychoanalysis is thoroughly humanistic. Although he admits that "the self as Freud depicts it is bound up not with secure possession but with instability and loss," he qualifies this by saying Freud's "vision of alienation" seems to "depend on the dream of authentic possession, even if that possession is never realized and has never been securely established." In spite of the rebuffs to "existential autonomy" delivered by the concepts of the unconscious and repression, for Greenblatt psychoanalysis nonetheless presupposes "the continuity of the subject," and, he adds, "along with the secret of incestuous fantasy, the Oedipus myth discloses the tragic inescapability of continuous selfhood." With reference to the case of Martin Guerre, Greenblatt's version of a psychoanalytic reading is that "the roots of Martin's identity lie deeper than society; they reach down . . . to the psychic experience of his infancy—the infancy only he can possess and that even the most skillful impostor cannot appropriate—and beneath infancy to his biological individuality" (213–14).

Although postmodernists would doubtless find much to quarrel with here, this summation of psychoanalysis is one with which I am in complete agreement. What is interesting from my standpoint is the way that Greenblatt's own understanding of psychoanalysis undermines his new historicist assumptions. The larger purpose of his essay is to argue that "the bafflement of psychoanalytic interpretation by Renaissance culture" (210) is the inevitable consequence of its imposition of "universalist claims" on an age in which they are "irrelevant to the point of being unthinkable" (215). What Greenblatt fails to appreciate is that if the essentialist conclusions he ascribes to psychoanalysis about the priority of biology over culture are sound—and he pronounces himself personally "quite comfortable" with them—then they continue to hold good even if, as he contends, they are not "drawn either explicitly or implicitly by anyone in the sixteenth century" (215).[1]

To compound this theoretical confusion, Greenblatt exaggerates the incommensurability of Renaissance and modern practices. In his opinion, "the crucial historical point is that . . . what is at stake in this case is not psychic experience at all but rather a communal judgment that must, in extraordinary cases, be clarified and secured by legal authority" (215). But his contention that identity in the Renaissance is entirely a function of "communal judgment" is refuted by his earlier statement that during the trial, Arnaud du Tilh took the stand and (presumably coached by the wife, who had become his conspirator) "recalled in great detail events from his childhood and adolescence that only the real Martin Guerre could have known" (211). If the trial proceeded by testing the memory of the man claiming to be Martin Guerre, this mode of inquiry indubitably links selfhood to "psychic experience."

Similarly, when Greenblatt claims that the appeals to Arnaud's body move "not from distinct physical traits to the life experience generated within, but outward to the community's determination" (216), he again inflates the novelty of Renaissance attitudes. Forensic evidence, whether provided by a fingerprint dusted at the scene of a contemporary crime or by the village shoemaker who, in Natalie Zemon Davis's

1. To draw an analogy, William Harvey put forward his theory of the circulation of the blood in 1628, but blood circulated in people before the discovery (people who may have held entirely different ideas), just as it circulates in people today. Largely because the Renaissance was a period of intense ideological turmoil, in which modern notions of subjectivity began to come into being, it has served as the focus for much of the recent new historicist scholarship that has flourished under Greenblatt's aegis.

words, "said that, if he were Martin Guerre, why had his feet grown so much smaller over the years?" (1983, 55), does not pretend to give access to inner "life experience" but simply aids in determining whether or not the story told by a given person is a credible one.

These links between Renaissance and modern habits of mind do not, of course, preclude the existence of genuine cultural differences. Combined with the theoretical contradictions in which Greenblatt's argument is enmeshed, they do, however, suffice to show how misguided is his attempt to banish psychoanalysis from Renaissance studies. His difficulties all stem from his unwillingness to face the crippling consequences for new historicism of his own admission that the roots of "biological individuality" do indeed go "deeper than society."

In seeking to meet the challenge to essentialist humanism of a politically oriented postmodernism, I have maintained that biology is a *primary* variable in human experience and history a *secondary* variable. The legitimacy of such a hierarchical distinction would be contested by deconstruction, the other dominant trend in postmodern thought, which attacks established values not from a political but from a linguistic standpoint. As is well known, the standard operating procedure of deconstruction is to take a pair of dialectically opposed terms—prototypically, speech and writing—and claim that the second term, held to be derivative or "supplementary" in Western metaphysics, in fact contaminates and subverts its ostensibly privileged counterpart.

In keeping with my focus on the Renaissance in the Martin Guerre story, I shall consider a specimen of deconstructive exegesis that pertains to the same period. Examining the polarity of nature and art as deployed in George Puttenham's *Arte of English Poesie* and other texts of the English Renaissance, Derek Attridge concludes that it is impossible to preserve a distinction between these terms or to assign nature any ontological priority. The threat of the "dangerous supplement of art" is that "since it belies its own secondariness in making good what is lacking in the nature it supplements, it constantly endangers nature's primariness" (1986, 270).

The rigor of Attridge's analysis is not in question, and I am even prepared to stipulate its validity for the particular texts he discusses. What I am *not* willing to concede is the radical deconstructionist claim that the antithesis between nature and art is wholly rhetorical or arbitrary. To do so would be to fall victim to what can only be described as madness (although deconstructionists would retort that the choice between sanity and madness is itself factitious). If we were to take the deconstructionist position seriously, we would have to tell someone with an artificial leg or attached to a respirator that there is no difference between these prosthetic devices and the bodily organs that they are intended to "supplement."

The case of an artificial limb is straightforward enough. Now I wish to extend the distinction between nature and art to the admittedly more nebulous region of the human psyche. It would not be difficult to imagine a deconstruction of Winnicott's opposition between the True Self and the False Self that would posit no occurrence of the True Self not already tainted by the False Self and hence no way of distinguishing spontaneity from compliance. But such logic chopping cannot be sustained in the face of human suffering. Anzieu lays bare how, like an allergy in the physical sphere, psychotic behavior entails an "anti-physiological reaction," in which "the signals of safety and danger are inverted." He elaborates: "Confidence in the natural functioning of the organism is either destroyed or has never been acquired. What is natural is experienced as artificial; the living is treated as mechanical; what is good for life is felt to represent a mortal danger" (1985, 107). Only someone prepared to equate "what is good for life" with "mortal danger"—and take the consequences—could convincingly dissent from Anzieu's extension of the notion of the "natural functioning of the organism" from the body to the mind.

The principles at stake in this discussion should already be clear: whether (in the words of my epigraph from Greenblatt) our "idea of nature" is anything more than "a cunningly wrought artifice" and whether "our property rights to ourselves" can be sustained. The connection between these principles is distilled with the utmost lucidity in the work of Oliver Sacks. In *The Man Who Mistook His Wife for a Hat*, Sacks recounts the case of Christina, the "disembodied lady" who lost her sense of proprioception, thanks to which "we feel our bodies as proper to us, as our 'property,' as our own" (1987, 43). Because Christina was unable to steer herself by her internal compass, she began through sheer force of will to learn to look at each part of her body as it moved. As Sacks puts it, "Nature having failed, she took to 'artifice,' but the artifice was suggested by nature, and soon became 'second nature'" (49–50).

Sacks does not underestimate the extraordinary courage of Christina or of his many other "unsung heroes, or heroines, of neurological affliction." Nor does he gloss over or romanticize the irreparable damage that Christina has suffered. Like a frog, she has been, in her own unforgettable epithet, *pithed.*

> She has lost, with her sense of proprioception, the fundamental, organic mooring of identity—at least of that corporeal identity, or "body-ego," which Freud sees as the basis of self. . . . She has succeeded in operating, but not in being. . . . Not all the spirit and ingenuity in the world, not all the substitutions or compensations the nervous system allows, can alter in the least her continuing and absolute loss of proprioception—that vital sixth sense without which a body must remain unreal, unpossessed. (52–53)

Like Anzieu, Sacks stresses the "organic mooring of identity," which enforces a distinction between "being" and "operating," or between what is living and what is mechanical. This distinction underlies Winnicott's polarity between the True Self and the False Self. Once again, only someone prepared to deny Christina's loss—and willing to stand in her stead—could validly question Sacks's generalization from the physiological to the psychological realm of the opposition between nature and the "second nature" of artifice.

The cardinal mistake of deconstruction is to assume that because the dichotomy between nature and art can be subverted in a textual analysis, it therefore has no basis in reality. This mistake reflects a prevalent contemporary shibboleth, that linguistic paradigms are the most important ones for comprehending not merely language and literature but all of human experience. According to Lacan, the "passion of the signifier" found in Ferdinand de Saussure and Freud unfolds "a new dimension of the human condition in that it is not only man who speaks, but that in man and through man *it* speaks (*ça parle*), that his nature is woven by effects in which is to be found the structure of language, of which he becomes the material" (1958a, 284).

Although Foucault is prominently identified with the political wing of postmodernism, much in his work reinforces the linguistic biases of Lacan and Derrida. In "What Is an Author?" Foucault maintains that contemporary writing "has freed itself from the necessity of 'expression'" and become instead "an interplay of signs" (1969, 116). Consequently, the goal of fiction is now "the total effacement of the individual characteristics of the writer" (117). In his peroration, Foucault insists that "the subject (and its substitutes) must be stripped of its creative role and analyzed as a complex and variable function of discourse." Rejecting the "tiresome repetitions" of inquiries into the "real author" of a text, Foucault holds up as an alternative the "murmur of in-difference" heard in Samuel Beckett's question: "What matter who's speaking?" (138).

This postmodern dismantling of the subject centers on what it means to use the pronoun "I." Typically, Lacan adheres to the "strictly linguistic" definition, whereby "I" is "nothing but the 'shifter' or indicative, which, in the subject of the statement, designates the subject in the sense that he is now speaking" (1960, 298). Barthes adds his spadefuls of dirt to the interment in his "Death of the Author," where he embraces "the necessity to substitute language itself for the person who until then had been supposed to be its owner" (1968, 143). Like Lacan, Barthes draws upon linguistics to posit that "the whole of the enunciation is an empty process, functioning perfectly without there being any need for it to be filled with the person of the interlocutors. Linguistically, the author is never more than the instance writing, just as *I* is nothing other than the instance saying *I:* language knows a 'subject,' not a 'person'" (145). Corroborating Derrida's notorious dictum "*There is nothing outside the text*" (1967, 158), Barthes concludes: "Life never does more than imitate the book, and the book itself is only a tissue of signs, an imitation that is lost, infinitely deferred" (1968, 147).

Issues of ultimate philosophical import cannot be settled by appeals to authority. Nonetheless, when confronted by the legions arrayed on the side of postmodernism, it is difficult for a defender of essentialist humanism not to feel embattled. Thus, in addition to mustering intellectual arguments, one of my aims in this chapter is simply to define a countertradition, to show that a body of contemporary thought of the highest order provides an alternative way of looking at the world. Apart from Winnicott and the Independent tradition of psychoanalysis, I have derived great inspiration from the work of Didier Anzieu, Daniel Stern, and Oliver Sacks.[2] I hope that others who share my sense that postmodernism is untrue to their own experience will take comfort from the knowledge that there are heroes also on our side.

The fallacy of reducing the self to an "interplay of signs" and the pronoun "I" to a linguistic "shifter" is betrayed by Foucault's supposi-

2. Among literary critics I would claim as allies Harold Bloom and Norman Holland. Holland's (1985) defense of the concept of identity draws upon the papers of Heinz Lichtenstein (1983). Most recently, I have encountered Charles Taylor's magisterial *Sources of the Self* (1989), to which the present study may be regarded as a psychoanalytic footnote.

tion that Beckett's question, "What matter who's speaking?" is imbued with a "murmur of indifference." As Daniel Gunn has noted with respect to the "misplaced gamesmanship" of Barthes, "the pronoun is an area of urgent, primordial *need*—and it is as such that Beckett and Proust allow the reader to experience it" (1988, 84). By hypostasizing language into an entity allegedly able to know its subjects, deconstruction trivializes subjectivity itself, in Paul Smith's trenchant post-Marxist critique, into "a mere passivity, a simple conductor of the hierarchy of semantic forces" (1988, 50). Hence, "Derrida holds no one responsible for the social history whose institutions we now inhabit," and his view of human agency is "limited in such a way that it could not be adapted to *any* oppositional politics" (53, 51).

Like Attridge's attempt to deconstruct the opposition between nature and art, the efforts of postmodernists to reduce the "I," or self, to a purely linguistic phenomenon exemplify the tendency to take an insight of limited validity and render it absurd and even dangerous by elevating it to the status of an absolute truth. Linguists may well be justified in analyzing an enunciation for their purposes as an "empty process," the pronouns as referring not to persons but to subjects, but this line of reasoning becomes demented when it is taken to mean that people do not exist or that language could "function perfectly" in the absence of interlocutors.

At the heart of the apocalyptic pronouncements of Barthes and company is a dichotomizing tendency that, as I argued in chapter 5, likewise mars the thought of both Lacan and Melanie Klein. Barthes supposes that if individuals are not the "owners" of language, then it is necessary "to substitute language itself for the person." But nowhere does he consider the intermediate possibility that subjects may indeed be shaped by the language they use while still retaining a degree of autonomy that allows them to shape language to their own expressive ends. As Jane Flax has commented of the "narcissistic premise" that governs Lacan's treatment of language, "He assumes that if something is not self-created, it must be alien and alienating" (1990, 96).[3]

Although the postmodern attempt to reduce human beings to "functions of discourse," lacking desire or agency, must be repudiated, my own brief on behalf of the self should not be construed as a denial of

3. See also John Ellis, who notes that deconstruction "is a victim of the restrictive binary logic that it likes to denigrate" (1989, 81).

the evident truth that human thought is dependent on language. My point again is simply that language emerges in an *intersubjective* context and that any proposal to sever it from its preverbal and psychological moorings is therefore doomed to failure. As Charles Taylor has put it, "the original situation of identity-formation" is one of "conversation with others," and in all our mental activities "we remain related to partners of discourse, either in real, live exchanges, or in indirect confrontations" (37–38).

Whereas postmodernists believe that human beings must be either the masters or the slaves of language, Taylor recognizes that "the drive to original vision will be hampered, will ultimately be lost in inner confusion, unless it can be placed in some way in relation to the language and vision of others" (37). Here he articulates an idea given a specifically hermeneutic inflection by Hans-Georg Gadamer, who maintains that "tradition is not simply a precondition into which we come, but we produce it ourselves, inasmuch as we understand, participate in the evolution of tradition and hence further determine it ourselves" (1960, 261). This philosophical dialectic is reformulated in psychoanalytic terms by Winnicott, who writes that "*it is not possible to be original except on a basis of tradition.*" As he explains, "the interplay between originality and the acceptance of tradition" in creativity is but "one more example" of "the interplay between separateness and unity" found in the relationship between "any one baby and the human (and therefore fallible) mother-figure who is essentially adaptive because of love" (1967d, 99–100).

From the perspective of object relations theory, no account of language—or of any other human phenomenon—can be accepted if it fails to take into account infantile dependence and the continuing need for good-enough environmental provision throughout life. For this reason developmental psychologists are unable to take seriously the disembodied speculations of postmodernism. Stern, the leading psychoanalytic researcher in the field, identifies volition as "the most fundamental invariant of core self-experience," without which "an infant would feel what a puppet would 'feel' like, as the nonauthor of its own immediate behavior" (1985, 76–77). Greenblatt, by contrast, invokes Thomas Hobbes's definition that "a *Person* is the same that an *Actor* is" to bolster his own contention that "all men . . . are impersonators of themselves" (1986b, 222). If this were really the case—if Greenblatt himself were a puppet and not an autonomous human being—he would have been unable (in the incident recounted in the epilogue to *Renaissance Self-Fashioning*) to *refuse* to mime the words, "I want to die," as his distraught companion on the flight from Baltimore to Boston requested him to do (1980, 255).

The sense of self originates before language is acquired and continues to develop thereafter. Psychologists have debated the relative continuity or discontinuity between preverbal and verbal experience, and even Stern does not maintain a consistent position. On the one hand, in his fourfold schema of stages in the evolution of the self—emergent, core, subjective, and verbal—he emphasizes that with the advent of language the infant "gains entrance into a wider cultural membership, but at the risk of losing the force and wholeness of original experience" (1985, 177). The tools of language and symbolic thinking, he claims, "finally make possible the distortion of reality and provide the soil for neurotic constructs" (182). This premise that preverbal experience is characterized by "wholeness" and that "distortion" is first introduced by language is, however, contradicted elsewhere when Stern attributes a capacity for teasing, which depends on "shareable mental states" (131), to infants less than a year old, admits that the "intersubjective sharing of experience" between preverbal infants and their caretakers "can result in loss" (214), and concludes that "at the level of verbal relatedness . . . language becomes available to ratify the split and confer the privileged status of verbal representation upon the false self" (227). If language merely "ratifies" a split and the "false self" is preverbal, then it is incoherent to maintain that language, like the Fall, causes a "distortion of reality" and "neurotic constructs" where none had existed before. In his eagerness to accentuate the transformations that language acquisition brings about in the intellectual and emotional development of the child, Stern loses sight of the continuities with earlier stages.

Such minor inconsistencies, however, do not detract from the cogency of Stern's work as a whole or narrow the philosophical gulf that separates the outlook of object relations theorists and their allies from the outlook of the postmodernists. As I have stressed, both here and in chapter 5, one of Winnicott's seminal insights concerns the necessity for *continuity* in the achievement of mental health. Indeed, he defines trauma as "a break in life's continuity" (1967d, 97), provoked in the first instance by the absence of the mother for what is to her baby an insupportable length of time.

The implications of Winnicott's point have been extended by those spokesmen for essentialist humanism that I have ranged alongside him. Stern observes that the sense of a core self "would be ephemeral if there were no continuity of experience" and that "continuity or historicity is the crucial ingredient that distinguishes an interaction from a relationship, with self as well as with another" (1985, 90). For Anzieu, as we have seen, the skin likewise performs an indispensable function in preserving the living body both "in its individuality and in its spatiotemporal continuity" (1985, 15). He advances a more comprehensive formulation: "This Ego feeling comprises three constitutive elements: a sense of unity through time (i.e. of continuity), a sense of unity in space at the present moment (or, more precisely, of proximity), and lastly, a sense of causality" (91). And Sacks, in his inimitable fashion, quotes David Hume's declaration that "we are nothing but a bundle or collection of sensations, which succeed one another with an inconceivable rapidity," but points out that such a vision of "Humean" being finds its apotheosis in the person of Jimmie, the Lost Mariner suffering from Korsakov's syndrome, "a gruesome reduction of a man to mere disconnected, incoherent flux and change" (30). Adverting to the Humean (and also postmodern) claim that personal identity is a fiction, Sacks rejoins: "This is clearly not the case with a normal human being, because he *owns* his own perceptions. They are not a mere flux, but *his* own, united by an abiding individuality or self" (124).[4]

Especially noteworthy in the foregoing excerpts is Anzieu's collocation of "unity through time" and "unity in space" with a "sense of causality" in his specification of the constituents of the ego. By introducing the principle of causality, Anzieu highlights the base on which Winnicott's understanding of the importance of "the space-time continuum" in identity formation (1971c, 50) implicitly rests—what could be described in Kantian terms as a theory of the "transcendental conditions" of human experience.

The phrase "transcendental conditions" is used by Taylor (1989, 32), who clarifies the philosophical underpinnings for this essentialist line of thought. Positing that "to know who you are is to be oriented in

4. Compare Richard Wollheim, who likewise upholds the "non-constructionist" theory that "no event in a person's life, even taken singly, can be adequately described without introducing the person who has it" (1984, 16). "What should be required is that one and the same person enters into each and every event that belongs to the same life. Interrelatedness of event is supplemented by identity of person" (19).

moral space," Taylor holds that the link between moral and spatial orientation "lies very deep in the human psyche" (28). "One orients oneself in a space which exists independently of one's success or failure in finding one's bearings," and it "belongs to human agency to exist in a space of questions about strongly valued goods, prior to all choice or adventitious cultural change" (30–31). Invoking Heidegger, Taylor likewise asserts "the inescapable temporal structure of being in the world" (47). Finally, he argues that "making sense of one's life as a story is also, like orientation to the good, not an optional extra" and concludes that these moral-spatial, temporal, and narrative conditions are "connected facets of the same reality, inescapable structural requirements of human agency" (47, 52).

Taylor's analysis arises in the context of philosophical, not psychoanalytic, reflection. For that reason the convergence between his delineation and Anzieu's of the invariants, or transcendental conditions, of human existence becomes all the more compelling. In particular, whereas he acknowledges that "the very term 'identity' is somewhat anachronistic for premodern cultures," he nonetheless holds that the issue of "what kind of life is worth living" is "not an optional matter for us, in just the way that the orientation which defines our identity is not, and ultimately for the same reason" (42). In other words, although the *answers* offered by different individuals and cultures are subject to variation, it is impossible to escape from the "space of questions," and the view that would deny any abiding realities in human life "is equivalent to the notion that we invent the questions as well as the answers" (30).

Here, it seems to me, is as satisfactory a statement as we are likely to find of the essentialist position, one that properly raises the discussion of "the transhistorical core of being" from the biological to the metaphysical plane. Like science and hermeneutics, these two frames of reference should be viewed as complementary, not antagonistic. The capacity to beget offspring with other members of the same species, the "innate patterns" of emotional display, and the "transcendental conditions of interlocution" (Taylor 1989, 38) are all interconnected and help to define the "universal essence of man."

Human beings must be capable of apprehending temporal and spatial unity if one is to credit these concepts. Strikingly, both Anzieu and Stern appeal to the same venerable precedent in putting forward their contemporary versions of this argument. For Anzieu, the skin ego possesses the "function of *intersensoriality*, which leads to the creation of a 'common sense' (the *sensorium commune* of medieval philosophy) whose basic reference is always to the sense of touch" (1985, 103–4). Stern cites Aristotle, the authority for so much medieval thought, as the first to advance the doctrine of "the unity of the senses" and to suggest that there was a "sixth sense" that "could apperceive the qualities of sensation that are primary (that is, amodal) in that they do not belong to any one sense alone, as color belongs to vision, but are shared by all the senses" (1985, 154). This notion of an integrative sixth sense, or common sense, adumbrates what is known in the structural theory of psychoanalysis as the "synthetic function of the ego" (Nunberg 1930), which more recent thinkers have not hesitated to call the self.

The rehabilitation of essentialist humanism that emerges from object relations psychoanalysis has far-reaching aesthetic implications. As Taylor has written, "The rebellion against the canonical notion of the unity of a work of art is linked to rebellion against the dominant idea of the unity of the ego" (1989, 478). But, taking the infant at the mother's breast as a prototype, Winnicott shows that the need for a structure of a beginning, middle, and end is intrinsic to human life. As he explains, the process of feeding "has to include the excitement of anticipation, the experience of activity during the feed, as well as the sense of gratification, with rest from instinctual tension resulting from satisfaction" (1964a, 51), and this pattern is revived during sexual experience. With respect to his spatula game, in which an infant typically first examines the glittering tongue depressor, then puts it in his or her mouth, and finally throws it away, Winnicott points out that this is a "completed experience," with "a beginning, a middle, and an end," and that such a "total happening" is "*good for the baby*" (77).[5] If Winnicott is right, then the injunction that a work of art should exhibit "organic" features, originally propounded by Plato and Aristotle and transmitted through Coleridge to twentieth-century new critics, far from being adventitious, corresponds to a deep psychological requirement, although the form this requirement takes varies from culture to culture, nor do sophisticated works of art gratify it in an unproblematic way.[6]

5. See also Stern, who describes the "episode" as the "basic memorial unit," which enables infants to integrate the "diverse features of a lived experience" into a "completed structure" (1985, 94–95).

6. Like the new critics, Winnicott places a high valuation on paradox, calling for the ambiguous status of the transitional object between reality and fantasy "to be accepted and tolerated and respected, and for it not to be resolved"

As I acknowledged in chapter 6 with regard to Fredric Jameson's attempt to proscribe "individualistic categories of interpretation," at times it is doubtless appropriate to adopt a more collective perspective. Everything depends on the aims of the analysis. Winnicott, after all, places the individual in a social context with his famous apothegm *"There is no such thing as a baby"* (1952, 99), for he forces us to recognize that a baby is always *with someone* and hence cannot be understood apart from its relationship with its primary caretaker. But, as I noted in chapter 5, André Green, still under Lacanian influence, challenges Winnicott's model by contending that "there is no such couple formed by the mother and the baby, without the father," both because the child "is a figure of the union between mother and father" and because the father "is always somewhere in the mother's unconscious" (1975, 50). Green moves from the dyad to the triangle, but he remains within the psychoanalytic confines of the family. Consequently, Deborah Anna Luepnitz issues a feminist rebuke to both Winnicott and Green by insisting that *"nothing* that a mother does is comprehensible" if it is removed from the contexts of "class, race, and the culture of patriarchy" (1988, 194).

Since each of these approaches is valid on its own terms, the methodological problem, as I have suggested, becomes simply one of deciding when to deploy which. If we grant the virtue of Luepnitz's sociological perspective, are we therefore not allowed to examine the oedipal issues highlighted by Green? If Green's claim for the ubiquity of triangulation is valid, are we to cast aside Winnicott's meditation on the bond between mother and child? If we embrace Winnicott's proposition that "there is no such thing as a baby," are we to conclude that the individual is merely an epistemological fiction? The answer to each question is no. As John Rickman (1951) long ago recognized, psychology is simultaneously a one-, two-, three-, and multi-body discipline, and its practitioners need to be able to oscillate among these various frames of reference.

What we are dealing with, in other words, is a series of concentric circles, in which the insights generated by broader perspectives (including a universal one) must be borne in mind when focusing on a

---

(1971d, xii). Similarly, Winnicott's (1967d) notion that culture originates in the "potential space" of play between mother and infant provides a basis for reviving the Kantian thesis of the "disinterested" nature of aesthetic experience, which has been under siege by politically oriented postmodern critics.

smaller unit of analysis but in which each circle has its own autonomy. That autonomy must not be foreclosed by a premature assumption that the more general takes precedence over the more particular. Indeed, as I urged with respect to both Green and Klein in chapter 5, the leap from a developmental to a structural approach should be taken with caution, because the former accords better with the actual standpoint of the child than the latter. Winnicott memorably puts it in these terms: "The mother and the baby come to the point of mutuality in different ways," since "the mother has been a cared-for baby" and has had all sorts of other relevant experiences, whereas "the baby is being a baby for the first time" and brings to the relationship only "the sum of the inherited features and inborn tendencies toward growth and development" (1970a, 256).

Stern's schema for the development of the self, as we have seen, consists of four stages—emergent, core, subjective, and verbal. To synthesize the implications of my attempt to fashion a psychoanalytic theory of the self, I propose a fourfold conceptual model of my own encompassing biological, historical, structural, and deconstructionist perspectives. Its purpose is at once to pare away the excesses of post-modernism and to integrate what remains within a framework of essentialist humanism.

In keeping with my view of biology as a *primary* variable in human experience, I predicate that the journey to selfhood begins with the fetus in the womb. (This is not an argument against abortion. I reject the idea of an immortal soul and think it absurd to suppose that a newly fertilized egg has the status of a person.) This incipient self depends on its intrauterine environment for survival, but it possesses a genetically endowed tendency toward growth. Although the contribution of both factors is indispensable, the relative weight of each is made clear by Winnicott: "It is the innate tendencies toward growth and develop-ment that produce the health, not the environmental provision. Yet good-enough provision is necessary, absolutely at the beginning, and relatively at the later stages" (1962c, 68).

Thus, innate factors are ontologically prior to environmental ones, although the cooperation of the latter is required if the potential of the True Self is to be actualized. The magnitude of the environmental contribution even in the womb has been tragically underscored in recent years by the epidemic of crack babies born to mothers who have smoked this highly addictive derivative of cocaine during pregnancy.

In the words of Coryl Jones, a research psychologist at the National Institute of Drug Abuse, prenatal exposure to toxic drugs can have the effect of "interfering with the central core of what it means to be human" (Blakeslee 1989, 1). Drugs are a social problem of immense proportions, calling into play the entire panoply of issues of "class, race, and the culture of patriarchy." For the addicted infant, however, the problem is ultimately a biological one, a horrific example of Anzieu's "anti-physiological reaction," in which "the signals of safety and danger are inverted" and "the natural functioning of the organism" is thwarted by environmental pollution.

Upon the *biological* foundation of the self is overlaid the *historical* dimension. By history, I mean to imply everything that distinguishes humans from other animals, which lack our self-consciousness and capacity for language. To be human is, after all, to dwell in historical time, with a memory of one's past and (even more importantly) a foreknowledge of one's own death. By the same token, as Taylor has reminded us, to be human is to inhabit a "space of questions" and to be driven to make "sense of one's life as a story." Fittingly, the very word *history* captures this defining quality of human existence, since it ambiguously refers either to past events or to the narrative that records those events.

The fluidity of the human experience of time leads to the third perspective in my fourfold schema of the self—the *structural*. Structural analysis, pioneered in the domain of linguistics by Saussure and extended to culture as a whole by Claude Lévi-Strauss, regards time as having both synchronic (or reversible) and diachronic (or nonreversible) axes. Indeed, Saussure's *Course in General Linguistics* (1915), which was compiled from students' lecture notes and published two years after his death, heralded a revolt against the historicist assumptions of the nineteenth century, for it gave precedence to synchrony and argued, in Frank Kermode's (1985) words, that "the speaker of a language is confronted not with a history but with a *state*" (1985, 5). Thus, after Saussure's "linguistic turn," the preferred twentieth-century model of explanation is no longer *genetic* but *systematic*, and the pursuit of origins has been superseded by the description of rules of operation.

Both in undermining linear temporality and in relying on linguistic paradigms, structuralism prepares the way for the full-fledged attack on the self of the *deconstructionist* outlook. (Not for nothing is *poststructuralism* a synonym for *postmodernism*.) Here it is useful to invoke the concept of "deferred action" (*Nachträglichkeit*), which, though derived from Freud (1895), has become a touchstone for postmodern thought generally: "Everything begins with reproduction. Always already: repositories of meaning which was never present, whose signified presence is always reconstituted by deferral, *nachträglich*, belatedly, *supplementarily:* for the *nachträglich* also means *supplementary*. The call of the supplement is primary, here, and it hollows out that which will be reconstituted by deferral as the present" (Derrida 1966, 211–12). Synchrony makes time reversible, but deferred action, according to which a randomly occurring later event revives the memory of an earlier one and augments its meaning, takes this structuralist concept one step further. As Ned Lukacher has lucidly explained, the upshot of deferred action is "to undermine and divide the notion of linear causality that works in one temporal direction," because it "demands that one recognize that while the earlier event is still to some extent the cause of the later event, the earlier event is nevertheless also the effect of the later event" (1986, 35).

The outlined schema is meant to be heuristic, and its categories are not easily separable. But as with the concentric circles of baby, nursing couple, oedipal triangle, and society at large, although some flexibility is called for, it would be a grievous error to allow the more speculative interrogative modes of structuralism and deconstruction to usurp the conceptual primacy of the simpler biological and historical perspectives.

The decisive issue is causality. From a biological standpoint, the operation of cause and effect is unambiguous. The mother who uses crack will damage the fetus in her womb, and the fetus can do nothing to prevent this interruption of its continuity of being. Earlier events have irrevocable later consequences. From a historical standpoint, the principle of cause and effect still holds sway, since to explain something historically is by definition to trace its antecedents and to show how the past has shaped the present. By the same token, the maturational processes that begin in the womb never cease to regulate the cycle of growth and decay that is the lot of the human species no less than of all others, animal as well as vegetable.

Yet, as we have seen, the advent of consciousness and language in human beings does sunder nature and culture, since the meaning of events becomes inseparable from their narration. Throughout their lives, people look back on the past and reinterpret it in light of their later knowledge, a process of revision that must be taken into account in any properly historical explanation. Thus, cause and effect, necessary though the concept is to historical understanding, is not sufficient for it, and the dynamics of temporality are already extremely complex. Finally, cause and effect is, respectively, suspended and inverted, as diachrony becomes irrelevant or inimical to the forms of interpretation that structuralism and deconstruction sponsor.

A deconstructionist would, I am sure, protest against the strategy of recuperation inherent in my fourfold schema, arguing that the logic of the "supplement" precludes any such hierarchical ordering of explanations. But as in my earlier discussion of nature and art, the grounds for ajudicating the conflict between essentialism and postmodernism are ultimately pragmatic. The possibility of sabotaging the opposition between nature and art in a literary text does not mean that the distinction has no basis in reality—as my example of the artificial leg showed—and so, too, both synchronic analysis and deferred action are powerful and sometimes appropriate exegetical tools in the sphere of temporality, but they do not mean that we can do without cause and effect and continuity of being.

Seen in a certain light, an earlier event may be the effect as well as the cause of a later one. But were we really to confuse past and future or to think of ourselves as texts, we would be as psychotic as Kirk Allen, the mad scientist who is the subject of "The Jet-Propelled Couch" in Robert Lindner's *The Fifty-Minute Hour*. Allen, having identified as an adolescent with a fictional character with the same name as his own, became convinced that he was "remembering the adventures of himself as a grown man." As an adult, he began to practice "teleportation," by means of which, in his own words, he had miraculously "crossed the immensities of Space, broken out of Time, and merged with—literally become—that distant and future self whose life I had until now been remembering" (1955, 247, 251).

Thus, nature enjoys a metaphysical priority over art, and the space-time continuum abides as a transcendental condition of human experience. Deferred action is indeed a valuable concept, but the inversion of time would be unthinkable without the passage of time, and it is the better part of sanity not to allow a logical shell game to swindle us into abandoning our conviction that one is primary and the other secondary. Crediting Derrida's claim that the "supplement is primary" is to take a vertiginous step into madness.

APPENDIX A ◆ THE GENESIS OF THE OBJECT RELATION

Otto Rank

We have attempted to show how the mother (her breast) is originally regarded by the suckling as belonging to its own ego or self. And we have shown how the child, as it gradually learns to accept the mother as an object of the external world that can be denied it, tries to find an independent and permanent substitute for her on its own body (finger, genitals). This process of the narcissistic cathexis, valuation, and utilization of the ego might be described as the first real psychological manifestation. We have learned further that the mechanism of every object cathexis or object relation is a kind of maternalization. By this I mean that the relation of the object to the ego is manifested thus: the object is invested with libido originally transferred from the ego to the mother and later is taken back into the ego. This mechanism explains not only the libidinal cathexis of the outer world (Jung's "interest") and the loss of this cathexis in the psychotic idea of the end of the world; more important still, it explains the relation of the ego to other human beings in love life and in social life.

The withdrawal of the object leads, as we have seen, to the search for a substitute in one's own ego, but, on the other hand, every object cathexis definitely contains ego elements. By this I mean that the ego tries to find itself or part of its beloved self in the object. Moreover, the relation of the ego to the object is twofold, in the sense just described and in another sense, because of the child's original idea of the mother as both a good (vouchsafing) and a bad (depriving) object. We have shown how a substitute for the good mother, the mother as the source of pleasure gratification, is sought on one's own body (sucking, masturbation) or, later on, in psychical form in one's own ego. At the same time the depriving mother, through identification with the inner inhibitions, is set up in the ego as a feared and punishing element, which, in contrast to the narcissistic substitute gratifications, manifests itself as anxiety or a guilt feeling.

On the way to social adjustment in the biologically conditioned Oedipus situation, a boy, then, learns gradually to identify the bad, depriving, feared mother with the father. In the Oedipus situation he learns to recognize the father as the real possessor of the mother. In this progress from preoedipal rivalry with brothers and sisters at the biological mother stage to social rivalry with the father, the original picture of the good, protecting mother is definitely reestablished—a prerequisite to the establishment of a mature love and sex relation to a woman. On the way to the Oedipus situation a girl, on the contrary, finds again the interfering, denying mother, and she gradually has to learn to find in the father a substitute for the pleasure-giving (breast) mother. This comes about through the equation already mentioned, of breast and penis, which presupposes a "displacement from above downward" and with it a reestablishment in the vagina of the original (oral) sucking activity. The biological Oedipus relation can thus be completely established only if the positive and negative attitudes toward the mother, which manifest themselves in the ego as narcissism and guilt feeling, have become simultaneously projected again in an object relation. This new object relation at the Oedipus stage differs from the primary object relation to the mother in that now the two mother roles, the good and the bad, are divided up between the father and the mother, the role assigned to each depending on the sex of the child. The success of this division determines the kind and intensity of the child's later sexual and social relations. This is why the Oedipus complex has such an important bearing upon the later fate of the human being's object relations. But that should not blind us to the fact that the Oedipus complex is only a transient phase of development and that its success or failure has been decisively determined beforehand by the original relation to the mother.

The Oedipus situation compels the child to project onto both sexes the ambivalent attitude that originally referred to the mother only. This ambivalence it has already utilized and built up in its ego as narcissism and guilt feeling. Its projection in the Oedipus situation is for the infantile ego not so much a task as an unburdening, enabling the ego to find again in objects gratifications and inhibitions which the maternal deprivations had forced within the ego. The Oedipus situation and the love relations corresponding to it psychologically at a later stage thus enable the individual partially and temporarily to cancel earlier ego developments that involved a psychical expenditure. One can, so to speak, unburden oneself in the love relation because one can objectify in the partner parts and mechanisms of one's own ego. This explains also the definite, clear "object hunger" that we see manifested to a marked degree in the analytic transference situation. But the aim of this unburdening is not merely a reestablishment of the Oedipus situation as such, or even a reestablishment of the original libido relation to the mother; as analysis of the neurosis undoubtedly teaches us, it also serves to relieve the ego of anxiety and guilt feeling. This tendency of the ego to seize every available opportunity to unload itself of inner tensions through the object relation shows us that the ego is, as it were, built up against its own will by necessity, as a result of deprivations. And it shows us, too, that the ego is always ready to unravel its ego structure in object relations as soon as it finds objects and situations suitable for its purpose.

There are certain dangers in this unburdening tendency, which appear in the various forms of social and sexual maladjustments. Certainly this tendency as such is the psychological prerequisite to the establishment and maintenance of all human relationships. But if it goes too far in any one direction, as, for example, in the pathological forms of being in love or in paranoic projections, then it leads to a partial dissolution of the ego structure, which disturbs its social adjustment inasmuch as absorption in one object relation or pathological restriction to a definite kind of object relation makes social relations to other objects impossible. Another danger, that of narcissistic limitation, threatens the ego when it strives too much *against* the tendency to form object relations, that is, when it will not submit to any form of dependency on any kind of an object.

To understand all the processes and possibilities of outlet that come to attention in normal and pathological ways, we must not only consider the psychic mechanisms that are constructed on the biological mother relationship. We must also take into account the influences and disturbances of the given milieu, which are important besides for a therapeutic understanding of the individual case. In analysis we regularly find the picture of the strict, bad mother, which has its origins in the biological deprivations associated with the mother, quite irrespective of the parents' real attitude or their character type and educational influence on the child. From that time on, the image of the father and mother is *created* in the Oedipus situation. This image, as I have said, does not always represent their real character, but it plays a great part in analytic and educational situations. Thus the transference proves to be not so much a repetition of the real Oedipus situation as a projection of one's own inner parent image, which is often contrary to the actual facts. This conception of the transference is consistent with the fact that *it is a state of "being in love" and thus represents an attempt to solve one's ego problems by means of an object*. One must, therefore, in the analysis not only interpret all expressions of the transference as repetitions of infantile reactions, referring in the analytic situation to the analyst, but must also make them intelligible to the patient as expressions of ego tendencies.

The following picture of the genetic development of the object relation is somewhat average. Both sexes will form and model the image of the parents from their own attitudes toward the good and bad mother and in accordance with their need of it for later object cathexis and ego unburdening. In general the boy, as we have said, has to find in the Oedipus situation the bad mother in the father, irrespective of whether the father is or is not strict. The boy must, so to speak, make the father bad, in order to keep the picture of the good mother clear. This enables him later on to develop a proper love relation to a woman. This process is complicated not only by the child's actual relation to the parents and their real characters but also by the fact that the original mother relation has left behind its sediment in the ego and thus determined the ego's relation to other libidinal objects. We have already noted how the original use of the two mother images in the ego decides the formation of either a more narcissistic (positively inhibited) type or a more neurotic (negatively inhibited) type. In the boy, for instance, an especially intense disappointment in the mother will have as its consequence an inability to make an adequate displacement of the image of the bad mother onto the father. In life, too, he will continually have to look for and find the bad mother, which may lead to his being repelled by women and attracted to men. Playing the part of the good mother himself, he will either love himself solely and narcissistically or look for the good mother in other men. The same thing is true for the girl, who, as a result of holding on too tightly to the depriving mother, comes to play the ideal mother toward other girls (in whom she loves herself). Individual character types and behavior can thus be explained according to whether an individual plays in life the good mother or looks for her in the object, or plays the bad mother or looks for her in the object. This point of view throws light also upon those forms of behavior that one might designate negative object relations, that is, those in which hatred, anxiety, and especially the guilt feeling predominate. The guilt feeling betrays the important role played by the ego in object relations, part of it being present in all love relations.

All these negative emotional relations, which play such a large part in the love life, are intelligible only as attempts to solve conflicts in the ego, which seeks to free itself from inner tensions and inhibitions. At the same time such attempts at freeing bring a new, secondary guilt-feeling reaction with them, since the moral ego cannot bear the idea of making use of "the other" (in the Kantian sense) as a means to an end. In many human beings sensual gratification seems to bring about the same reaction, because they cannot bear to use the other (the other sex) as a means for narcissistic gratification. It is, therefore, no wonder that the guilt feeling is typically attached to the orgasm, which represents the climax of sexual gratification and hence something forbidden. This prohibition can regularly be traced back analytically to the earliest maternal deprivations of narcissistic pleasure gratifications on the individual's own body and reaches its climax in the masturbation conflict. This conflict proves to be a conflict in one's own ego, which is now independent of outside deprivations and prohibitions and is intelligible in genetic terms only in connection with the early biological privations imposed by the mother. The projection of these ego conflicts explains also why in crises through which the ego passes, the love object is frequently made the representative or, as it were, scapegoat of one's own inner inhibitions and conscience. We find the same attempt to solve an ego conflict on the object in analysis in the relation of the patient to the analyst. This explains the strong guilt feeling that necessarily develops from the analytic situation. Getting rid of this guilt feeling involves many great difficulties.

Again we learn that every relation to an object consists of projections of parts of one's own ego and ego conflicts, rather than the mere repetition of a biological situation. Certainly this ego that is projected into the object relation was originally built up and developed on the basis of an object relation— mainly on its biological relation to the mother, the development of which we have already sketched as far as the Oedipus situation. The primary deprivations imposed by the mother compel the child to go back again to its own ego and so create narcissism, which, in later object relations, is again split up into its original components. The degree of narcissism is a decisive factor in these later object relations, since it determines whether the original *object* is sought and found or whether one's own *ego* is objectified. This not only leads in extreme cases to homosexuality but also determines whether the heterosexual relation represents a reestablishment of the original object relation or an attempt to find one's own ego again. I have stated elsewhere that in every object choice and love relation the two components, the object and the ego, are operative side by side [1926b, 141–54]. I should only like to add that the greatest difficulties in the real love choice are to be explained by these two tendencies working against each other and also that most love conflicts arise when a development of the ego disturbs a previously gratifying object relation.

Postponing the discussion of this highly complicated influence of the ego development on the object relation, let us turn back to the simpler situation of the original object relation to the mother. We shall try first to work out certain typical consequential phenomena of this relation as manifested in character types. One masculine type retains the negative attitude to the mother and, side by side with this maternal superego, develops later an inadequate paternal superego. Either he is narcissistic in the positive sense of wanting to be loved and thus playing the child who looks outside for the good, ideal mother but never finds her, or he himself plays the good, ideal mother to other human beings, whom he helps, whom he must save (savior fantasy). His sex life is rather a protest against the strict mother than a reestablishment of the libidinal relation to the protecting mother and accordingly suffers from the restricting influence of guilt feeling. The other masculine type builds up the paternal inhibitions over the maternal prohibitions and so identifies himself with the father, not the mother, but at the same time he projects everything negative onto the father. He is more manly, active, and heterosexual than the first type, who often enough projects his negative attitude toward the father back again on the mother and in this way arrives at homosexuality or impotence. In such cases it is the task of analytic therapy to bring the patient to recognize this primal image of the bad mother, whom he tries to deny by himself playing the part of the ideal, good mother. This succeeds only if he can work off the suppressed revenge toward the strict mother in the analytic situation, instead of in the real relation to the woman (Don Juan, impotency, homosexuality).

This disappointment in the mother is an essential factor also in the boy's later negative attitude to the father and in the girl's to the man. It rests on all the deprivations from birth, weaning, and training in cleanliness to the Oedipus situation, and it is essentially aggravated through the advent of brothers or sisters, who interfere with the relation to the mother. In this preoedipal phase, in which the other children and not the father interfere with exclusive possession of the mother, the mother is, as it were, made responsible for the additional children, as well as for all the deprivations suffered at her hands. At the stage of the training in cleanliness this fact often comes to light in the infantile theory of the anal child. From analysis one gets the impression that the whole anal-birth theory belongs to this preoedipal stage, in which the father as procreator plays no part, the forbidden deed being perpetrated by the mother alone. The idea of the anal child often has the added implication that the child can be thrown away as a worthless waste product and no longer be a disturbance.

The later disappointment of the boy on finding the mother has no penis is neither his first nor his most important disappointment in her; indeed, it is possible only because of the earlier disappointments. She is, first, a narcissistic disappointment, because the boy, who for a long time accepted her as a part of his own ego (identification) now finds her to be unlike his ego, that is, unsuitable for identification and the narcissistic ideal formation based on it. Again, as we have already noted, it is not only fear of the father that holds the boy back from the mother but also his own fear of ego difference (lack of penis), which he gradually has to accept as he has all the previous disappointments. This kind of disappointment he learns to recognize at the genital stage as a consequence of the anatomical difference in sex. At the same time, the father is recognized as the owner of the penis, and his part in the procreation of children is imagined or learned from experience. Then the mother's lack of a penis can be felt as an advantage in a double sense. On the one hand, it absolves her from sole responsibility for the advent of other children; on the other hand, the recognition of her feminine sex role frees her from the ego (and identification), so she can become a real object in the sense that she can be possessed sexually. This is the progressive side of the Oedipus situation, although, to be sure, the powerful father is still recognized as the possessor of the mother.

At this stage the boy completes his real biological adjustment, because he definitely gives up the mother as an ego object (part of the ego) and accepts a real (libidinal) object in harmony with his later sexual role. He has to effect this change and adjustment independently of the father, and the father, in playing the inhibiting part, helps on the process by making it possible for the boy to project a great part of his disappointment in the mother, as well as his own inner difficulties, onto the father; in other words, the boy makes the father responsible for all these disappointments and frustrations—it is no longer the strict, punitive mother who keeps him from herself and sex but the father, who represents all external and internal hindrances. This makes it possible for the boy to desire the mother again instead of fearing her.

But even at the biological stage of the sex-object relation, the woman cannot be taken purely as an object. This new object relation is made possible only through the establishment of a new ego relation, which we recognize in the complicated psychic process of *being in love*. This being in love is an ego problem pure and simple and seems to have the function of bringing the demands of the biological sex role into harmony with the ego tendencies. This becomes particularly clear in an analytic study of so-called homosexuality, in which psychoanalysis long ago recognized a narcissistic ego problem. But here again psychoanalysis stopped with the libidinal explanation, characterizing the homosexual object choice as narcissistic; that is, one loves oneself in the same sex, as the mother loved (or should have loved) one. But this is only one form of narcissistic object choice; the ego mechanism lying at its base is just as active in the heterosexual object relation. In order to understand this, however, one must go beyond the libidinal explanation and take up the genetic, evolutionary point of view. It then becomes evident not only that one always looks for or hopes to find the ideal mother or the ideal ego in the love object, which is always chosen narcissistically, but that object relations in general are a kind of dumping ground for outworn phases of one's own ego development. Depending upon the experience and the mechanism that comes into play, at one time it may be a matter of wanting to find again the original object or one's own ego, at another time of wanting the idealized object or ego or even the depreciated object or ego. This last case, that of seeking the despised object or ego, which is so important for an understanding of pathogenic development, makes it clear that all object relations represent attempts to solve ego conflicts. That is, the object relation, in every sense, serves as a dumping ground for some former phase of the ego, which has to be given up, which one wants to keep in the object or in the relation to the object, and from which, on the other hand, one tries to free oneself by objectifying it. This explains most of the conflicts connected with object relations, which become more complicated and destructive as this process of ego deposit continues, as it does during the whole course of the object relation, so that the real depreciation and the final renunciation of this part of one's ego development is accomplished only through a depreciation and renunciation of the object itself.

This mechanism of the ego deposit is clear in homosexuality, which involves a second self who represents one's own ego (or higher or lower self) sexually, as well as in other ways. In the heterosexual object choice, the same mechanism is operative, but there it is complicated by the factor of sex differentiation, which disturbs the ego tendencies. Psychoanalysis has attempted to account for this by means of the castration complex but without taking into consideration the important mechanism of the ego psychology involved. For the girl, in accordance with her infantile adjustment to her biological sex role, the man has the importance of an ideal ego, which she wants for herself (envy of the penis) and with which she can identify herself in a positive sense if she is able to deposit her ego ideal in the man. But if she herself is, or wants to become, this ideal—that is, cannot sufficiently project this part of her wish-ego—then all the conflicts and difficulties that psychoanalysis has included under the concept masculinity complex will follow. As for the boy, we have already seen how he learns to give up the mother as an ego object and accept her as a sexual object if he is able to renounce narcissistic identification with her and accept a love object that obviously is different (castrated) from his own physiological self.

But the psychological problem is, How can human beings, with their narcissistic disposition and development, love another sex different from their own, that is, from themselves? The answer would be very simple if its practical application did not encounter all the difficulties that we find in the love conflicts of humankind. The answer would be, namely, that individuals arrive at a sexual object relation because of their biological sexual role and the natural attraction of the sexes for each other. This would be the case if individuals did not have to make such interminably complicated detours and to build up such elaborate justifications to fit themselves psychologically for their natural part and to adjust themselves to it without conflict. It is their ego and its development that oppose the demands of their biological sex role and that need the complicated apparatus of love to justify sensuousness, to compensate for sadism by tenderness, and finally to admit, in the unavoidable guilt feeling, that sex and love are a highly egoistic affair, which is resisted by one's moral ego.

For the man, as a condition and a result of his acceptance of the woman as a love object, two possibilities are open, similar to those that we have already described for the woman. Whereas the more favorable possibility generally results for the woman, namely, that she accepts the man as her ideal ego, the man seems more inclined or compelled to objectify the woman as a kind of lower self (previously described). This has its foundation not only in the idea of castration, which causes the man to identify the woman with the anxiety-charged part of his own ego and to see in her, as it were, his own feared fate. But his disappointment, that is, discovering the woman's lack of a penis, is, as we have noted, only the last in a series of earlier disappointments that go to form the picture of the bad, destructive, objectionable mother. So the woman's object choice, considered from the point of view of that ego, represents rather an idealization, a finding of the desired ego ideal in the other sex. This is only partly the case for the man, since, although he also desires the ideal mother, he can no longer find her because of his ambivalent attitude toward her. To the girl, on the other hand, the father appears irreproachable, although this ideal attitude, too, can be interfered with through the penis envy aroused by her brothers.

In this whole process of ego finding, ego projection, and ego depositing, two possibilities offer themselves, each in turn involving three possible mechanisms and outlets. From the mother-child or object-ego relationship, in conjunction with the narcissistic ego cathexis, one may project and objectify either more of one's own ego or more of the original mother object. In either case, one may project as true an image as possible, an idealized image, or a depreciated image. In both men and women, the various types of object choice and relations of the ego to the object depend upon which of these possibilities eventuate. But the development of this ego relation to the object also determines the character of the individual, whose object choice is only a symptom of his ego development. Thus from the beginning the libidinal object relations, in every form and at every stage, are attendant phenomena and sediments of the development of the ego. This explains not only changes in object relations, but also the difficulties involved in and attending such changes. In the most favorable cases the ego grows and develops in biological harmony with and for the children, in whom one deposits large parts of one's past (depreciated) and future (ideal) ego development. At the same time, the parents enable the children, through identification, to develop their own egos and to build up their own ego structure. Every object relation nevertheless holds destructive elements within it, since the deposit of overcome and renounced ego phases always involves a breaking up and reorganization of the ego structure, which we know and fear as the destructive side of love.

APPENDIX B ♦ INTERVIEW WITH

CLARE WINNICOTT, JUNE 1983

Tape 1

MICHAEL NEVE: Was he a Plymouth Brother?

CLARE WINNICOTT: Oh, no, no. Heavens, no.

MN:That's what [Masud] Khan told me.

CW: What? Everybody . . . [*Both laugh*]

MN: But he did. He swore he was a Plymouth Brother.

CW: No, absolutely not. He couldn't possibly have been. No, they were Methodists. His father was a Methodist. His mother was Anglican church, but when she married the father, they both settled in the Methodist church, which was ten minutes' walk away from where they lived. And they were very much leading lights in the church. The father was treasurer of it; he sang in the choir. And the whole family went to church every Sunday morning.

And I think it wasn't in the least a repressive religion, in their home.

MN: Interesting. That seems unusual.

CW: Unusual. I think the Methodists are a bit difficult—different. [*MN laughs*] Different.

MN: Different.

CW: Not difficult. I mean, I think they're different from some nonconformists. I really do. No, I remember him saying one day, he always walked home from church with his father. That was his privilege, because he was very much the youngest in the family. This was the important thing about him.

His two sisters were six and seven years older than he. So he was like an only child almost, at the bottom of the family tree, surrounded by a lot of people who thought he was wonderful: two sisters, mother, a nanny, sometimes a governess in the house, Aunt Delia, another aunt living in the house for a lot of the time.

And father was a very busy businessman and became wealthy and was the mayor, Lord Mayor of Plymouth, was knighted, et cetera—a friend of the Astors and all that.

MN: Really.

CW: Got Lady Astor into Parliament. When Astor became Lord Astor, it was

Sir Frederick that said to Lady Astor: "Why don't you stand? And we'll get you in." So he was really connected with all that.

But I think that nonconformism meant a lot to them all, and bound them in a way. It sort of was a binding force within the family, their religion; but it wasn't a hard, strict religion. They were very . . . very free.

Walking home one day with his father from church, Donald started to get him to talk about religion—asked him about something—and his father replied, "Listen, my boy. You read the Bible—what you find there. And you decide for yourself what you want, you know. It's free. You don't have to believe what I think. Make up your own mind about it. Just read the Bible."

And then they were very profoundly religious, but it's not obvious. They've all got a terrific sense of humor, and that is really an important thing about Donald. There aren't disasters in the Winnicott home; there are just funny episodes.

And it makes a lot of difference. And I would say that the religion wasn't in the least oppressive. Donald was religious. His first, when he got to Cambridge, I think—no, I don't think he did join the SCM [Student Christian Movement]. But he certainly spoke to medical students very much on Christian lines. You know, wanting to help people and save people. Not save people, help people. It's not a strict religion somehow. It's just a rather loving religion. Based on love, based on helping people.

So I think it was important to him. It allowed him to question. I mean, this is the point about nonconformists anyway. [MN makes agreeing noise] He was allowed to question, and he did.

When he married, his wife—first wife—was an Anglican, and he became confirmed at the age of twenty-six or -seven, something like that. And I think, you know, went to church a bit, but gradually this dropped off. Gradually he just didn't want to do it.

MN: Did he ever lose it? I mean, do you think he ever became, as it were . . .

CW: He was never anti-religion! Ever, ever. He was only too thankful if anybody could believe in anything! [MN laughs] He would say: "The point is, can they believe? I don't care what it's about. The capacity to believe is much more important than what you believe."

MN: And then he read medicine in Cambridge.

CW: He was at school in Cambridge. He went away at thirteen. From home. His father sent him away from home at thirteen. He was at a prep school in Plymouth—day prep school—and his father made a sudden decision to send him away to boarding school, to the Leys School in Cambridge, which is a nonconformist prep school. Which he simply loved! I mean, he had that immense vitality and capacity to enter into things and enjoy himself. I've never known anyone who could enjoy himself more.

This didn't mean he wasn't serious or concerned about people and the world generally—he was tremendously concerned. But he'd got the way of playing.

And his whole development of this theory of playing, which I've written about—you'll have to read that sometime [*MN makes agreeing noise*]—really is very much a part of him.

MN: People make distinctions about playing and games. He didn't really mean games, did he? He meant play.

CW: He meant play.

MN: What is play and what's a game? What's the difference between playing . . .

CW: Well, games are something organized that you accept the rules about, that you play according to the rules with a group of people. Play in itself is a quality of living, which is playful. Playful. Playfulness.

MN: Is it tactile? Is it sensual?

CW: It can be anything! I mean, it doesn't . . . It can be nothing. It can be just ideas. It can be concerned with any medium—just talking. I mean, this is in what I've written, but somebody came to our house one day—stayed a weekend in our house—and said to me, "You and Donald play, don't you?"

So I said, "Do we? I have not thought of it in that way."

He said, "Oh, yes you do. You play with me. You play with all kinds of things. My wife and I, we don't play."

And I thought a lot about it, and I could see what he meant. We did play with arranging our furniture—chucking this out or . . . with books, with reading, with—and going out. We had our Saturdays always for play. No work was done by either of us on Saturdays, except enjoying ourselves and thinking what to do. We worked on Sundays, sometimes.

MN: Two of the things that seem to have been momentous were Darwin, and then Freud.

CW: He met Darwin when he was at school. He found the books of Darwin on the secondhand bookstalls that Cambridge is famous for, in the market. And there are letters from him to his mother, saying, "If you ask me what I want for my birthday, it's money—to buy some of those wonderful books I pass every day."

And he collected Darwin. I've got the books here. And it was a revelation to him. It changed his whole life. It really changed his attitude to religion—began to change it. And he just felt, "There's a scientific way of working and that's where I am. That's what I want to do. I want to make discoveries and I want to understand them."

MN: Do you think he thought of Freud as a scientist?

CW: I think we must use the word *broadly* scientific. Scientific for him meant investigation and observation and trying to understand and—what's the word I want?—not codify, but . . .

MN: Organize? Or collate?

CW: What you've seen, your observations. And a very good example of his very simple technique, which has been mentioned by a lot of people—people who are really good researchers, top medical researchers, have said, "This paper of his is a perfect example of quite high-powered research in the simplest possible way." And that's the paper on "The Observation of Infants in a Set Situation," which is in *Collected Papers*. A very simple technique for making something available to the infant and watching what happens. And noting it.

MN: It seems a very simple question, but why children?

CW: Why did he become a pediatrician?

MN: Yes.

CW: Oh, I think he didn't quite know what to do. He intended to be a G.P. He'd always had his eye on being a G.P. and had promised his first wife that he would be. Her father was. But he began to be—he got two appointments in 1923 as a physician.

Why did he become a pediatrician? is what you asked me. I think it's because he knew he must stay in London. He wanted to get psychoanalysis, and it was available only in London. Therefore being a G.P. in London wasn't what he wanted to do.

He became more and more interested in the psychological factors in physical illness and played around with it a bit on his own, just as a student and a young doctor. Then I think he was impressed by certain people. Now I'm not going to remember their names, but they were quite famous people and one of them *was* a pediatrician. And he became his house surgeon for a time and just thought, you know, this is perhaps something I'd like to do. And he applied for two jobs in hospitals—there was no pediatric course to go to then, in those days—and he set up practice as a pediatrician in Harley Street.

I think it was really the influence of people, people he admired, who were doing the kind of work that he was interested in. I think it's perhaps also that he's naturally easy with children. And all the family are. His eldest sister, who is the only one alive now—and she is ninety—still has children, nine-, ten-year-olds, who come to visit her. They knock at the door, "I've come to see the old lady."

And she takes them very seriously. I heard her talking last time with a nine-year-old, about a new piece of music this child had just learned. She played it to her on the piano. And she discussed the music with her.

But they've all got a way with children, all of them. The middle sister, who has died, ran all the Brownies for miles around, for years and years. You know, really loved them. So I think they've all had a natural facility with children. Must come from their parents! And their own experience.

But this may be too rambling for what you want!

MN: No, no! It's good. I mean, because in some way it seems—intuitive. In other words, this wasn't a program. This was intuitive or he liked somebody's personal style or sense of worth and therefore would follow it or intuit it. [*CW makes agreeing noises*] And it seems very familial, the whole thing. It was not, as it were, a big decision, made theoretically.

cw: No, I think not. The biggest decision made was not to go into his father's business. You see, he was the only son, and there was a very prospering business—wholesale in hardware. And, you know, all the navy was there to fit up.

And it was a very family business. The two brothers were in it, the brothers Winnicott, and they knew all their staff and they were very much patriarchal figures to their staff. And they very much wanted Donald to come into the business—his father, terribly much.

His father was really the brains of the business, I think. Highly intelligent person. And very dignified. And the real blow was not going into the business—making that decision. He tried to make himself go into the business to please his father. I've got a letter about it here. But only his friend said to him, "What are you doing? You're absolutely mad. Do what you want to do."

And he said, "How wonderful! Do you think I really can?" I mean, he did square it up with his father, and went to the head[master] and said, "I want to be a doctor."

And the head looked at him and said, "Boy—." Donald takes him off. "Not brilliant, but will do." And that's it.

Tape 2

MN: There seems to me to be some sense in which there's an absent person in Winnicottian theory, and that is the father.

cw: Mmm.

MN: Did he see himself as maternal in some way within himself, with these children? And where is the father in the theory? He seems to be the ghost at the feast.

cw: Yes, I think perhaps one of the things to be said about this is that a lot of his writing is about early infancy, isn't it? And, in a sense, the father is a duplicate mother at that point. He's not a separate person.

But he has written on the father. I mean, there are papers on "Where Does Father Come In?" in his broadcasts. "What About Father?" But I know people do say this about him; but *I* think it's partly because—this is what I've said—he's dealing with early infancy, when father is a duplicate mother. And the father . . . He hasn't written about father—he's written about father in relation to children.

He's also written about marriage and creative living in marriage, and this isn't published yet. It's all going to be published. We're doing it, working on it.

Yes, all right. In a sense, I see what people mean. He doesn't spell it out perhaps enough. But I think in his clinical work with children father was an immensely important part of the total situation. He wanted to be in touch with fathers. Very much.

MN: Because he seems to think—isn't that one of the famous asides?—that he's never seen a child. In other words, he'd always seen a child with somebody. An aunt, a parent.

cw: Mmm. And he would go into the whole—particularly when you get an eight- or nine-year-old child. He would always ask, "Well, how much of a role does father play in this child's life?" I remember one very well known surgeon who came to him with a child, a young boy about eight or nine. And Donald said to him, "Look, it's you. He wants you; he wants contact with you."

And this man put everything off and took this kid out to the zoo, out to Regent's Park one day. And the only comment from the child was, "There are not enough lions." [*Laughter*]

But Donald made a real point of bringing the fathers in on a consultation— on the work he was doing. Without any question. I don't know if you've read *The Piggle*, have you? Well, I mean the father is very important in all that. I think Donald didn't see enough of his own father. Father was—but it was very typical of that social class and that kind of person—working in the town, taking on huge responsibilities locally. He was a J.P. as well. And he was always out at meetings.

So he says, "I was left too much to all my mothers. Thank goodness I was sent away at thirteen!"

mn: Given all his thoughts about the facilitating environment and so on, did he think it was a good thing he'd gone away then? I mean, good for him psychologically.

cw: He would think so. He simply loved it! Mind you, I'm sure he had a difficulty in breaking from home, but he didn't hesitate. The minute he was given a chance he didn't hesitate. And when he *got* to school, he simply loved it. I mean, plunged into it! But always wrote. I've got piles of letters of his from home, that they've saved, which show his liveliness and interest. In them. He always sends his love to the cat and everybody's mentioned, right through—all the maids and all the cast of characters.

mn: Were there any contexts where a child might be happy other than family life?

cw: In what situation?

mn: Well, in terms of becoming a happy child. I mean, was he quite conservative in that sense about the family structure, do you think? That that was where individuation and maturation would absolutely have to take place?

cw: The richness of life, he thought, really did depend tremendously on the early environmental factors. I mean, people can find richness for themselves later on, if they're lucky, if they meet the right people. But I think he did feel, you know, for quality of living family gave the security, which gave you the freedom to explore everything. And I think his own family life did give him a great freedom. I mean, there was nothing he wouldn't look at or explore, if you wanted to, if you'd got the time.

I think there's one famous episode in his life, when he was nine, and he looked in the mirror and he said, "I'm too nice." And really, from this point he started coming bottom of the class. Blotting everything, blotting his copybook, shoving things around, torturing flies, pulling their wings off. You know, just doing naughty things.

MN: Did he like naughtiness? Was he in favor of naughtiness?

CW: He wanted to find this other dimension in himself. "I'm too good! I'm coming top all the time! Everybody likes me too much! I must find the nastiness in myself!" And, you know, he smashed—another famous episode—a doll that belonged to his sister, because father teased him about this doll. His father teased him. So he simply took a mallet and smacked the doll.

And he was very pleased at this event. Frightfully pleased that he had smashed it! But quite glad when father melted the wax of the doll's face and put it together again.

Mmm. Now what are we on to? You want to go on about the family, do you?

MN: Not really. No, no.

CW: No, no.

MN: No, we can think about other things.

CW: I don't . . .

MN: Let's try optimism and pessimism. Freud in some sense is a pessimistic thinker. He [Winnicott] doesn't seem to have been a pessimist.

CW: Hardly.

MN: That seems an enormous difference.

CW: Enormous difference.

MN: Is that to do with Judaism as against Methodism [*laughs*] or . . .

CW: I don't . . .

MN: There's a way in which he's a kind of non-Jewish Freud, isn't there [*laughs*]?

CW: Yes, very, very, very, very, very non-Jewish indeed. Very English, actually. Really brought up in an English traditional way, but a liberal English way. I think the difference between him and a great many other psychoanalysts—in fact, almost everybody—is that he came at psychoanalysis from pediatrics. From a study of normal families who are ill, with ill children, but seeing . . . He saw sixty thousand cases in his clinics, in his three clinics, by the time he retired. He'd seen sixty thousand mothers with children, parents with children. He ran three clinics.

And he studied the whole family, always took the whole family into account, because he just couldn't do it just with the child. He made very quick contact with the child, but it was the family structure that he tried to support in his clinical work. Very much so. So that he got experience of normality, normal families—poor, poverty-stricken—he worked in the East End and Paddington Green, which are both very poor areas.

But he would go and visit the families if he felt like it. Go out and visit them.

Often did. Round about Paddington Green. And I think this experience of normal family working and how it can work he brought in with him to psychoanalysis. And it comes with something positive. It comes at psychoanalysis from health, rather than from illness, from pathology. It doesn't get at it from pathology.

He discovers pathology as he goes along. And he had no illusions about pathology and the effect of serious illness on people. In fact, I'd often be surprised that he'd pick up—you know, from a contact with somebody—when we left them he'd say, "Well now, I wonder how long he's been on drugs." Or whatever. And I thought, "My goodness, you know, he doesn't miss a thing really." He had very, very acute powers of observation—about everything.

MN: But take the Freudian death instinct. He doesn't seem to . . .

CW: He doesn't believe in it. He's written about that. I don't know if you know. He doesn't go along with it at all. He doesn't. He thinks death is a disaster, which you have to put up with, because you're human. No, he didn't like the idea of death at all.

MN: What about loneliness? He talked wonderfully about, as we know, the capacity to be alone. What's the difference between being alone and being lonely?

CW: Being lonely is you're—you feel incomplete. You're missing somebody. There's a bit of depression and pathology in it perhaps. Not necessarily. Yes, perhaps to some extent.

The capacity to be alone is an achievement of good experiences—enough good experiences to keep your own inner world good. Loneliness is being without your good object, in a sense. Being alone with the bad, you know, you *are* alone then. There's a great deal of difference. Mrs. [Melanie] Klein, of course, wrote on loneliness. Soon after he'd written his paper. And they're very different papers.

But I think for him loneliness has got depression—illness perhaps—and the capacity to be alone has got health in it.

MN: What about waiting?

CW: Waiting for the patient, you're talking about?

MN: Well, he says something very interesting about just waiting.

CW: For development to happen?

MN: Yes.

CW: For things to happen?

MN: Yes. Or a child waiting for the meal, knowing the meal will come. Learning that the meal will be coming and waiting, as against demanding or screaming or whatever.

CW: Yes.

MN: That seems very . . .

CW: Yes, he does make that an important issue. That when the child's intellectual powers are developing, he knows the sound means there's something happening, and can rationalize and can wait. For a certain length of time. Can keep the good thing going for a certain length of time. If it's over that edge, then there's disaster.

But this is very much according to age and stage of development. Yes, emotional development. I mean, how far have you gotten in the waiting game? And that's really according to how you've experienced it. If you've not been left waiting too long, till the thing snapped. Then it's very hard to mend it again. It's like being brought out tight and then the elastic snaps and can't be put together. And there are stages when it's gone too far.

But timing for him was tremendously important in all developmental processes. The right time for the right thing, you know. And that people have got a time and a rhythm of their own, in themselves, which he would work to free or let develop.

MN: One thing that seems quite strangely different from Freud is the stuff on infantile sexuality. I mean, he doesn't seem to think that sexuality is absolutely primary in infantile development but comes when other cognitive capacities or whatever have matured. Is that right?

CW: Yes.

MN: Because that seems quite an important difference, doesn't it?

CW: Yes.

MN: From classic Freudian theory?

CW: Yes. In a way, Freud, of course, pioneered all that, didn't he? So Donald could take it for granted. I mean, he knew about it. He didn't have to discover it. Freud did. So perhaps that's why Freud—the emphasis is there. But I think he thought that it would happen. There was no denying it. This happened. It had to be dealt with by parents.

It would be discussed with parents. He had many of these sexual problems always. He would use it in his work with children. I should think it comes into *Therapeutic Consultations*. And it does with *The Piggle*, definitely. But I think for him perhaps it hadn't got the importance that it had for Freud.

Or the central position, let's say. It isn't importance. It's important, all right. But it had a central position for Freud, did it not? I mean, Freud developed his other theories around this one, quite a lot. But I think Donald could take it for granted, and it was a part of a deep, developmental process. He believed deeply in the developmental process. There was always a drive towards health—a biologically backed drive towards health. And that includes mental health. That was his conviction.

MN: Which might be Darwinian. Or did he read Piaget?

CW: Yes, but not well. That was very—yes, I think, Darwinian. But that started him off on this.

Another thing—I'm jumping a bit. Another person who influenced him a great deal during his medical training was Lord Horder. He was then Dr. Thomas Horder, training medical students in Bart's [St. Bartholomew's Hospital]. Now, he was attached to Tommy Horder at some points. And it was Horder who said to him, "Listen to your patient. Don't you go in with your wonderful knowledge and apply it all. Just listen. They'll tell you quite a lot of things. You'll learn a lot if you listen."

And Horder practiced this himself. And he watched Horder work. And he cottoned on immediately to this and found how fascinating it was to hear people talk about themselves. Now, this is very unusual in medical practice.

MN: To listen to the patient?

CW: Very much so. [MN laughs] It really is. I mean [CW laughs], I don't know. You're in the history of medicine, but I'm a very experienced patient. Anyhow it was said to me the other day, "Well, we didn't believe you when you said this—that if you stopped taking these pills, your temperature would go up. We didn't believe you."

I said, "I know you didn't. But there it is. I was right."

MN: So that the analyst is not lording it over the patient, as it were [CW makes agreeing noises], in Winnicott's scheme.

CW: He would very much feel that. It's what we can do together.

Tape 3

MN: Henry James? I mean, really? It seems rather . . .

CW: Rather what?

MN: Ascetic or fastidious.

CW: Mmm. Well, he was at Cambridge. He went from Cambridge onto a destroyer in the First World War, as the medical officer in charge. He was only a student in his first year. He knew nothing. Fortunately, there was a good medical orderly, who taught him.

But he writes back to his mother, saying, "I'm only here so that the men can write home and tell their mothers that there's a doctor on board."

MN: But he's a sort of object, isn't he [laughs], a comforting object?

CW: Yes. I mean, he had some very important experiences on that destroyer. They saw enemy action and death, because people died. And he had to take action. He had to do what he could do.

But he had a lot of free time and read the novels of Henry James, as far as I can tell, most of the time. He had a lot of time for reading. Meredith, the whole of Meredith. He's read a great many people. And we always, when he and I met, had a book between us that he was reading aloud to me. And he read aloud, interestingly enough, to the boys in his dormitory at school. He read a book aloud.

MN: And he would read to you aloud?

CW: He would read to me aloud. If I read to him aloud, he'd go to sleep, so I let him do the reading. I never went to sleep. I sewed or did something. But there was always a book on the go. Always. We'd read it whenever we could. But certainly we were reading all the time.

MN: Music?

CW: He was very musical indeed. Very. He could have done something with it. Played the piano. I mean, there are stacks of music. Go through a Brahms sonata. He'd rush up and play the piano between patients. And at the end of the day a musical outburst fortissimo. No question about that. He loved music.

And the whole family was musical. One of the sisters plays and sings. Used to sing; she can still play the piano, though she's blind and ninety. She unfortunately cannot read the music any more.

Yes. What else did he read? Biographies mostly.

MN: Any heroes? I mean, Freud admires Hannibal and . . .

CW: Freud?

MN: And Napoleon [*laughs*] and so on. Yes. Freud obviously loves the men who conquer the world, which is quite telling. Did he admire Napoleon or . . .

CW: No.

MN: Or any kind of all-conquering figure?

CW: No. No. I wouldn't say so, no. He much preferred the—I mean, he liked Virginia Woolf. He liked the intricate things. He liked the stream of consciousness stuff, you know? Interested in the lot. He liked poetry, but that's a thing that I'm into more than he was. I could say a Shakespeare sonnet on demand, you know, which he enjoyed.

MN: Any historical heroic figures he . . .

CW: Darwin! Darwin was the great person in his life. And Freud. Were the great influences in his life. He read all of Darwin when he was quite young and was always reading Freud. Never without a book of Freud.

MN: Did he follow Freud's style at all? Did he like the style of writing?

CW: He admired tremendously Freud's clear thinking and ability to put things down and to change his mind. He admired that a lot. But I don't know. I think he did admire Freud's way of writing. He often queried the translations. But then the new translation came along. And he did quite a lot to facilitate that new translation. It was while he was chairman of the Publications Committee [of the International Psychoanalytical Association].

MN: Did he think changing your mind was an important capacity?

CW: Very important. To be able not to defend your position. Once you're defending your position, you've lost sight of science, he would say. I mean, he would imply that. Once you're defending a position, you watch out. You're on to something different.

MN: Defense.

CW: Yes, defense.

MN: You're getting to the manic defense, probably.

CW: Well, no. He wouldn't say manic defense. He would say you're defending a position, which you've perhaps no right to defend. This new evidence doesn't fit into your defended position. Why are you defending your position? What's wrong with it? There's new evidence here that you've got to consider; your position may not be valid.

MN: It seems an odd question, but he seems possibly to have had the rather wonderful insight that intelligence isn't the only thing. Is that right? I mean, that there are more things in the life of a person than, as it were, being clever.

CW: Mm-hmm. Yes. I would think it comes back to this quality of living. The capacity to play with ideas. The capacity to treat things lightly and seriously at the same time, on the other hand. This isn't answering your question, though.

MN: There's some way in which you might think of the history of someone being very, very clever as a loss.

CW: Mm-hmm.

MN: They've lost the capacity to enjoy life [laughs], like many academics, or be sensual, be gay, just not worry too much. You know, all the things that seem very attractive about his playfulness. That there are more things than being a smarty-pants.

CW: Absolutely. And he has often said in public—you know, and been criticized for saying it—that intelligence, a high I.Q., can be a very great handicap. Because it's going to be exploited—by you or somebody else. The intelligence has got to serve the capacity for living and experiencing. Experiencing. And observing.

He was tremendously observant. That has something to do with intelligence, I know. But it also is the capacity to relate what you're observing to something you already know. Make the connections to build up a theory.

He was permanently engaged in building up his theories. I mean, being influenced by other people's theories, but it was really his own, out of his clinical experiences, that was his lifelong quest. Building up his own theory from experience.

MN: Did he like puns?

CW: No. On the whole, not.

MN: Did they annoy him?

CW: No. Not annoy. No, he could laugh at puns. I mean, he could pun; he could definitely pun. But he would often say, "A sense of humor is not teasing." Or punning, really. A sense of humor is something different: it's being light with things. It's being able to play with things. And the capacity to play . . . The capacity to deal with life's experience is very much related to the capacity to play.

He says this very clearly in his work, in his papers on playing. The capacity to contain experience and integrate it into yourself is very much related to the capacity to play with.

MN: So, in a way, punning might be merely clever, whereas . . .

CW: Clever, clever! And that's fun, that's a game! Yes. Let's play it. He and Sir Peter Tizard (as he is now), who is a pediatrician—president of the International [Psychoanalytical Association] now, I think—somewhere high up. He and Peter would have comic letters going between each other. There were always funny letters, sometimes in poetry.

MN: Any favorite painting in all the world? A Vermeer?

CW: Hmm. I can't think of any particular painting. He always loved going to see pictures. Hmm. Wait a moment. He was never sure of Picasso. We went and saw all the Picassos in France.

MN: Was he doubtful about modernism? About the modern?

CW: I think he was always interested in what they were doing and why they were doing it. But I think his favorite paintings would be more classical. [Walter] Sickert and people like this he liked very much. You know, something elusive, something that leads you on.

MN: That seems so interesting.

CW: Something magical that leads you on.

MN: But James and Sickert, you would never have thought. You'd have thought something bolder, more, as it were, crudely realistic. But he seems not to have . . .

CW: Do you?

MN: I don't know.

CW: But do you feel that Henry James is very bold?

MN: No, he's very, very refined.

CW: Yes. And so is Sickert surely. Mmm. Yes, I think his tastes were very refined, really. And, of course, in music the late Beethoven quartets. Particularly towards the end of his life. Bach, in a way, he played. He loved to play Bach. If he sat down without music, he would always play Bach automatically. In a sense, he was perhaps his favorite composer, although towards the end of his life he was permanently listening to late Beethoven quartets. Fascinated by them and their structure.

MN: Did he die in a way he would like to have done?

CW: Yes, I would say, on the whole. We'd been listening to music that day, and he died suddenly. At least to me. I don't know to him. I looked at him the day before he died. And he was sitting on the floor. (We never sat on chairs. We always sat on the floor.) I was looking at him and I thought, "If I really loved him, I wouldn't want him to go on too much longer. He's too tired." Because he was ill—had got heart failure.

But then he'd had about six coronaries and recovered from them and kept himself going. And didn't stop himself doing a thing. When he went down to his home in Devon, he'd be up at the top of a tree, in the last year of his life. A few months before he died. He was at the top of a tree, cutting the top off. I said, "What the hell are you doing up there?"

He said, "Well, I've always wanted the top of this tree off. It spoils the view from our window." Which it did. And he got it off.

And I thought, "I must get him down. He's absolutely crazy." And I thought, "No, it's his life and he's got to live it. If he dies after this, he dies."

But this was him. He wanted to live. He had started his autobiography, you see. And it was going to be called *Not Less Than Everything*. And he quotes [T. S.] Eliot. And then he's put at the bottom: "Prayer: Oh, God, may I be alive when I die."

And he was, really. We'd looked at a film. It was a very comic film of old cars, a very amusing film. I'd spotted that it was on, and I said, "I think you'll like this." We looked at this, and he said, "What a happy-making film!" and went to sleep. And I woke up on the floor, and he was already dead, on the floor.

MN: But you used to sit on the floor. He liked the floor.

CW: We always liked the floor. It wasn't in this house; it was in another house. Further along in Chester Square. Yes, we always sat on the floor—him on one side, me on the other. We all had—we had our places. We had a rug that we sat on.

MN: Did he like rolling in the grass?

CW: Yes.

MN: Rolling around?

CW: And riding his bicycle. You know, with his feet on the handlebars. Till very late in life. And a policeman stopped him and said, "Fancy an old man like you setting an example to everybody." Coming down Haverstock Hill with his feet on the handlebars.

And also I've known him drive his car, sitting with his head through the roof and a walking stick on the accelerator. Oh, I've really driven with him like that. He'd try anything, if you . . . He was the most spontaneous thing that ever lived. But I don't, I don't know . . .

◆ REFERENCES

References are listed under each author in order of the date of original publication. That date appears in text citations and footnotes. The edition consulted is the one listed in the bibliographic entry.

Abarbanel, J. 1983. The Revival of the Sibling Experience during the Mother's Second Pregnancy. *Psychoanal. Study Child*, 38:353–79.

Abraham, K. 1922. "The Trifurcation of the Road" in the Oedipus Myth. In *Clinical Papers and Essays on Psychoanalysis*. Tr. H. Abraham and D. R. Ellison. New York: Basic Books, 1955, pp. 83–85.

Andreas-Salomé, L. 1964. *The Freud Journal*. Tr. S. A. Leavy. New York: Basic Books, 1976.

Anzieu, D. 1985. *The Skin Ego: A Psychoanalytic Approach to the Self*. Tr. C. Turner. New Haven: Yale Univ. Press, 1989.

———. 1986. *A Skin for Thought: Interviews with Gilbert Tarrab on Psychology and Psychoanalysis*. Tr. D. N. Briggs. London: Karnac, 1990.

Aristotle. 1941. *Nicomachean Ethics*. In *The Basic Works of Aristotle*. Ed. R. McKeon. New York: Random House.

Attridge, D. 1986. Puttenham's Perplexity: Nature, Art, and the Supplement in Renaissance Poetic Theory. In Parker and Quint 1986, pp. 257–79.

Atwood, G. E., and R. D. Stolorow. 1984. *Structures of Subjectivity: Explorations in Psychoanalytic Phenomenology*. Hillsdale, N.J.: Analytic Press.

Bacal, H. A. 1987. British Object-Relations Theorists and Self Psychology: Some Critical Reflections. *Int. J. Psycho-Anal.*, 68:81–98.

———. 1989. Winnicott and Self Psychology: Remarkable Reflections. In Detrick and Detrick 1989, pp. 259–71.

Balint, M. 1932. Character Analysis and New Beginning. In Balint 1952, pp. 159–73.

———. 1937. Early Developmental States of the Ego. Primary Object-love. In Balint 1952, pp. 90–108.

———. 1952. *Primary Love and Psycho-Analytic Technique*. London: Maresfield Library, 1985.

———. 1968. *The Basic Fault: Therapeutic Aspects of Regression*. New York: Brunner/Mazel, 1979.

Barthes, R. 1968. The Death of the Author. In *Image/Music/Text*. Ed. and tr. S. Heath. New York: Hill and Wang, 1977, pp. 142–48.

Bion, W. R. 1950. The Imaginary Twin. In *Second Thoughts: Selected Papers on Psycho-Analysis*. London: Maresfield Library, 1967, pp. 3–22.

Blakeslee, S. 1989. Crack's Toll among Babies: A Joyless View of Even Toys. *New York Times*, Sept. 17.

Bloom, H. 1973. *The Anxiety of Influence: A Theory of Poetry*. New York: Oxford Univ. Press.

Bollas, C. 1987. *The Shadow of the Object: Psychoanalysis of the Unthought Known*. New York: Columbia Univ. Press.

———. 1989. *Forces of Destiny: Psychoanalysis and Human Idiom*. New York: Columbia Univ. Press.

Bowlby, J. 1969. *Attachment*. 2nd ed. New York: Basic Books, 1982.

Brandschaft, B. 1989. Klein, Balint, and Fairbairn: A Self-Psychological Perspective. In Detrick and Detrick 1989, pp. 231–58.

Buckley, P., ed. 1986. *Essential Papers on Object Relations*. New York: New York Univ. Press.

Casement, P. 1985. *On Learning from the Patient*. London: Routledge, 1990.

———. 1990. *Further Learning from the Patient: The Analytic Space and Process*. London: Routledge.

Chodorow, N. 1978. *The Reproduction of Mothering: Psychoanalysis and the Sociology of Gender*. Berkeley: Univ. of California Press, 1979.

———. 1989. *Feminism and Psychoanalytic Theory*. New Haven: Yale Univ. Press.

Clancier, A., and J. Kalmanovitch. 1984. *Winnicott and Paradox: From Birth to Creation*. Tr. A. Sheridan. London: Tavistock, 1987.

Clément, C. 1981. *The Lives and Legends of Jacques Lacan*. Tr. A. Goldhammer. New York: Columbia Univ. Press, 1983.

Copjec, J., ed. 1987. Dossier on the Institutional Debate. *October*, 40:51–135.

Crews, F. 1986. *Skeptical Engagements*. New York: Oxford Univ. Press.

Darwin, C. 1872. *The Expression of the Emotions in Man and Animals*. Chicago: Univ. of Chicago Press, 1965.

Davis, M. 1985. Some Thoughts on Winnicott and Freud. *Bull. Brit. Assn. Psychotherapists*. 16:57–71.

———. 1987. The Writing of D. W. Winnicott. *Int. Rev. Psycho-Anal.*, 14:491–501.

Davis, M., and D. Wallbridge. 1981. *Boundary and Space: An Introduction to the Work of D. W. Winnicott*. Harmondsworth, Eng.: Penguin Books, 1983.

Davis, N. Z. 1983. *The Return of Martin Guerre*. Cambridge: Harvard Univ. Press.

Deri, S. K. 1984. *Symbolization and Creativity*. New York: International Univ. Press.

Derrida, J. 1966. Freud and the Scene of Writing. In *Writing and Difference*. Tr. A. Bass. Chicago: Univ. of Chicago Press, 1978, pp. 196–231.

————. 1967. *Of Grammatology*. Tr. G. C. Spivak. Baltimore: Johns Hopkins Univ. Press, 1976.

————. 1978. Coming into One's Own. Tr. J. Hulbert. In *Psychoanalysis and the Question of the Text*. Ed. G. Hartman. Baltimore: Johns Hopkins Univ. Press, pp. 114–48.

Detrick, D. W., and S. P. Detrick, eds. 1989. *Self Psychology: Comparisons and Contrasts*. Hillsdale, N.J.: Analytic Press.

Deutsch, H. 1937. Absence of Grief. *Psychoanal. Q.*, 6:12–22.

Dollimore, J. 1984. *Radical Tragedy: Religion, Ideology and Power in the Drama of Shakespeare and His Contemporaries*. Chicago: Univ. of Chicago Press.

Eagle, M. N. 1984. *Recent Developments in Psychoanalysis: A Critical Evaluation*. Cambridge: Harvard Univ. Press, 1987.

Eigen, M. 1981a. The Area of Faith in Winnicott, Lacan and Bion. *Int. J. Psycho-Anal.*, 62:413–33.

————. 1981b. Guntrip's Analysis with Winnicott: A Critique of Glatzer and Evans. *Contemp. Psychoanal.*, 17:103–12.

Engel, G. L. 1975. The Death of a Twin: Mourning and Anniversary Reactions. Fragments of Ten Years of Self-Analysis. *Int. J. Psycho-Anal.*, 56:23–40.

Ellis, J. M. 1989. *Against Deconstruction*. Princeton: Princeton Univ. Press.

Fairbairn, W. R. D. 1941. A Revised Psychopathology of the Psychoses and Psychoneuroses. In Fairbairn 1952, pp. 28–58.

————. 1944. Endopsychic Structure Considered in Terms of Object-Relationships. In Fairbairn 1952, pp. 82–136.

————. 1946. Object-Relationships and Dynamic Structure. In Fairbairn 1952, pp. 137–51.

————. 1949. Steps in the Development of an Object-Relations Theory of the Personality. In Fairbairn 1952, pp. 152–61.

————. 1951. A Synopsis of the Development of the Author's Views Regarding the Structure of the Personality. In Fairbairn 1952, pp. 162–79.

————. 1952. *Psychoanalytic Studies of the Personality*. London: Routledge and Kegan Paul, 1986.

————. 1954. Observations on the Nature of Hysterical States. *Brit. J. Med. Psychol.*, 27:105–25.

————. 1958. On the Nature and Aims of Psycho-Analytical Treatment. *Int. J. Psycho-Anal.*, 39:374–85.

Ferenczi, S. 1912. The Symbolic Representation of the Pleasure and Reality Principles in the Oedipus Myth. In *Sex in Psychoanalysis*. Tr. E. Jones. New York: Basic Books, 1950, pp. 253–69.

————. 1923. *Thalassa: A Theory of Genitality*. Tr. H. A. Bunker. New York: Norton, 1968.

————. 1927. Review of O. Rank, *Technik der Psychoanalyse: I. Die analytische Situation* (Technique of psychoanalysis: 1. The analytic situation). *Int. J. Psycho-Anal.*, 8:93–100.

———. 1930. The Principles of Relaxation and Neocatharsis. In Ferenczi 1955, pp. 108–25.

———. 1933. Confusion of Tongues between Adults and the Child. In Ferenczi 1955, pp. 156–67.

———. 1955. *Final Contributions to the Problems and Methods of Psycho-Analysis.* Ed. M. Balint. Tr. E. Mosbacher et al. New York: Brunner/Mazel, 1980.

———. 1988. *The Clinical Diary of Sandor Ferenczi.* Ed. J. Dupont. Tr. M. Balint and N. Z. Jackson. Cambridge: Harvard Univ. Press.

Ferenczi, S., and O. Rank. 1923. *The Development of Psycho-Analysis.* Tr. C. Newton. New York: Dover, 1956.

Flax, J. 1990. *Thinking Fragments: Psychoanalysis, Feminism, and Postmodernism in the Contemporary West.* Berkeley: Univ. of California Press.

Foucault, M. 1969. What Is an Author? In *Language, Counter-Memory, Practice: Selected Essays and Interviews.* Ed. D. F. Bouchard. Tr. D. F. Bouchard and S. Simon. Ithaca: Cornell Univ. Press, 1977, pp. 113–38.

Freud, A. 1936. *The Ego and the Mechanisms of Defense.* Rev. ed. Tr. C. Baines. New York: International Univ. Press, 1970.

Freud, S. 1895. *Project for a Scientific Psychology.* In *The Standard Edition of the Complete Psychological Works.* Ed. and tr. J. Strachey et al. 24 vols. London: Hogarth Press, 1953–74. (hereafter *S.E.*), 1:295–397.

———. 1900. *The Interpretation of Dreams. S.E.,* vols. 4 and 5.

———. 1905. *Three Essays on the Theory of Sexuality.* In *S.E.,* 7:125–245.

———. 1907. The Sexual Enlightenment of Children. In *S.E.,* 9:131–39.

———. 1913a. The Theme of the Three Caskets. In *S.E.,* 12:291–301.

———. 1913b. *Totem and Taboo.* In *S.E.,* 13:1–161.

———. 1914. *On the History of the Psycho-Analytic Movement.* In *S.E.,* 14:7–66.

———. 1916. Some Character Types Met With in Psycho-Analytic Work. In *S.E.,* 14:311–33.

———. 1916–17. *Introductory Lectures on Psycho-Analysis. S.E.,* vols. 16 and 17.

———. 1917. A Childhood Recollection from *Dichtung und Wahrheit.* In *S.E.,* 17:147–56.

———. 1918. *From the History of an Infantile Neurosis.* In *S.E.,* 17:7–122.

———. 1919a. A Child Is Being Beaten. In *S.E.,* 17:179–204.

———. 1919b. The "Uncanny." In *S.E.,* 17:219–56.

———. 1920. *Beyond the Pleasure Principle.* In *S.E.,* 18:7–64.

———. 1921. *Group Psychology and the Analysis of the Ego.* In *S.E.,* 18:69–143.

———. 1923. *The Ego and the Id.* In *S.E.,* 19:12–66.

———. 1924a. The Dissolution of the Oedipus Complex. In *S.E.,* 19:173–79.

———. 1924b. Letter to Fritz Wittels. In *S.E.,* 19:286–88.

———. 1926. *Inhibitions, Symptoms and Anxiety.* In *S.E.,* 20:87–172.

———. 1930. *Civilization and Its Discontents.* In *S.E.,* 21:64–145.

———. 1933. *New Introductory Lectures on Psycho-Analysis.* In *S.E.,* 22:7–192.

———. 1937. Analysis Terminable and Interminable. In *S.E.,* 23:216–53.

———. 1939. *Moses and Monotheism.* In *S.E.,* 23:7–137.

———. 1940. *An Outline of Psycho-Analysis.* In *S.E.,* 23:144–207.

Freud, S., and J. Breuer. 1895. *Studies on Hysteria. S.E.,* vol. 2.

Fromm, E. 1956. *The Art of Loving.* New York: Harper.

Fromm, M. G., and B. L. Smith, eds. 1989. *The Facilitating Environment: Clinical Applications of Winnicott's Theories.* New York: International Univ. Press.

Gadamer, H.-G. 1960. *Truth and Method.* Tr. G. Barden and J. Cumming. New York: Crossroad, 1982.

Gallop, J. 1985. *Reading Lacan.* Ithaca: Cornell Univ. Press.

Glatzer, H. T., and W. N. Evans. 1977. On Guntrip's Analysis with Fairbairn and Winnicott. *Int. J. Psychoanal. Psychotherap.,* 6:81–98.

Green, A. 1966. Logic of Lacan's *objet (a)* and Freudian Theory: Convergences and Questions. Tr. K. Kleinart and B. Schlossman. In Smith and Kerrigan 1983, pp. 161–91.

———. 1975. The Analyst, Symbolization and Absence in the Analytic Setting. Tr. K. Lewison and D. Pines. In A. Green 1986, pp. 30–59.

———. 1983. The Dead Mother. Tr. K. Aubertin. In A. Green 1986, pp. 142–73.

———. 1986. *On Private Madness.* London: Hogarth Press.

———. 1987. Oedipus, Freud, and Us. Tr. C. Coman. In *Psychoanalytic Approaches to Literature and Film.* Ed. M. Charney and J. Reppen. Rutherford, N.J.: Fairleigh Dickinson Univ. Press, pp. 215–37.

Green, H. 1964. *I Never Promised You a Rose Garden.* New York: Holt, Rinehart and Winston.

Greenberg, J. R., and S. A. Mitchell. 1983. *Object Relations in Psychoanalytic Theory.* Cambridge: Harvard Univ. Press.

Greenblatt, S. 1980. *Renaissance Self-Fashioning: From More to Shakespeare.* Chicago: Univ. of Chicago Press.

———. 1986a. Fiction and Friction. In *Reconstructing Individualism: Autonomy, Individuality, and the Self in Western Thought.* Ed. T. C. Heller, M. Sosna, and D. E. Wellbery. Stanford: Stanford Univ. Press, 1986, pp. 30–52.

———. 1986b. Psychoanalysis and Renaissance Culture. In Parker and Quint 1986, pp. 210–24.

Grolnick, S. 1990. *The Work and Play of Winnicott.* New York: Jason Aronson.

Grolnick, S., L. Barkin, and W. Muensterberger, eds. 1978. *Between Reality and Fantasy: Transitional Objects and Phenomena.* New York: Jason Aronson.

Grosskurth, P. 1986. *Melanie Klein: Her World and Her Work.* Cambridge: Harvard Univ. Press, 1987.

Grünbaum, A. 1984. *The Foundations of Psychoanalysis: A Philosophical Critique.* Berkeley: Univ. of California Press.

Gunn, D. 1988. *Psychoanalysis and Fiction: An Exploration of Literary and Psychoanalytic Borders.* New York: Cambridge Univ. Press.

Guntrip, H. 1961. *Personality Structure and Human Interaction.* London: Hogarth Press, 1982.

———. 1968. *Schizoid Phenomena, Object Relations and the Self.* London: Hogarth Press, 1986.

———. 1971. *Psychoanalytic Theory, Therapy and the Self.* London: Maresfield Library, 1985.

———. 1975. My Experience of Analysis with Fairbairn and Winnicott (How Complete a Result Does Psycho-Analytic Therapy Achieve?) In Buckley 1986, pp. 447–68.

———. 1978. Psychoanalysis and Some Scientific and Philosophical Critics. *Brit. J. Med. Psychol.,* 51:207–24.

———. N.d. *Psycho-Analytical Autobiography: A Study of the "Dream Process" over Thirty Six Years, Showing the Effects of an Amnesia for an Infancy Trauma.* 2 vols. Unpublished manuscript.

Habermas, J. 1968. *Knowledge and Human Interests.* Tr. J. J. Shapiro. Boston: Beacon Press, 1972.

Hamilton, V. 1982. *Narcissus and Oedipus: The Children of Psychoanalysis.* London: Routledge and Kegan Paul.

Hay, J. 1979. Oedipus Tyrannus: *Lame Knowledge and the Homosporic Womb.* Washington: Univ. Press of America.

Hegel, G. W. F. 1817. *Logic.* Tr. W. Wallace. Oxford: Clarendon Press, 1978.

Heimann, P. 1950. On Counter-Transference. *Int. J. Psycho-Anal.,* 31:81–84.

———. 1956. Dynamics of Transference Interpretations. *Int. J. Psycho-Anal.,* 37:303–10.

Hermann, I. 1933. Zum Triebleben der Primaten (On the instinctual life of primates). *Imago.* 19:113–25.

———. 1936. Clinging—Going-in-Search: A Contrasting Pair of Instincts and Their Relation to Sadism and Masochism. Tr. M. Nunberg and F. R. Hartman. *Psychoanal. Q.,* 45 (1976): 5–36.

Holland, N. N. 1985. *The I.* New Haven: Yale Univ. Press.

Howard, J. E. 1986. The New Historicism in Renaissance Studies. In *Renaissance Historicism: Selections from English Literary Renaissance.* Ed. A. F. Kinney and D. S. Collins. Amherst: Univ. of Massachusetts Press, 1987, pp. 3–33.

Hughes, J. M. 1989. *Reshaping the Psychoanalytic Domain: The Work of Melanie Klein, W. R. D. Fairbairn, and D. W. Winnicott.* Berkeley: Univ. of California Press.

Jacobson, E. 1964. *The Self and the Object World.* New York: International Univ. Press.

Jameson, F. 1981. *The Political Unconscious: Narrative as a Socially Symbolic Act.* Ithaca: Cornell Univ. Press.

Jones, E. 1925. Introduction to the Congress Symposium. *Int. J. Psycho-Anal.,* 6:1–4.

———. 1953. *The Life and Work of Sigmund Freud.* Vol. 1. New York: Basic Books.

————. 1955. *The Life and Work of Sigmund Freud.* Vol. 2. New York: Basic Books.

————. 1957. *The Life and Work of Sigmund Freud.* Vol. 3. New York: Basic Books.

Jung, C. G. 1912. *Psychology of the Unconscious: A Study of the Transformations and Symbolisms of the Libido.* Tr. B. M. Hinkle. New York: Moffat and Yard, 1916.

Kermode, F. 1985. Freud and Interpretation. *Int. Rev. Psycho-Anal.,* 12:3–11.

Kerr, J. 1988. Beyond the Pleasure Principle and Back Again: Freud, Jung, and Sabina Spielrien. In *Freud: Appraisals and Reappraisals: Contributions to Freud Studies,* vol. 3. Ed. P. E. Stepansky. Hillsdale, N.J.: Analytic Press, pp. 3–79.

Khan, M. M. R. 1972. The Becoming of a Psycho-Analyst. In *The Privacy of the Self.* London: Hogarth Press, 1974, pp. 112–28.

————. 1975. Introduction to D. W. Winnicott 1958b, pp. xi–l.

Klein, D. B. 1981. *Jewish Origins of the Psychoanalytic Movement.* Chicago: Univ. of Chicago Press, 1985.

Klein, G. S. 1976. Freud's Two Theories of Sexuality. In *Psychology vs. Metapsychology: Essays in Memory of George S. Klein.* Ed. M. M. Gill and P. S. Holzman. *Psychol. Issues,* 36:14–70.

Klein, M. 1930. The Importance of Symbol-Formation in the Development of the Ego. In M. Klein 1984, 1:219–32.

————. 1932. *The Psycho-Analysis of Children.* M. Klein 1984, vol. 2.

————. 1935. A Contribution to the Psychogenesis of Manic-Depressive States. In M. Klein 1984, 1:282–311.

————. 1937. Love, Guilt, and Reparation. In M. Klein 1984, 1:306–43.

————. 1945. The Oedipus Complex in the Light of Early Anxieties. In M. Klein 1984, 1:370–419.

————. 1946. Notes on Some Schizoid Mechanisms. In M. Klein 1984, 3:1–24.

————. 1952. The Origins of Transference. In M. Klein 1984, 3:48–56.

————. 1984. *The Writings of Melanie Klein.* 4 vols. Ed. R. Money-Kyrle, B. Joseph, E. O'Shaughnessy, and H. Segal. New York: Free Press.

Kohut, H. 1959. Introspection, Empathy, and Psychoanalysis: An Examination of the Relationship between Mode of Observation and Theory. *J. Amer. Psychoanal. Assn.,* 7:459–83.

————. 1971. *The Analysis of the Self: A Systematic Approach to the Treatment of Narcissistic Personality Disorders.* New York: International Univ. Press.

————. 1977. *The Restoration of the Self.* Madison, Conn.: International Univ. Press, 1986.

————. 1979. The Two Analyses of Mr. Z. *Int. J. Psycho-Anal.,* 60:3–27.

————. 1980. Reflections on *Advances in Self Psychology.* In *Advances in Self Psychology.* Ed. A. Goldberg. New York: International Univ. Press, pp. 473–554.

————. 1984. *How Does Analysis Cure?* Ed. A. Goldberg with P. E. Stepansky. Chicago: Univ. of Chicago Press.

Krüll, M. 1979. *Freud and His Father.* Tr. A. J. Pomerans. New York: Norton, 1986.

Lacan, J. 1948. Aggressivity in Psychoanalysis. In Lacan 1977, pp. 8–29.

———. 1949. The Mirror Stage as Formative of the Function of the I as Revealed in Psychoanalytic Experience. In Lacan 1977, pp. 1–7.

———. 1953. The Function and Field of Speech and Language in Psychoanalysis. In Lacan 1977, pp. 30–113.

———. 1954. La topique de l'imaginaire (The topic of the imaginary). In *Ecrits.* Paris: Seuil, 1966, pp. 87–103.

———. 1954–55. *Le seminare: Livre II. Le moi dans la théorie de Freud et dans la technique de la psychanalyse* (The Seminar: Book 2. The ego in Freud's theory and in the technique of psychoanalysis). Paris: Seuil, 1978.

———. 1955. The Freudian Thing, or the Meaning of the Return to Freud in Psychoanalysis. In Lacan 1977, pp. 114–45.

———. 1958a. The Direction of the Treatment and the Principles of Its Power. In Lacan 1977, pp. 226–80.

———. 1958b. The Signification of the Phallus. In Lacan 1977, pp. 281–91.

———. 1960. The Subversion of the Subject and the Dialectic of Desire in the Freudian Unconscious. In Lacan 1977, pp. 292–325.

———. 1966. Intervention on Transference. In Mitchell and Rose 1985, pp. 61–73.

———. 1973. *The Four Fundamental Concepts of Psycho-Analysis.* Ed. J.-A. Miller. Tr. A. Sheridan. New York: Norton, 1981.

———. 1975. Seminar of 21 January 1975. In Mitchell and Rose 1985, pp. 162–71.

———. 1977. *Ecrits: A Selection.* Tr. A. Sheridan. New York: Norton.

Laing, R. D. 1959. *The Divided Self: An Existential Study in Sanity and Madness.* Harmondsworth, Eng.: Penguin Books, 1970.

Landis, B. 1981. Discussions with Harry Guntrip. *Contemp. Psychoanal.,* 17:112–17.

Leavy, S. A. 1980. *The Psychoanalytic Dialogue.* New Haven: Yale Univ. Press.

———. 1985. Demythologizing Oedipus. *Psychoanal. Q.,* 54:444–54.

Lesser, S. O. 1967. *Oedipus the King:* The Two Dramas, the Two Conflicts. In *The Whispered Meanings: Selected Essays.* Ed. R. Sprich and R. W. Noland. Amherst: Univ. of Massachusetts Press, 1977, pp. 149–80.

Lichtenstein, H. 1983. *The Dilemma of Human Identity.* New York: Jason Aronson.

Lidz, T. 1988. The Riddle of the Riddle of the Sphinx. In Rudnytsky 1988a, pp. 35–49.

Lieberman, E. J. 1985. *Acts of Will: The Life and Work of Otto Rank.* New York: Free Press.

Lindner, R. 1955. *The Fifty-Minute Hour: A Collection of True Psychoanalytic Tales.* New York: Rinehart.

Little, M. I. 1985. Winnicott Working in Areas Where Psychotic Anxieties Predominate: A Personal Record. *Free Associations,* 3:9–42.

Loewald, H. W. 1962. Internalization, Separation, Mourning, and the Super-ego. In Loewald 1980, pp. 257–76.

———. 1979. The Waning of the Oedipus Complex. In Loewald 1980, pp. 384–404.

———. 1980. *Papers on Psychoanalysis*. New Haven: Yale Univ. Press.

———. 1985. Oedipus Complex and Development of Self. *Psychoanal. Q.*, 54:435–43.

Luepnitz, D. A. 1988. *The Family Interpreted: Feminist Theory in Clinical Practice*. New York: Basic Books.

Lukacher, N. 1986. *Primal Scenes: Literature, Philosophy, Psychoanalysis*. Ithaca: Cornell Univ. Press.

Mahler, M. 1968. *On Human Symbiosis and the Vicissitudes of Individuation*. Vol. 1: *Infantile Psychosis*. New York: International Univ. Press.

———. 1972. On the First Three Subphases of the Separation-Individuation Process. In Buckley 1986, pp. 222–32.

———. 1988. *The Memoirs of Margaret S. Mahler*. Ed. P. E. Stepansky. New York: Free Press.

Mannoni, M. 1967. *The Child, His "Illness," and the Others*. New York: Pantheon, 1976. Translated from the French.

Marcus, S. 1986. The Psychoanalytic Self. *Southern Rev.*, 22:308–25.

Mark, D. In press. The Third Generation of Analysis Tests Freud's Theories. In *Freud and Forbidden Knowledge*. Ed. J. Kerr and P. L. Rudnytsky. New York: New York Univ. Press.

Masson, J. M. 1984. *The Assault on Truth: Freud's Suppression of the Seduction Theory*. New York: Farrar, Straus, and Giroux.

———, ed. 1985. *The Complete Letters of Sigmund Freud to Wilhelm Fliess, 1887–1904*. Cambridge: Harvard Univ. Press.

McGuire, W., ed. 1974. *The Freud/Jung Letters: The Correspondence between Sigmund Freud and C. G. Jung*. Tr. R. Manheim and R. F. C. Hull. Princeton: Princeton Univ. Press.

Meisel, P., and W. Kendrick, eds. 1985. *Bloomsbury/Freud: The Letters of James and Alix Strachey, 1924–1925*. New York: Basic Books.

Meissner, W. W. 1984. *Psychoanalysis and Religious Experience*. New Haven: Yale Univ. Press.

Menaker, E. 1982. *Otto Rank: A Rediscovered Legacy*. New York: Columbia Univ. Press.

Michels, R. 1986. Oedipus and Insight. *Psychoanal. Q.*, 55:599–617.

Milner, M. [J. Field, pseud.] 1950. *On Not Being Able to Paint*. New York: International Univ. Press, 1979.

———. 1952. The Role of Illusion in Symbol Formation. In *The Suppressed Madness of Sane Men*. London: Routledge, 1988, pp. 83–113.

———. 1968. *The Hands of the Living God: An Account of a Psycho-Analytic Treatment*. London: Hogarth Press.

———. 1978. D. W. Winnicott and the Two-Way Journey. In Grolnick, Barkin, and Muensterberger 1978, pp. 37–42.

Milrod, D. 1968. Summary of D. W. Winnicott, "The Use of an Object" and discussions by Edith Jacobson, Bernard D. Fine, and Samuel Ritvo. New York Psychoanalytic Society, November 12. Unpublished manuscript.

Mitchell, J., and J. Rose, eds. 1985. *Feminine Sexuality: Jacques Lacan and the Ecole Freudienne.* Tr. J. Rose. New York: Norton.

Nin, A. 1931–34. *Diary.* Vol. 1. Ed. G. Stuhlmann. New York: Harcourt Brace Jovanovich, 1966.

———. 1939–44. *Diary.* Vol. 3. Ed. G. Stuhlmann. New York: Harcourt Brace Jovanovich, 1969.

Nunberg, H. 1930. The Synthetic Function of the Ego. *Int. J. Psycho-Anal.*, 12 (1931): 123–40. Translated from the German.

Parker, P., and D. Quint, eds. 1986. *Literary Theory / Renaissance Texts.* Baltimore: Johns Hopkins Univ. Press.

Phillips, A. 1988. *Winnicott.* London: Fontana Press.

Phillips, J. 1987. Grünbaum on Hermeneutics. *Psychoanal. and Contemp. Thought*, 10:585–626.

Pontalis, J.-B., D. Anzieu, and G. Rosolato. 1977. A propos du texte de Guntrip (Notes on the text of Guntrip). *Nouvelle Rev. de Psychanal.*, 15:29–37.

Progoff, I. 1956. *The Death and Rebirth of Psychology.* New York: McGraw-Hill, 1973.

Rangell, L. 1982. Transference to Theory: The Relationship of Psychoanalytic Education to the Analyst's Relationship to Psychoanalysis. *Annual of Psychoanal.*, 10:29–56.

Rank, O. 1907. *Der Künstler: Ansätze zu einer Sexual-Psychologie* (The artist: Preliminaries to a sexual psychology). Vienna: Heller.

———. 1909. *The Myth of the Birth of the Hero.* Tr. F. Robbins and S. E. Jelliffe. New York: Journal of Nervous and Mental Disease Publishing Co., 1914.

———. 1912. *Das Incest-Motiv in Dichtung und Sage* (The incest theme in literature and legend). Leipzig: Deuticke.

———. 1914. *The Double.* Tr. H. Tucker. Chapel Hill: Univ. of North Carolina Press, 1971.

———. 1924a. *The Don Juan Legend.* Tr. D. G. Winter. Princeton: Princeton Univ. Press, 1975.

———. 1924b. *The Trauma of Birth.* New York: Harcourt, Brace, 1929. Translated from the German.

———. 1926a. The Genesis of Genitality. *Psychoanal. Rev.*, 13:126–44.

———. 1926b. *Sexualität und Schuldgefühl* (Sexuality and the sense of guilt). Leipzig: Internationaler Psychoanalytischer Verlag.

———. 1926c. *Technik der Psychoanalyse: I. Die analytische Situation* (Technique of psychoanalysis: 1. The analytic situation). Leipzig: Deuticke.

———. 1927a. *Grundzüge einer genetischen Psychologie auf Grund der Psychoanalyse der Ichstruktur. I Teil* (Fundamentals of a genetic psychology based on the psychoanalysis of ego structure. Part 1). Leipzig: Deuticke.

————. 1927b. Psychoanalytic Problems. *Psychoanal. Rev.,* 14:1–19.

————. 1927c. Review of S. Freud, *Hemmung, Symptom und Angst* (Inhibitions, symptoms, and anxiety). *Mental Hygiene,* 11:181–86.

————. 1929a. Beyond Psychoanalysis. *Psychoanal. Rev.,* 16:1–11.

————. 1929b. The Psychological Approach to Personal Problems. *J. Otto Rank Assn.,* 1, no. 1 (1966): 12–25.

————. 1929c. *Truth and Reality.* Tr. J. Taft. New York: Norton, 1978.

————. 1929–31. *Will Therapy.* Tr. J. Taft. New York: Norton, 1978.

————. 1930a. Literary Autobiography. *J. Otto Rank Assn.,* 16, nos. 1 and 2 (1981), pp. 3–38.

————. 1930b. *Psychology and the Soul.* Tr. W. D. Turner. New York: Barnes, 1961.

————. 1932a. *Art and Artist.* New York: Knopf. Translated from the German.

————. 1932b. *Modern Education.* Tr. M. Moxon. New York: Knopf.

————. 1941. *Beyond Psychology.* New York: Dover, 1958.

Richardson, W. J. 1983. Lacan and the Subject of Psychoanalysis. In Smith and Kerrigan 1983, pp. 51–74.

Ricoeur, P. 1977. The Question of Proof in Freud's Psychoanalytic Writings. *J. Amer. Psychoanal. Assn.,* 25:835–71.

Rickman, J. 1951. Number in the Human Sciences. In *Selected Contributions to Psycho-Analysis.* Ed. W. C. M. Scott. New York: Basic Books, 1957, pp. 218–23.

Roazen, P. 1969. *Brother Animal: The Story of Freud and Tausk.* New York: Knopf.

————. 1971. *Freud and His Followers.* New York: New American Library, 1976.

Rodman, F. R., ed. 1987. *The Spontaneous Gesture: Selected Letters of D. W. Winnicott.* Cambridge: Harvard Univ. Press.

Róheim, G. 1934. *The Riddle of the Sphinx.* Tr. R. Money-Kyrle. New York: Harper Torchbooks, 1974.

Roith, E. 1987. *The Riddle of Freud: Jewish Influences on His Theory of Female Sexuality.* London: Tavistock.

Roudinesco, E. 1986. *Jacques Lacan and Co.: A History of Psychoanalysis in France, 1925–1985.* Tr. J. Mehlman. Chicago: Univ. of Chicago Press, 1990.

Roustang, F. 1976. *Dire Mastery: Discipleship from Freud to Lacan.* Tr. N. Lukacher. Baltimore: Johns Hopkins Univ. Press, 1982.

Rudnytsky, P. L., ed. 1984. *Otto Rank: A Centennial Tribute. Amer. Imago,* 41 (Winter).

————. 1987. *Freud and Oedipus.* New York: Columbia Univ. Press.

————, ed. 1988a. *The Persistence of Myth: Psychoanalytic and Structuralist Perspectives.* New York: Guilford.

————. 1988b. Redefining the Revenant: Guilt and Sibling Loss in Guntrip and Freud. *Psychoanal. Study Child,* 43:423–32.

Sachs, H. 1944. *Freud: Master and Friend.* Cambridge: Harvard Univ. Press, 1945.

Sacks, O. 1987. *The Man Who Mistook His Wife for a Hat.* New York: Harper and Row.

Saussure, F. de. 1915. *Course in General Linguistics.* Tr. W. Baskin. London: Collins, 1974.

Schneiderman, S. 1983. *Jacques Lacan: The Death of an Intellectual Hero.* Cambridge: Harvard Univ. Press.

Schur, M. 1972. *Freud: Living and Dying.* New York: International Univ. Press.

Seidenman, E. W. 1978. In Therapy with Otto Rank, 1936–38. *J. Otto Rank Assn.,* 13, no. 1: 51–64.

Shakespeare, W. 1601. *The History of Troilus and Cressida.* In *The Riverside Shakespeare.* Ed. G. B. Evans et al. Boston: Houghton Mifflin, 1974.

Sophocles. 1974. *Oedipus Tyrannus.* In *Fabulae.* Ed. A. C. Pearson. Oxford: Oxford Univ. Press. In Greek.

Smith, J., and W. W. Kerrigan, eds. 1983. *Interpreting Lacan.* New Haven: Yale Univ. Press.

Smith, P. 1988. *Discerning the Subject.* Minneapolis: Univ. of Minnesota Press.

Spence, D. P. 1976. *Narrative Truth and Historical Truth: Meaning and Interpretation in Psychoanalysis.* New York: Norton.

Spitz, E. H. 1988. The Artistic Image and the Inward Gaze: Toward a Merging of Perspectives. In Rudnytsky 1988a, pp. 111–28.

———. 1989. Conflict and Creativity: Reflections on Otto Rank's Psychology of Art. *J. Aesthetic Ed.,* 23:97–109.

Sprengnether, M. 1990. *The Spectral Mother: Freud, Feminism, and Psychoanalysis.* Ithaca: Cornell Univ. Press.

Stärcke, A. 1921. The Castration Complex. Tr. D. Bryan. *Int. J. Psycho-Anal.,* 2:179–201.

Stern, D. 1985. *The Interpersonal World of the Infant: A View from Psychoanalysis and Developmental Psychology.* New York: Basic Books.

Stolorow, R. D., and G. E. Atwood. 1979. *Faces in a Cloud: Subjectivity in Personality Theory.* New York: Jason Aronson.

Sutherland, J. D. 1989. *Fairbairn's Journey into the Interior.* London: Free Association Books.

Suttie, I. D. 1935. *The Origins of Love and Hate.* London: Free Association Books, 1988.

Swales, P. J. 1982. Freud, Minna Bernays, and the Language of Flowers. Privately published by the author.

Swan, J. 1974. *Mater* and Nannie: Freud's Two Mothers and the Discovery of the Oedipus Complex. *Amer. Imago,* 31:1–64.

Taft, J. 1958. *Otto Rank: A Biographical Study.* New York: Julian Press.

Taylor, C. 1989. *Sources of the Self: The Making of the Modern Identity.* Cambridge: Harvard Univ. Press.

Turkle, S. 1978. *Psychoanalytic Politics: Freud's French Revolution*. New York: Basic Books.

Viderman, S. 1979. The Analytic Space: Meanings and Problems. Tr. P. Gross. *Psychoanal. Q.*, 48:257–91.

Winnicott, C. 1978. D. W. W.: A Reflection. In Grolnick, Barkin, and Muensterberger 1978, pp. 17–33.

———. 1989. D. W. W.: A Reflection. In D. W. Winnicott 1989, pp. 1–18.

Winnicott, D. W. 1941. The Observation of Infants in a Set Situation. In D. W. Winnicott 1958b, pp. 52–69.

———. 1945. Primitive Emotional Development. In D. W. Winnicott 1958b, pp. 145–56.

———. 1948. Paediatrics and Psychiatry. In D. W. Winnicott 1965b, pp. 157–73.

———. 1949. Birth Memories, Birth Trauma, and Anxiety. In D. W. Winnicott 1958b, pp. 174–93.

———. 1950. Some Thoughts on the Meaning of the Word "Democracy." In D. W. Winnicott 1986, pp. 239–59.

———. 1952. Anxiety Associated with Insecurity. In D. W. Winnicott 1958b, pp. 97–100.

———. 1953. Transitional Objects and Transitional Phenomena. In D. W. Winnicott 1971d, pp. 1–25.

———. 1954. Metapsychological and Clinical Aspects of Regression within the Psycho-Analytical Set-up. In D. W. Winnicott 1958b, pp. 278–94.

———. 1956a. The Antisocial Tendency. In D. W. Winnicott 1958b, pp. 306–15.

———. 1956b. Primary Maternal Preoccupation. In D. W. Winnicott 1958b, pp. 300–5.

———. 1957. The Mother's Contribution to Society. In D. W. Winnicott 1986, pp. 123–27.

———. 1958a. Psycho-Analysis and the Sense of Guilt. In D. W. Winnicott 1958b, pp. 15–28.

———. 1958b. *Through Paediatrics to Psycho-Analysis*. New York: Basic Books, 1975.

———. 1959. Nothing at the Centre. In D. W. Winnicott 1989, pp. 49–52.

———. 1959–64. Classification: Is There a Psycho-Analytic Contribution to Psychiatric Classification? In D. W. Winnicott 1965b, pp. 124–39.

———. 1960a. Ego Distortion in Terms of True and False Self. In D. W. Winnicott 1965b, pp. 140–52.

———. 1960b. The Theory of the Parent-Infant Relationship. In D. W. Winnicott 1965b, pp. 37–55.

———. 1961. Psychoanalysis and Science: Friends or Relations? In D. W. Winnicott 1986, pp. 13–18.

———. 1962a. Ego Integration in Child Development. In D. W. Winnicott 1965b, pp. 56–63.

———. 1962b. A Personal View of the Kleinian Contribution. In D. W. Winnicott 1965b, pp. 171–78.

———. 1962c. Providing for the Child in Health and Crisis. In D. W. Winnicott 1965b, pp. 64–72.

———. 1963a. Communicating and Not Communicating Leading to a Study of Certain Opposites. In D. W. Winnicott 1965b, pp. 179–92.

———. 1963b. Dependence in Infant-Care, in Child-Care, and in the Psycho-Analytic Setting. In D. W. Winnicott 1965b, pp. 249–59.

———. 1963c. The Development of the Capacity for Concern. In D. W. Winnicott 1965b, pp. 73–82.

———. 1963d. From Dependence towards Independence in the Development of the Individual. In D. W. Winnicott 1965b, pp. 83–92.

———. 1963e. Morals and Education. In D. W. Winnicott 1965b, pp. 93–105.

———. 1963f. Psychiatric Disorder in Terms of Infantile Maturational Processes. In D. W. Winnicott 1965b, pp. 230–41.

———. 1963g. Psychotherapy of Character Disorders. In D. W. Winnicott 1965b, pp. 203–16.

———. 1963h. Training for Child Psychiatry. In D. W. Winnicott 1965b, pp. 193–202.

———. 1964a. *The Child, the Family, and the Outside World.* Harmondsworth, Eng.: Penguin Books, 1978.

———. 1964b. This Feminism. In D. W. Winnicott 1986, pp. 183–94.

———. 1965a. *The Family and Individual Development.* London: Tavistock, 1984.

———. 1965b. *The Maturational Processes and the Facilitating Environment: Studies in the Theory of Emotional Development.* New York: International Univ. Press, 1966.

———. 1967a. The Concept of a Healthy Individual. In D. W. Winnicott 1986, pp. 21–38.

———. 1967b. D. W. W. on D. W. W. In D. W. Winnicott 1989, pp. 569–82.

———. 1967c. Delinquency as a Sign of Hope. In D. W. Winnicott 1986, pp. 90–100.

———. 1967d. The Location of Cultural Experience. In D. W. Winnicott 1971d, pp. 95–103.

———. 1967e. Mirror-Role of Mother and Family in Child Development. In D. W. Winnicott 1971d, pp. 111–18.

———. 1968a. Children Learning. In D. W. Winnicott 1971d, pp. 142–49.

———. 1968b. Clinical Illustration of "The Use of an Object." In D. W. Winnicott 1989, pp. 235–40.

———. 1968c. *Sum,* I Am. In D. W. Winnicott 1986, pp. 55–64.

———. 1969. The Use of an Object and Relating through Identifications. In D. W. Winnicott 1971d, pp. 86–94.

———. 1970a. The Mother-Infant Experience of Mutuality. In D. W. Winnicott 1989, pp. 251–60.

———. 1970b. The Place of the Monarchy. In D. W. Winnicott 1986, pp. 86–94.

———. 1971a. Creativity and Its Origins. In D. W. Winnicott 1971d, pp. 65–85.

———. 1971b. Dreaming, Fantasying, and Living. In D. W. Winnicott 1971d, pp. 26–37.

———. 1971c. Playing: A Theoretical Statement. In D. W. Winnicott 1971d, pp. 38–52.

———. 1971d. *Playing and Reality.* London: Tavistock, 1984.

———. 1971e. *Therapeutic Consultations in Child Psychiatry.* London: Hogarth Press, 1985.

———. 1974. Fear of Breakdown. In D. W. Winnicott 1989, pp. 87–95.

———. 1977. *The Piggle: An Account of the Psychoanalytic Treatment of a Little Girl.* Ed. I. Ramzy. New York: International Univ. Press.

———. 1986. *Home Is Where We Start From: Essays by a Psychoanalyst.* Ed. C. Winnicott, R. Shepherd, and M. Davis. New York: Norton.

———. 1988. *Human Nature.* New York: Schocken.

———. 1989. *Psycho-Analytic Explorations.* Ed. C. Winnicott, R. Shepherd, and M. Davis. Cambridge: Harvard Univ. Press.

Winnicott, D. W., and M. M. R. Khan. 1953. Review of W. R. D. Fairbairn, *Psychoanalytic Studies of the Personality.* In D. W. Winnicott 1989, pp. 413–22.

Wollheim, R. 1984. *The Thread of Life.* Cambridge: Harvard Univ. Press.

Wordsworth, W. 1850. *The Prelude.* Ed. E. de Selincourt. 2nd ed. Ed. H. Darbishire. Oxford: Clarendon Press, 1959.

DATE DUE